One Submarine's Secret War Against the Axis

One Submarine's Secret War Against the Axis

HMS *Triumph*, SOE and MI9 in the Mediterranean, 1941

Gav Don

Pen & Sword
MARITIME

First published in Great Britain in 2025 by
Pen & Sword Maritime
An imprint of Pen & Sword Books Limited
Yorkshire – Philadelphia

ISBN 978 1 03613 251 4

A CIP catalogue record for this book is available from the British Library.

Typeset by Mac Style
Printed in the UK by CPI Group (UK) Ltd, Croydon, CR0 4YY.

MIX
Paper | Supporting responsible forestry
FSC® C013604
FSC www.fsc.org

The Publisher's authorised representative in the EU for product safety is Authorised Rep Compliance Ltd., Ground Floor, 71 Lower Baggot Street, Dublin D02 P593, Ireland.
www.arccompliance.com

For a complete list of Pen & Sword titles please contact

PEN & SWORD BOOKS LIMITED
47 Church Street, Barnsley, South Yorkshire, S70 2AS, England
E-mail: enquiries@pen-and-sword.co.uk
Website: www.pen-and-sword.co.uk
or
PEN AND SWORD BOOKS
1950 Lawrence Road, Havertown, PA 19083, USA
E-mail: uspen-and-sword@casematepublishers.com
Website: www.penandswordbooks.com

To John McGregor, without whom this would have remained just a nice idea.

Contents

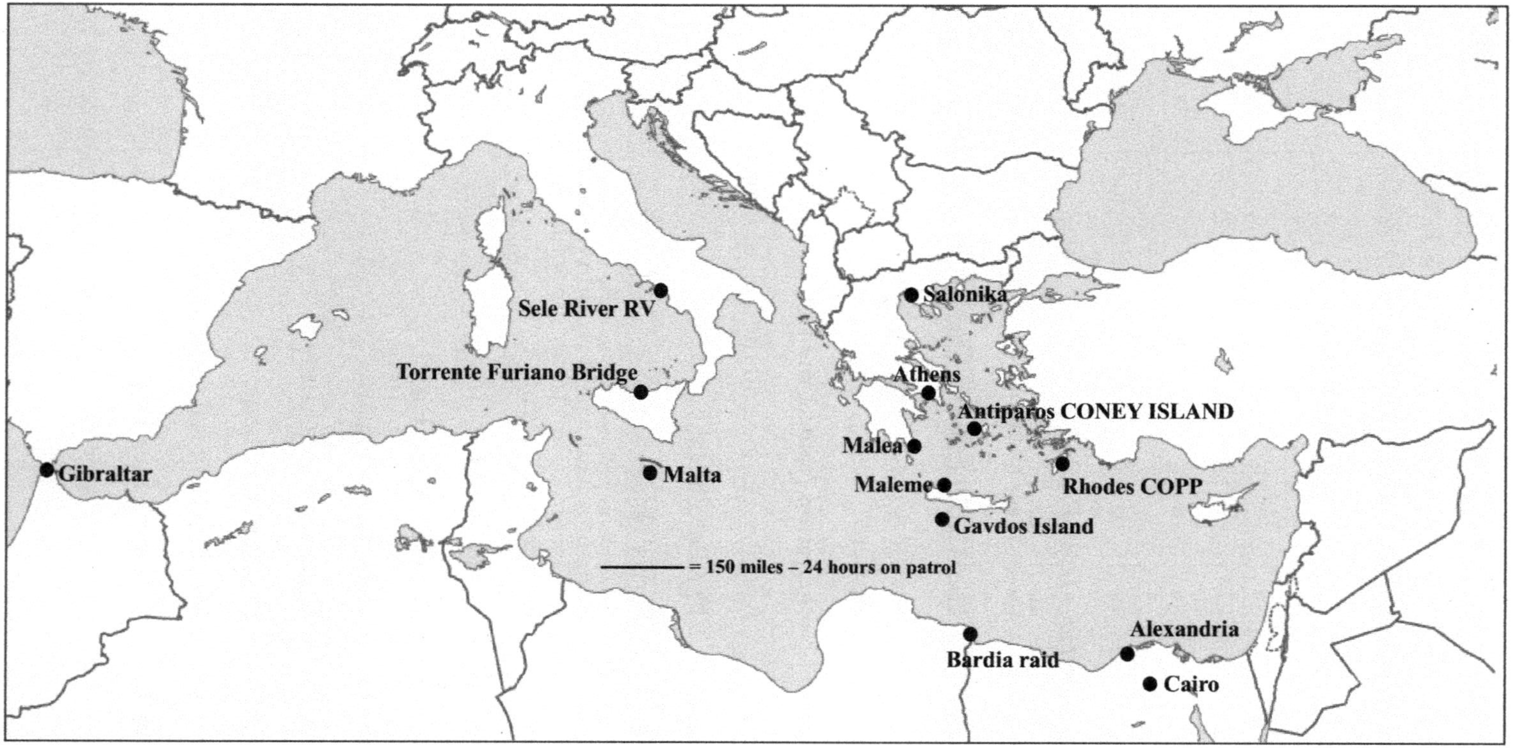

Mediterranean Sea.

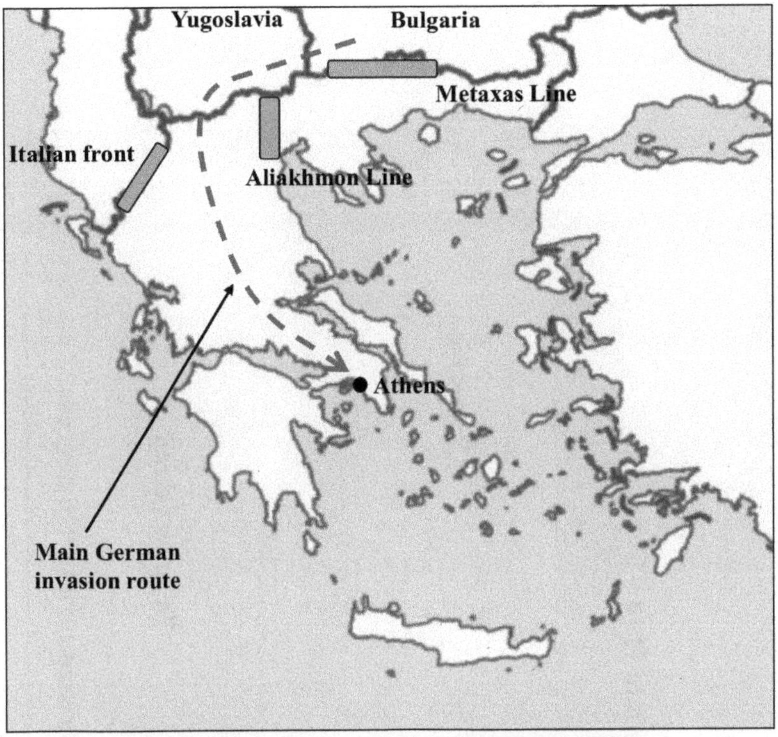

Operation Marita.

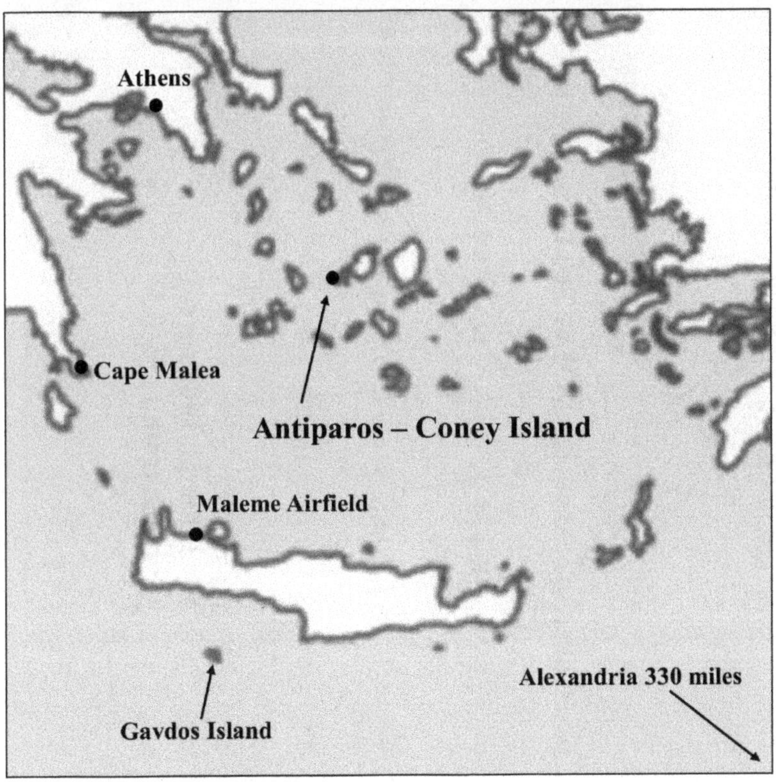

Triumph's operations in the Aegean Sea.

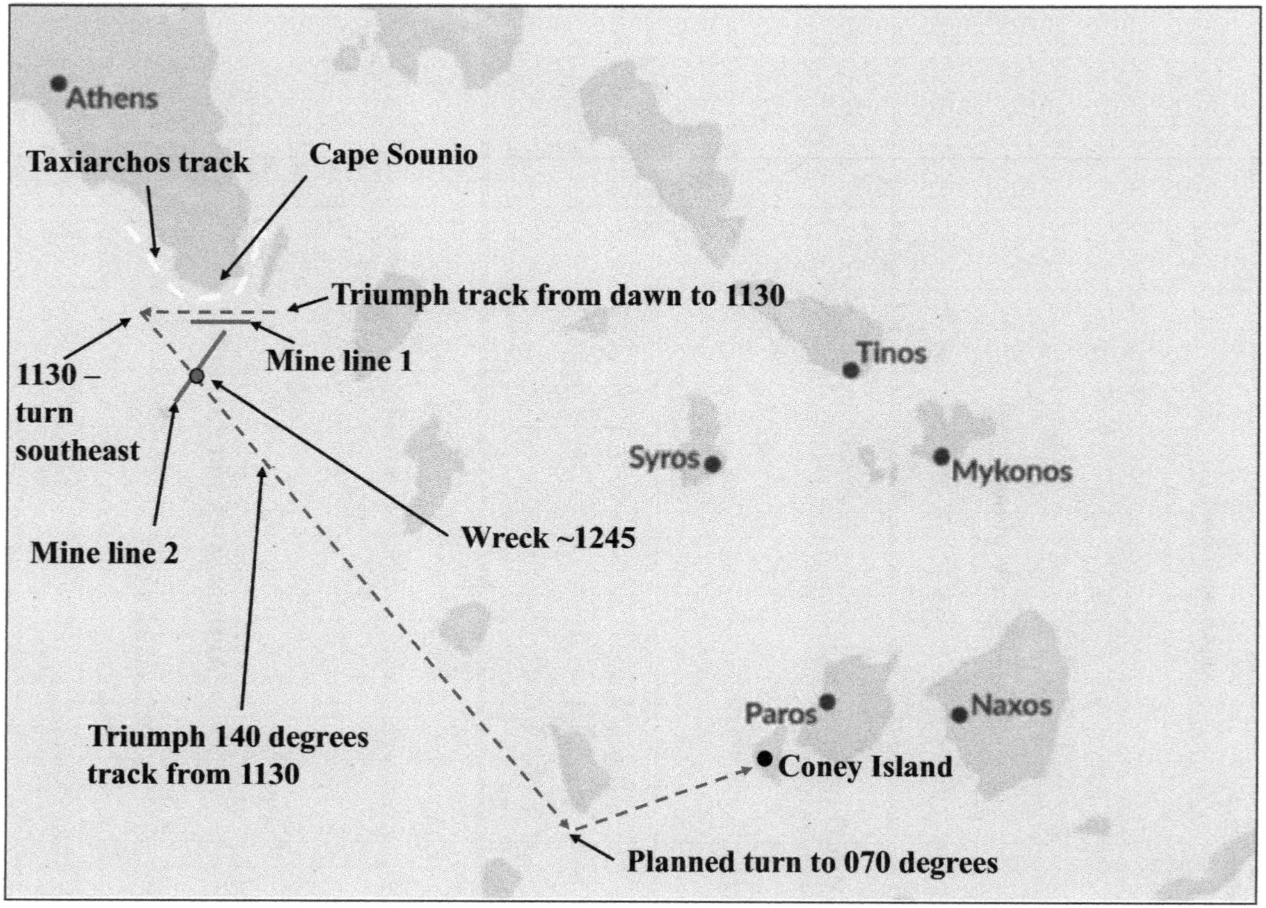

Triumph's last day.

Foreword

The disappearance of the British submarine HMS *Triumph* in 1942 is part of my family's story. My father's younger brother Michael was on board and his loss, felt by my grandparents and my parents to their dying days, was compounded by having no knowledge of how, where and when Michael had died. The long silence surrounding HMS *Triumph* was the silence of unresolved grief and of families growing up only with fragments of memory, poignant letters, faded photographs and many, many unanswered questions.

This is the fascinating story of the life of *Triumph* over the course of 1941, before her disappearance without trace and with the loss of all on board in January 1942. It tells this story on several levels – the role of the British submarines in the wider geopolitical context of the early years of the war in the Mediterranean; how a submarine operated day to day; how despite very high attrition rates they had a vital part in disrupting Italian naval movements and Axis supply routes to Rommel's army in North Africa; and how they became key to Special Operations in the Mediterranean theatre, particularly after the fall of Greece. Above all it describes what it was like for those on board, bringing to life the special qualities required to be on patrol in dangerous and testing conditions for weeks on end, with the sudden complexities of an attack and the cold courage of sitting out the enemy's response. It also tells the story of some of the brave and colourful men drawn into the clandestine world of Special Operations – of feuding agencies and of the acutely hazardous mix of resistance, espionage and aiding Allied escapers in occupied Greece.

This meticulous account is the result of a lifetime's journey by Gav Don, also a nephew of one of those lost, to research into the unanswered questions surrounding the disappearance of HMS *Triumph*, not only by piecing together the story of the submarine's loss but also by searching out the relatives and descendants of the crew, bringing us together in a community united in the memory of those who died. The discovery of the wreck in 2023, combined with the author's painstaking reconstruction of *Triumph*'s final hours, brought to me a profound sense of closure, one I know I share with the families of all those who died.

For us, this book is in itself an act of remembrance. More widely, it is the gripping story of the life and death of one submarine – unembellished, un-romanticized and unique. I believe few readers will remain unmoved.

Lord Janvrin
August 2025

Introduction

How It All Began

I grew up in a large and boisterous family, as the fourth of six children, but to one side of the noise and commotion of family life lay a gap – one family member was always visibly absent. This was my uncle Robert Douglas-Don, my father's elder and only brother. Absent, at least, in person. Robert's portrait, painted when he was twelve, hung in our dining room and presided over every family meal. His medals rested in a case on the dining room windowsill beside a small pewter model of his submarine. And his officer's sword and Midshipman's dirk lay in our attic, where, of course, I found them on one or other exploration. The medal case had a label with the date and position of his loss: January 1942, somewhere in the Aegean. Nothing more.

A submarine is a small part of a war – just sixty men and a thousand tons of steel, brass and rubber – and it usually features less prominently in written war histories that tell of the struggles of millions. As an adult, four decades of distraction by education, work, and my own family led Robert's submarine to feature less prominently in my attentions too. He made his presence known occasionally – first when I spent a happy summer at the age of eighteen sailing a yacht around the Aegean, wondering in quiet moments if I was sailing over his grave, and later, when I entered the Royal Navy and wore his officer's sword on parades. In 2010, I found myself with time and resources to try and find out what had happened to him, where, and most importantly, why. So began the journey which has ended with this book.

Along the way I found some 250 other descendants and relatives of Robert's shipmates, who all suffered from the same sense of absence, of a gap, in their family's stories. My journey revealed a rich narrative of the life of a single submarine and the men who sailed her. The level of detail astonished me. Over fifteen years of searching I found thousands of pages of documents, reports, narratives, war diaries, memoirs, signals, photographs, memoranda, contemporary film, letters, telegrams and verbal history, in archives, libraries, bookshops and attics scattered from New Zealand via South Africa to Greece and Britain, and on to Canada. This treasure trove, carefully collected, catalogued and analyzed, revealed *Triumph*'s story, one I felt was worth telling. It's not just the story of one submarine and her people, but the story of the campaigns in which she fought and of the agents, spies and saboteurs she carried to and from those campaigns. The heart of this book is 'why' as much as 'what'. It is also, in a way, the story of all seventy-eight submarines lost by the Royal Navy during the war, written for their descendants and family members, as well as *Triumph*'s.

Everything that follows is factual. Nothing is embellished or fictionalized. There are no invented people or places, or events. Neither is anything left out. I have written this story as an accurate and comprehensive record of *Triumph*'s war on the Axis. I have, though, taken two liberties. I have occasionally added snippets of dialogue between the players in *Triumph*'s tragedy. Some of this is drawn from details recorded in documents. Some reflects dialogue recorded in personal memoirs of men who were there. Some is lifted verbatim from contemporary film and recordings. The rest is drawn from my personal experience of life in a warship as an officer in the modern Royal Navy, adjusted for the passing of time. I think that *Triumph*'s crew would find the dialogue familiar, and I hope that the reader will feel that it adds a real-life quality to facts recorded at the time for military record only.

My second liberty is that I have treated *Triumph*'s crew in 1941 as if it was exactly the same group of men throughout the year – the men who were lost in January 1942. In fact, men left and joined individual submarines as the requirements of the service demanded, but most of the men lost in *Triumph* were in her for most of the preceding year, and to honour their memory, I have 'frozen' her 1941 crew as it was on the day they died. It would have been pointlessly complicated and distracting to have tracked men in and out, apart from the unlucky (or lucky) Petty Officer Taffy Telfer and his CO Commander (later Admiral Sir) Wilfrid Woods.

It is to the sixty-four men, now lying on the bed of the Aegean Sea, to whom this book is dedicated.

Chapter 1

Salpa, June 1941

Lieutenant Renato Guagni, commander of His (Italian) Majesty's submarine *Salpa*[1] lowered the binoculars from his eyes to draw deeply on his cigarette. His boat had surfaced thirty miles north of the British naval base at Alexandria some hours after the intense east Mediterranean sun had begun to beat down on the choppy sea. Guagni's skin was crawling – the surface was no place for a submarine in daylight, but after crossing hundreds of miles of open sea from Taranto his navigating officer had demanded time to fix *Salpa*'s position with an accurate sunsight with his sextant before nosing in towards the enemy base. *Salpa*'s little bridge was crowded – Guagni, the navigator and three lookouts jostling for space. However, the danger would soon pass – *Salpa* would dive back to safety in a few minutes. Just time for one more smoke.

A mile away Lieutenant Alf Peterkin, navigating officer of His Britannic Majesty's Submarine *Triumph*, lowered his eyes to the binocular lenses of her search periscope for what felt like the thousandth time that year. A second earlier the periscope had risen slightly above the surface of the Mediterranean Sea into the intense early morning sunlight, for *Triumph* too was just north of her home port of Alexandria, sailing towards the open sea at a depth of eighteen feet. She was at the start of her sixteenth war patrol and working to get clear of the coast before turning west to her patrol area across the Afrika Corps' supply lines. Through his lenses Peterkin could see that the sea was moderately rough, but here in *Triumph*'s control room there was no motion and little noise, apart from the soft whine of hydraulics under pressure and the hum of a ventilation fan. Peterkin began to walk the periscope briskly in a circle to scan the horizon and then froze.

'Captain in the control room. Starboard twenty, steer zero nine zero. Down periscope'.

Just eight feet away Peterkin's commanding officer, Lieutenant Commander Wilfrid Woods, came instantly awake from his doze and shot out of his tiny cabin to Peterkin's side.

'What have you got, Pilot?'

Woods used Peterkin's designation, that of the boat's navigator or 'pilot' instead of his name or rank.

'Submarine, Sir, on the surface, track about south, one mile, Italian, definitely.'

'Diving Stations.'

These two crisp words were all that was needed to bring *Triumph* to a fighting pitch – diving stations being submariner-speak for 'action'. The order, quickly repeated over the internal loudspeakers, tore every man in the boat from his sleep to his fighting station.

As men arrived in the control room and took over their duties, Woods raised the periscope for his first look. He already had it trained on the approximate bearing of the target, which he found within seconds. He lingered for a moment, his mind racing with the trigonometry of a possible torpedo attack.

'Down.'

The periscope slid into its well at Woods' feet while his brain calculated at a high pitch. The ideal place from which to fire a torpedo was abeam or just ahead of the target, but this one was already sailing away from him at a fine angle. She had clearly surfaced in the few minutes between Peterkin's last look and this one. The target was making ten knots on her diesel engines, while *Triumph* could safely make only four or five knots on her electric batteries. The range was opening at three yards per second. Both the fine angle and the opening range meant that by the time he had turned his boat through half a circle to follow her, taken the extra periscope sights he needed to work out a possible firing solution for his torpedoes, and lined his boat up on the firing track, the target would be out of range.

Luckily *Triumph* had another powerful weapon to bring to the fight.

'Alarm Alarm Alarm. Stand by Gun Action. Gun's crew close up. Group up, half ahead together, make your speed five knots. Steer one eight zero.'

Men once again sprang to follow Woods' orders. Now, instead of preparing to fire a torpedo at the target, *Triumph* would leap to the surface like a broaching whale while ten men raced up three separate ladders to man her four-inch deck gun and a pair of Lewis machine guns. Two of the ladders, side by side, led up the gun tower onto the gun's rotating platform. At the head of one of these was Petty Officer Robert Theobald. At thirty-six he was two years older than his captain and a veteran submariner of ten years standing. Theobald was the gunlayer – responsible for adjusting the vertical aim of the gun and pulling the trigger. His action position was a small seat on the gun's right-hand side. On the other side of the gun was the gun trainer, whose job it was to keep the gunsight centred on the target. Crammed in behind and next to him was Able Seaman Luther Jones, who set the range wheel on the sight to the target's range and added left and right deflections under the orders of the gunnery officer, Lieutenant Robert Douglas-Don, on the bridge above and behind him. Behind Luther were two men, each cradling a live four-inch shell. More men clustered on the gun tower ladders below were ready to form a human chain to pass additional shells up to the gun platform as needed and to replace any man who was injured or killed by gunfire coming from the target, for she too was armed with a deck gun of about the same size as *Triumph*'s. Woods was setting up a quick-draw western shootout. The element of surprise was on his side, but a frighteningly large number of things could go wrong and turn him from predator to prey.

Ten feet above Woods' head, at the head of the ladder leading to the bridge, and with his hand on the last remaining clip that held it shut against the sea outside, crouched Douglas-Don. His job was to watch the fall of shot and call corrections down to Luther Jones. He and Robert Theobald had already snatched a look at the target through the attack periscope to familiarize themselves with its track and range. To make the ambush swift and deadly it was necessary to 'bounce' *Triumph*'s 1,000 tonnes violently to the surface as quickly as possible. In charge of her trim and buoyancy was her First Lieutenant (and her second-in-command), Lieutenant Michael Janvrin. The son of a Gloucestershire vicar, Janvrin had an almost impish face which was quick to laugh. Aged twenty-three, Janvrin was a career officer who had volunteered for submarines in the spring before the war.

In order to get *Triumph* from periscope depth to opening fire as fast as possible he ordered her ballast tanks be filled with compressed air, pushing water out and lightening the boat, while simultaneously ordering the men on the fore and after planes to set them both 'hard to dive' and increasing her speed. With this combination *Triumph* was held underwater for a few seconds while straining to reach the surface, until Janvrin ordered 'planes hard to rise, blow ones, twos and sixes, surface'.

Released from her natural home underwater by the air rushing into her main ballast tanks *Triumph* shot into the sunlight, her gun platform reaching the surface just four seconds after the order. The bridge and gun-tower hatches were still under water when Douglas-Don gave the order 'off clips'. Half a tonne of lukewarm June Mediterranean seawater cascaded down over the waiting men while the boat finished her ascent, but they shouldered their way past the flood to their stations. Just five seconds later, and only ten seconds after Janvrin's order, *Triumph*'s gun was already swinging onto the target's bearing and Douglas-Don was calling range and deflection orders down to Jones on the sight setting wheels, his voice nearly strangled with the tension, his heart racing and his mouth dry.

'Range oh one three.[2] Deflection four right. Point of aim – conning tower. Independent.'

'On' from Theobald.

'On' from the trainer.

The gun's breech snacked home behind its first shell.

'Ready' from Luther Jones.

'Shoot.'

Half a second later Theobald pulled the firing lever and the first shell was away before the gun deck was clear of streaming sea water. Douglas-Don watched the shell as it flew towards the target and splashed into the sea. A little over and a little astern of the target.

'Down fifty, right two.'

'On.'

'On.'

In seconds the breech was cleared of the empty shell casing, a new shell was loaded, and the breech shut.

'Ready.'

'Shoot.'

Repeat, repeat, repeat, a shell crashing out every five seconds.

Behind him Douglas-Don was dimly aware of the light chattering of the port Lewis Gun spraying the target's bridge and gun deck with .303 rounds.

Guagni did not know he was under attack before *Salpa* was hit. The flash and blast of *Triumph*'s shell made the men on the bridge flinch into cover, stunned and deafened. Five seconds later another shell arrived. As *Triumph*'s fire crashed into them in a nightmare of flame, shrapnel and noise, Guagni shouted down the bridge voice-pipe the order to bring his own gun into action. He could not risk a dive – because the shells crashing into his boat had almost certainly damaged his pressure hull, and because in the thirty seconds it would take him to dive, six more shells would hit, guaranteeing that his boat would sink when she fled underwater. The only thing to do was fight back. His gun's crew straggled onto the bridge and down to *Salpa*'s own gun. They managed to fire five rounds, but the stark terror and shock of what was happening to them, compounded by the storm of machine gun bullets whipping past them, caused them to aim wildly. With their nerve broken, they sought shelter inside their boat.

Triumph was closing the range all the time. As soon as her hatches were open, Woods had ordered the engine room to start her diesel engines, and she was now sailing at twelve knots towards the target. Woods, who had reached the bridge, could see his shells hitting just half a mile away, but he could not guarantee that they were inflicting lethal damage. The target might still dive at this point and escape, or counterattack. Closing the range to 500 yards. and aiming with a naked eye, Woods called down the voice pipe.

'Fire one.'

Two seconds later a torpedo leapt from its tube at forty knots.

'Fire two.'

Two were enough. Woods could see the first torpedo's trail of exhaust bubbles streaking out from his bows towards *Salpa*, and he watched as it ended right under the target's conning tower fifteen seconds later. For everyone on *Triumph*'s bridge and gun platform this was a unique experience – normally not even the captain of a submarine would watch his torpedoes hit for he was too busy working on keeping his boat alive by evading a counterattack. This time a dozen men saw, for the first time, what a torpedo hit looked like up close: 660 pounds of Torpex explosive detonated in a massive flash producing a towering cloud of smoke, water and debris which shot 200 feet into the air. *Salpa*, cut in half, sank like a stone. No one escaped.

Janvrin too was now on the bridge. He had looked the target up in his confidential ship recognition book on the chart table.

'She was Italian, Sir. *Salpa*. Search for survivors?'

Woods looked at the disordered patch of sea that had a few seconds before been the home of forty submariners, men like himself and his crew, fighting for their country, asking not why, just when and how. A spreading patch of oil and random wreckage was all that showed where, just a few seconds before, there had been a thousand tonnes of steel and forty men, like him.

'Not much chance of those, Number One. Let's get below at double time. Well done everyone. Secure the bridge, Guns, dive the boat please.'

It was 0808. The action had lasted seven minutes.

Chapter 2

The Mediterranean Theatre, January 1941

Six months earlier

'Bridge, three miles to run.'

Lieutenant Alf Peterkin's voice sounded tinny as it echoed up the voice pipe to Lieutenant Commander Wilfrid Woods on His Majesty's Submarine *Triumph*'s small bridge. Ahead of him Woods could see his boat's bow in the starlight, smoothly cutting through black water in these last hours of a dark winter's night, white foam sliding down her saddle tanks on each side. As *Triumph*'s navigating officer, her 'pilot' to his fellow officers in her tiny wardroom, Peterkin had plotted her position by dead reckoning from a star sight five hours earlier. She was now just fifteen minutes from her ordered rendezvous with one of the Royal Navy's small minesweepers off the Maltese port and capital city of Valletta.

Woods disliked his first name – a Victorian hangover – and was known to all in the submarine service as 'Sammy', after a famous golfer of the time who shared his surname.

'Very good.' Woods' reply was a reflex, the standard acknowledgement of a report from a junior of any rank, not a judgement on Peterkin's pilotage.

'Yeoman to the bridge.'

Twelve feet below his feet, in the warm, red-lit control room, Leading Signalman Tom Kilty slung the strap of his black metallic signal projector over his shoulder as he climbed the bridge ladder. It banged slightly on the narrow hatches as he emerged on the bridge deck at Woods' feet. Tom was known to all on the boat by his traditional job title – yeoman – usually shortened to 'yeo' to rhyme with 'low'. A Welshman from Glamorgan, at twenty-four Tom was one of the older junior men in the boat, and a pre-war submariner. His wide-set eyes, slight overbite and bouffant hair gave him a goofy appearance, but as a signaller he was recognised as a man of knowledge by his shipmates.

'All set with the recognition signal, yeo?' asked Woods.

'Yes, Sir, ready.'

Tom laid the buff-coloured flimsy book on the little bridge chart table, anchoring it with the coffee mug he had precariously brought with him. It was open at the page for the day, 12 January 1941. Orderly columns of three-letter codes with times and dates were just visible in the soft red light of a torch propped on the chart table. Tom plugged in his signal projector, pressed its glass lens against his thick bridge coat to hide its glare, and gave its venetian blind shutters a test flick.

To protect her on her approach to Malta *Triumph* had been allocated an escort, the minesweeper, to meet her and guide her into Valletta. This was a moment of acute danger. Allied ships and aircraft tended to shoot first and ask questions later when they saw the low threatening silhouette of a surfaced submarine at night. The exhausts from her twin diesel engines made a barely audible, steady, quiet whooshing noise astern of the bridge, but the attention of the five men clustered on it was focussed intently ahead and to the west, searching the complete darkness for the sharp blinking signal light that would mark the presence of her escort.

Even though relative safety lay only a few miles ahead, all on board *Triumph* were tense. Here, a few miles outside Valletta's entrance, her life was in the balance. The Italian fleet, with over a hundred submarines (nearly double the number in the Royal Navy), knew well that there was only a single entrance to Valletta's twin harbours,[1] and that to wait in ambush off that entrance offered a good chance of a target. The Italian naval base at Taranto lay just 300 miles north and east of Malta – a scant twenty hours' sailing. *Triumph*'s four lookouts scanned their quarters of the horizon intently through large naval binoculars, whose lenses gathered every tiny piece of available light into a lesser gloom. A surface action was a quick-draw gunfight – he who saw and shot first usually lived to tell the tale.

Italian submarines were not the only threat, or even the worst. In the eight months since joining the war on the German side, Italian minelaying ships and fast-attack craft had been busy. The waters around Malta were already a web of deadly mines, floating on long steel cables a few feet below the sea surface or sitting on the seabed waiting for a ship to pass overhead. While Malta was blessed with a small and busy flotilla of minesweepers, the Italians regularly sent fast motor boats out from Sicily at night, just fifty miles north, to lay fresh mines on the obvious approach track to Valletta's entrance.

Nor was the enemy *Triumph*'s only problem. The Royal Air Force ran anti-submarine patrols whose pilots and observers were none too skilled in distinguishing friendly submarines from hostile ones, or in keeping an accurate plot of their position to avoid known allied submarine patrol areas. While it would be another year before the RAF actually sank a British submarine, there had already been several attacks by friendly aircraft. Even the Royal Navy's own ships and submarines were potentially deadly – the first British submarine sunk in the war, late in 1939,[2] had been torpedoed in error at night by one of her sisters when she had failed to see and reply to the flashing light of a challenge because her yeoman had allowed the power cable of his signal projector to become entangled in the dark. Here, in this very position on the approaches to Valletta, *Triumph*'s sister HMS *Truant* had miraculously escaped being torpedoed by the submarine HMS *Upholder* when she had completely failed to see the coded challenge, flashed from the latter at night. She had been lucky: *Upholder*'s commanding officer, David Wanklyn, was blessed with excellent night vision and through his binoculars correctly identified the silhouette of a British T-class submarine in time to cancel the attack a few seconds before he fired.[3]

Every man in *Triumph* knew that the last hour of an approach to Valletta was pregnant with disaster, and that in the event of a disaster the common outcome was no survivors. All aboard were depending on Tom Kilty doing his job correctly. Even a slight error in the code, or a slight misalignment of his signal lantern might be answered by a salvo of shells or a torpedo.

A few minutes later the signal lights stabbed to and fro in the dark, friend acknowledging friend with relief.

'Escort signalling, Sir. Welcome to Malta. Take station astern of me at half a cable, speed one zero, base course two six five. Hope you've brought some gin.'

Thirty minutes later *Triumph* and the sixty men inside her slipped gratefully between Valletta's breakwaters in the sharpening light of a Mediterranean winter's dawn. To their right lay the hump of Manoel Island, whose nearest end was occupied by a Venetian quarantine hospital now employed as Malta's submarine base. Shelter, comfort, baths and rest lay just a few minutes away. To their left was the ancient fortress of Valletta. Already a scattering of water taxis hung around their track, their owners looking forward to the fares to come from *Triumph*'s thirsty and curious crew when leave began.

Sammy Woods had every reason to be delighted with his new command. Commissioned in 1939, *Triumph* was the fifth boat in the latest class of Royal Navy ocean-going submarines designed just before the war. At 273 feet long and weighing just over a thousand tonnes, *Triumph* was at her simplest a single eighteen-foot wide tube of steel onto which were welded various external tanks, platforms and structures to allow men to work on her deck. The tube formed a watertight 'pressure hull' which could withstand water pressure down to at least 400 feet, and possibly much deeper, though no one aboard was keen to test just how deep.

Almost everything that *Triumph* needed to operate was inside her pressure hull. At her fore ends were six torpedo tubes which were permanently loaded. These opened inboard to a compartment with six reload torpedoes – the fore ends – and outboard to the sea. Next astern came four cramped messes, one for her twenty-three junior sailors, one each for her nine petty officers and six artificers, and finally one for her four officers. The artificers were a community of highly trained non-commissioned engineers, men whose years of training allowed them to recreate, from raw metal, almost any of the ten thousand moving parts that filled *Triumph* using just the lathe and drills in her engine room and their long experience. These three messes were crammed into a total space just eighty feet long by ten feet wide – about the size of a London underground carriage. At the aft end of this space was a tiny cupboard of a cabin for Sammy Woods, smaller than a railway sleeper compartment but the only private living space in the boat.

At the mid-point of the pressure hull was the control room, the boat's nerve centre. Two periscopes occupied much of the cramped space available. The rest of the compartment was filled with controls for steering and diving, valves for moving compressed air or seawater into her dozen ballast tanks, her chart table, an electromechanical computer for calculating the firing angles for her torpedoes, and a novel sonar set for detecting mines. In action the control room had no fewer than eleven men at work in about 150 square feet.

Astern of the control room came first the signals office with multiple radio sets and a safe containing the boat's codes and cyphers. The signals office was both the most spacious and the quietest workspace in the boat, but not the most fragrant, for across the passageway was the galley, in which

Triumph's single chef turned out sixty cooked meals twice a day with cold meals and snacks in between.

Aft of the galley the pressure hull was filled with machinery. The first compartment contained a pair of 900 kw diesel engines so large that there was just space to walk between them. Here the artificers ruled supreme, with stokers to help them manage supplies of fuel, water and lubricating oil, and to do the grunt work of lifting and shifting heavy components when repairs were needed. Next in line came the Motor Room, in which the power from a large bank of lead acid batteries, which ran below most of the boat's internal deck, flowed through massive copper breakers into two 1,000 kw electric motors beneath its deck plating. *Triumph* was propelled by her diesel engines while surfaced, and her electric motors while dived. Astern of the Motor Room was another sailors' mess, this time for the boat's sixteen junior stokers and her chef, Cornelius O' Brien. Astern of that lay a small space, whose deckhead sloped down to deck level, containing her steering motors, the watertight glands through which her propellor shafts reached the sea, and a set of air compressors used to top up the high-pressure air tanks she used to reach the surface after each dive.

Inside her pressure hull *Triumph* contained all she needed to float, move and fight, for up to five weeks at a time. For most of her crew this little world would be all they'd see on patrol, for only her officers and a handful of seamen would spend time on the bridge while she recharged her batteries. Stoker George Woodward of HMS *Thule* later wrote 'if you're in the control room you know what's going on, but in the engine room you haven't an idea. That's the worst part of it. Your mind starts working'.[4] Whether dived or surfaced *Triumph* was like a burrow – permeated with a warm fragrant fug of diesel fuel, cooking, cigarette smoke, bilge water, sharp-scented gases flowing off the batteries, and of course the combined scent of sixty largely unwashed men wearing the same clothing for weeks at a time. These men formed small tribes – the seamen, the artificers (tiffs, in naval vernacular), the stokers, the senior rates and the wardroom officers. It was said that one could detect a submariner ashore by smell from thirty yards, though the men in the boat quickly became acclimatized to their atmosphere. One of the reasons men volunteered for the dirty and dangerous work of a submariner was that they had to set aside their tribal loyalties to work as a highly integrated team, because they knew that a single mistake by a single man was enough to sink the boat and kill everyone.

Outside the pressure hull, *Triumph*'s electric motors were connected to a pair of bronze propellers. *Triumph* had no gearboxes – her electric motors drove the propellers directly. On the surface, diesel power was provided by clutching the diesel motors to the forward ends of the shafts. The diesels could only be operated in one direction – ahead – so if *Triumph* wanted to go astern, she had to de-clutch her diesels from the shafts and work with her electric motors, which could run in both directions. Placed at her bow and stern were two pairs of small hydroplanes which acted as underwater wings to direct the hull up or down while dived. The effect of these planes on *Triumph*'s depth was extremely sensitive. They were operated by hydraulic pressure from large wheels in the control room. Using them, the two planesmen (one operating the aft pair, the other the forward pair) could keep *Triumph* within six inches of an ordered depth in even rough seas. Above the control room were two additional torpedo tubes; they were there to give an extra two shots that could be fired ahead if a sufficiently valuable target appeared. These tubes were loaded in harbour, and, once fired, remained empty until she returned to reload.

Higher still were *Triumph*'s bridge and gun platform, for use when surfaced. Both were reached by ladders from inside her pressure hull. Strong pressure-tight hatches were placed at the upper and lower ends of the ladder spaces. The bridge was used as a command position when *Triumph* was surfaced and was also the place where four lookouts took station in wartime to search intently for surface and air contacts. Forward of the bridge, and a few feet below it, *Triumph*'s four-inch gun was a significant weapon. It sat in a small rotating turret to protect its crew from weather and shrapnel, which could be aimed swiftly to port or starboard. The gun threw a twenty-two-pound high explosive shell accurately out to four miles – the maximum distance that a man on the bridge could see before the earth's curve dipped the surface out of sight. With her gun's crew well worked up, *Triumph* could surface and fire six aimed shots in less than sixty seconds, with the first shot getting away just five seconds after she broke surface. Armed with torpedoes and guns and trained to perfection, *Triumph* was an apex ambush predator, both dived and surfaced.

Back inside the pressure hull the main deck ran at approximately the widest part of the circular hull, giving a maximum headroom inside of eight feet but more often five or six feet. Below this deck a 150-tonne bank of lead-acid batteries stored power to drive her electric motors and other equipment. Also below the main deck were her magazine, with 100 four-inch shells, her food stores, and miscellaneous auxiliary equipment spaces, including one for her electrical gyro compass.

At war, *Triumph*'s normal routine was to spend nights on the surface running her two diesel engines, one to drive the boat at about ten knots, the other to drive one of her electric motors as a generator to feed fresh current into her battery bank. A couple of hours before dawn each day she would shut off her diesels and dive, to spend the day moving at a walking pace on her two electric motors, waiting for a target to present itself. *Triumph* had no alternative to staying dived in daylight, for the Mediterranean was well patrolled by Axis aircraft, and to stay on the surface under air attack would be suicidal. Also, if her position was known and reported, no Axis ships would come within reach of her torpedoes. This routine left enough spare charge in her batteries for an attack, when she might extravagantly consume battery power to move quickly to a firing position, or to escape a counterattack, and for a few extra hours in reserve for emergencies.

Electric power was always a scarce resource. The other scarce resource was breathable air. *Triumph* had compressed air tanks for pushing water out of her ballast tanks (to surface) but no air tanks dedicated to life support. Her batteries could not provide enough electrical power to run an electrolyser to extract oxygen from seawater. So, when she shut her bridge hatch and dived in the twilight of each day on patrol, her crew just had the half million litres of air she took down with her to last them until she next surfaced. The critical factor was not so much the amount of oxygen available in *Triumph*'s air, but the amount of carbon dioxide her crew breathed out. On diving, *Triumph*'s air contained less than 0.5 per cent of carbon dioxide. Humans can work more or less normally with concentrations of carbon dioxide up to about three per cent (the exact maximum level is personal to each person, older people have less tolerance). At higher percentages, men lose consciousness, and at higher levels still, they die. An average man breathes out nineteen litres of carbon dioxide per hour. In *Triumph* it took just seventeen hours for the percentage of carbon dioxide in her air to reach the critical three per cent level.[5] A couple of additional hours could be claimed by spreading a carbon dioxide absorbent chemical, Protosorb, on gauze trays in her messes, but in essence, on each dive, *Triumph* took and held a giant breath.

These circumstances combined to mean that *Triumph* could, at a stretch, stay dived for seventeen hours and still operate efficiently, but at the end of that period, much of her crew's attention would be focussed only on breathing and staying conscious. In consequence, smoking (almost every man aboard smoked, since cigarettes were supplied duty free) was banned when dived. In any case, after several hours underwater, there was too little oxygen in the air to light a match.

If air, electricity and living space were in short supply, diesel fuel was not. *Triumph*'s tanks could hold 130 tonnes of diesel, enough to sail 8,000 miles on the surface over a month or more. In the Mediterranean, fuel was never a problem. The base at Malta lay within 500 miles of its target patrol areas. Alexandria and Gibraltar were within 1,000 miles. *Triumph*'s range would have allowed her to sail the Mediterranean end to end twice on a single refuel. And supplies of diesel, even at Malta under siege, were equally unworrying, at least during 1941; 1942 was another matter. Malta was so well-supplied with diesel that Mediterranean submarines were sometimes used as tankers to carry aviation fuel to Malta in their half-empty fuel tanks.[6]

Triumph was a large modern submarine and therefore built with freshwater tanks large enough to provide some twenty litres per man per day. Even her crew's addiction to tea made little dent in the provision, leaving a generous supply for personal hygiene, but the culture of the submarine service was formed a generation before, in much smaller submarines, with no spare freshwater; that culture included a belief that a proper submariner should be a stranger to soap while on patrol. Hence, *Triumph*'s crew took the minimum clothing to sea, wore it without change, and washed only their hands and faces. Uniform rules did not apply on patrol (officers were expected to dress slightly more smartly, though no more cleanly). In any case, living cheek by jowl with a large amount of machinery constantly leaking diesel, oil and grease would have made cleanliness a losing battle.

Triumph's arrival at Malta in January 1941 was a small part of a large concentration of forces, initiated by the Admiralty across the whole Mediterranean Sea, after Mussolini had joined Germany's war in June 1940. Up until that point, the Mediterranean had been one segment of the long sea route that connected Britain with the eastern parts of her Empire. Until June 1940 troops, food and raw materials flowing from Australia, India, the Persian Gulf and Burma to Britain's shops, factories, refineries and training grounds took the short cut through the Suez Canal and sailed the 2,000-mile length of the Mediterranean to the strait of Gibraltar, from where it was a shorter 1,300-mile dash to Liverpool. The alternative route, around South Africa, added 7,000 miles to the voyage home – twenty days through waters well within reach of the Kreigsmarine's larger U-boats.

Italy's entry into the war closed the short cut, for it passed only 100 miles south of Sicily – within easy range of attack from aircraft, surface ships and submarines, and vulnerable throughout to the thousands of mines Italy swiftly laid in Mediterranean waters around Malta and Sicily (over 10,000 in the first month of the war, and many thousands more later on).[7] No amount of escort could guarantee the safe passage of merchant ships along the Mediterranean.

The normal east-west Mediterranean traffic was immediately replaced by three new sea routes, all vital to Italy's war. In 1911, Italy had won the provinces of Cyrenaica and Tripolitania on Africa's northern coast from the Ottoman Empire, to form the colony of Italian North Africa or Italian Libya. Here, two Italian armies of a quarter of a million men were available for an Axis attack on Egypt. If the offensive was successful, the British would be driven out of Egypt, losing the large secure port of Alexandria and the Suez Canal in the process, and have no base from which to resist a follow-on attack further east to the Anglo-Iranian Oil Company's fields which lay at the head of the Persian Gulf. Axis success there would put Anglo-Iranian's oil production (200,000 barrels per day)[8] into German and Italian hands. Even today, Axis daily oil consumption during the war is a question of uncertainty, but it is fair to say that Anglo-Iranian's fields were capable of supplying the whole Axis war machine on land, in the air, and at sea. These fields were less important to Britain because most of Britain's oil was produced in America and Venezuela, but the Mediterranean fleet and the Allied troops and aircraft in Egypt depended on Anglo-Iranian oil, transported west to Egypt by a single pipeline, for their survival.

The possible prize was impressive, but Mussolini's first moves were not. After declaring war, Italian forces crossed the border into Egypt, but only just, for they swiftly dug themselves into desert fortifications and stopped to await events. Waiting was not as passive a strategy as it seems today. The British position in Egypt was politically far from secure. Nominally, Egypt was an independent semi-constitutional kingdom with its own government of Egyptian ministers, working under what the Empire considered a 'protectorate'. Most of Egypt's underclass and middle class – professionals, managers, workers, peasants and the poor – wanted the British gone. It would have taken very little in the way of setbacks for Britain's tenuous hold on Egypt to have been upset by a mass independence movement.

From the start of the war Egypt's Prime Minister, Ali Maher, had been equivocal over whether he preferred Britain or the Axis as an overlord: 'The [British] Embassy soon realized that Ali Maher's actions were designed to tell the Axis powers that, although forced to cooperate with Britain, he was covertly thwarting them wherever possible.'[9] That said, Egyptians were wary of falling under Italian rule as well, having watched the literal rape of Libya and Libyans by Count Graziani's army when it suppressed a rebellion in Fezzan in 1930.

The Egyptians were not Britain's only problem in the Middle East. A considerable contingent of French civilians was present in Egypt (French interests owned a majority of the shares in the Suez Canal), and in the port of Alexandria lay the French battleship *Lorraine* and her escorting destroyers. Just across Palestine's northern border, in Syria, a French army of 37,000 men had declared for Vichy. The Vichy government was nominally neutral but highly amenable to pressure from Germany. A new and powerful squadron of Vichy battleships lay at the naval base of Oran. When this fleet refused to defect from Vichy to the Allied cause, Churchill ordered its destruction, swiftly carried out by Admiral Cunningham and his Mediterranean fleet on 2 July 1940. Naturally provoked by Britain's aggression, other Vichy forces became a significant threat. Admiral Cunningham reached an *entente* of neutrality with Admiral Godefroy, commander of the French squadron in Alexandria, whose men spent the war living aboard their ships with full pay and shore leave in exchange for a studied inactivity, but Godefroy's ships remained in full fighting order and might have changed sides to Vichy at any moment. The garrison in Syria was another matter, until neutralized in the middle of 1941.

Italian success in Africa might also persuade neutral Turkey to join the Axis, and if Britain coerced the King of Egypt into declaring war on the

Axis the inevitable resultant bombing of Muslim Cairo might lead other Muslim states (including Turkey) to blame Britain for bringing the war to Islam and to take the Axis side. So, for Britain, Egypt was a powder keg threatened by a large Italian force in the west, a possible Vichy force to the north, and a more distant Turkish threat north of that. Italy's desert army was supplied by sea along the short north-south route from Sicily to Tripoli, which quickly became Italy's most vital sea corridor.

Italy had two other vital sea routes. A month after beginning his offensive towards Egypt in the Western Desert, Mussolini had ordered the Italian forces, then occupying Albania, to attack Greece. The arrival of fuel, food and ammunition for this force depended on ships making a 100-mile hop across the Adriatic Sea – short but vulnerable to attack by the Royal Navy. And finally, Italy had no indigenous supplies of oil. Every gallon of fuel burned by her tanks, air force and navy had to come from somewhere else. With Suez and Gibraltar closed to her, the only practical sources of oil were the fields on Romania's Black Sea coast and at Baku in Soviet Azerbaijan. Oil arrived from both sources by ship after sailing 1,000 miles through waters within easy reach of British ships and aircraft based at Alexandria and Malta.

One belligerent almost completely absent from the Mediterranean scene in 1940 was Germany. At the end of 1940, the French Mediterranean coast was controlled by Vichy France and was in practice neutral, though it favoured Germany. Spain was also tenuously neutral, as were France's colonies in Algeria, Tunisia and Syria. Austria had lost its Adriatic coast with the fall of the Austro-Hungarian Empire in 1919. Germany's only access to the Mediterranean was through the straits of Gibraltar – intensely patrolled by the Royal Navy and the RAF. In any case, Germany's navy was fully engaged elsewhere, and Hitler felt comfortable relying on Italy's large and modern fleet, centred on its six new powerful battleships. In a nod to the Roman emperors he admired and wished to emulate, Mussolini called the Mediterranean 'Mare Nostrum' – 'our sea' – and Germany's Ober Kommando der Wermacht was happy to leave it that way.

Mussolini's decision to attack Greece in October 1940 flowed from a muddled cocktail of pride, pragmatism and a desire to show Hitler that Italians too could take the 'living space' they needed. The pride was born from the fact that Mussolini had become dictator of Italy a full ten years before Hitler had reached the same position in Germany. Mussolini thought of Hitler as the junior partner in the fascist 'firm', but he could see that Hitler did not agree. Looking around for a short, sharp victory with which to show that Italy's leader was the equal to Germany's, he thought he had found it in Albania and Greece.

The pragmatic component of Mussolini's decision was founded in Italy's distaste for Greece's Anglophilic nature. Greece allowed its merchant fleet to be used to supply Britain and allowed the Royal Navy ready access to the Aegean Sea, Italy's main supply route for Russian and Romanian oil. In addition, Italy already possessed the Dodecanese Islands (Rhodes and Kos) on the far side of the Aegean, whose distance from Italy rendered them vulnerable to both Greek and British attack. Mussolini concluded that Greece should be brought under the firm political control of the Axis, and perhaps even fully occupied if necessary. Topping off Mussolini's cocktail of ambitions was a strident belief in Rome that Greece, with roughly one-tenth of Italy's population and economic power, would be an easy victim. After all, Italy had overrun neighbouring Albania in just three days. Greek politics were fractured by internal division, and its army was weakened by political purges and a poor economy.

Mussolini expected Greece to fall quickly and painlessly, but his invasion of Greece was delayed by the demands of the advance towards Egypt, and by other debates between himself and Hitler over priorities and agendas, so it was not until October 1940 that the date was set, in a general staff meeting that has been described as 'one of the most superficial and dilettantish discussions of high-risk military strategy ever recorded'.[10] When the attack began, on 28 October 1940, Greece fell neither quickly nor painlessly. Shelving their bitter domestic disputes, Greeks immediately unified against the Italian invasion. The attack, launched into Greece's Pindus Mountain range at the onset of winter, failed quickly and completely. A drive through the Pindus today reveals why. The frontier runs across steep, rocky, roadless mountains rising to 8,000 feet and divided by deep, sheer valleys and gorges. Every bluff and saddle can be turned into a strong point. Vehicles are of limited use. Greek troops found they could outflank Italian forces by using the high ridges to move on foot and mule behind Italian forces in the valleys and outflank them. Winter in the Pindus feels remarkably un-Mediterranean. Deep snow prevents all road movement, while strong winds freeze the blood. Even in May, snow still covers the tops.

In October 1940 the Italians attacked into a gathering winter which would turn into one of the coldest in memory. After a week of fighting, the deepest Italian advance was a thirty-mile salient on a front of about six miles. Elsewhere along the frontier the average advance was between three and six miles. Italy's attack ground to a frozen halt after a month, and by the end of 1940 Greek forces were advancing into Albania, and almost everywhere had pushed Italian forces back at their start lines. By 6 January 1941, when *Triumph* was leaving Gibraltar for her voyage to Malta, the battle had died away as men turned their attention to surviving the freezing weather and bringing supplies up through the white wilderness. Both sides were waiting to see what the thaw might bring.

The Allies' three bases in the Mediterranean were fully equipped with dockyards or floating docks, technicians and workshops to support ships of all sizes, from a submarine to a battleship. Gibraltar, 1,000 miles from Italy's mainland, was out of range of an Italian air attack. Alexandria was a little nearer, with Rhodes less than 400 miles away, but so far had suffered little from the attentions of Italy's air force, the Regia Aeronautica. Malta was on Italy's doorstep. Its first air raid arrived the day after Italy entered the war but was light and ineffectual. Air attacks continued to be a minor distraction until January 1941, when the Tenth Flying Corps of the Luftwaffe (Fliegerkorps X) began to arrive in Sicily to increase the pressure. At the start of 1941, as *Triumph* was sailing from Gibraltar for Malta, 200 German aircraft arrived in Sicily. Their first large raid took place two days before *Triumph*'s arrival, when they tried to finish off the aircraft carrier *Illustrious*, which had limped into Grand Harbour at the end of the Operation Excess convoy which *Triumph* had been escorting. Malta was to suffer almost daily raids for the next three years and become the most-bombed place on the planet,[11] but the dockyard continued to operate throughout the war.

The Allied strategy was to keep hold of Egypt, protect the Anglo-Persian oil fields, keep Turkey neutral, and keep Greece free from Axis control. Those goals required the Allies to contest control of the Mediterranean, not for use as a trade route but to isolate Italian forces in Libya and Greece, and to cut Italy's oil supply line, defend the base in Malta and maintain Allied positions in Egypt and Palestine, whose loss would lay the Persian Gulf open to Axis occupation.

In 1939, only three of the Royal Navy's sixty submarines were based on Malta. The Admiralty quickly ordered ten large submarines of the Fourth Submarine Flotilla to move from their peacetime base in Hong Kong to Alexandria, as a precautionary measure. This force compares with a total Italian submarine force of 120, of which no less than forty-nine were on patrol in the Mediterranean on the day Italy entered the war in June 1940. The submarine war quickly drew blood, most of it British. Through 1940, Britain lost no fewer than nine submarines in the Mediterranean, out of seventy-eight departures on patrol from Mediterranean bases – a mortality rate of almost twelve per cent per departure. Of the 498 men manning those nine boats, 446 died and fifty-two were captured. This appalling mortality rate was not a uniquely Mediterranean feature. In home waters, the Royal Navy lost thirteen submarines in 1940, and 393 men out of their total crew of 563. By the end of 1940, the Navy had lost over a third of its 1939 submarine fleet and a quarter of its submarine personnel either to death or capture.

This rate of loss meant that if a typical boat was in commission for a year and carried out fourteen patrols during that year, its chances of survival were slightly less than one in five. *Triumph*'s crew, bringing her alongside the submarine base at Malta in the pale morning light of 12 January 1941, knew these statistics all too well. Submarine losses were publicly reported in the press, and in any case, the men lost were mostly friends and shipmates, for the whole Royal Navy's seagoing submarine service in 1939 contained just over 2,500 men. One-third of those were already dead. Sammy Woods and his crew can only have thought that their year in the Mediterranean was tantamount to a suicide mission.

It was not all bad news. One item on the strategic to-do list – find and sink Italy's Battle Fleet – had effectively been ticked off six weeks earlier when Admiral Cunningham's twenty-one Fairey Swordfish torpedo bombers had disabled three of Italy's six battleships at Taranto and proved to the other three that they were fatally vulnerable to air attack if they dared put to sea. But Italy's submarines and mine-layers were still busy everywhere.

It was into this busy but lethal arena that *Triumph* sailed in January 1941. As she went alongside her berth at the Malta submarine base on Manoel Island on 12 January, her ship's company undoubtedly felt as much apprehension as excitement for their coming year under the wine-dark sea. For one man, Stoker Harry Hague, the year was to end too quickly. A few days after arriving at the Manoel Island base *Triumph* was docked for a regular inspection in Grand Harbour. She was both unlucky and lucky. The dock was in the naval dockyard, close to the carrier *Illustrious* and the merchant ship MV *Essex*. Fliegerkorps X was determined to finish the job it had started by sinking *Illustrious*. On 16 January, about a hundred Luftwaffe dive bombers flew in to attack *Illustrious*. Remarkably, the aircraft carrier survived without being hit, but *Essex* was less lucky, receiving a bomb hit in her engine room, setting her on fire. In her cargo holds lay 4,000 tonnes of ammunition, vital to Malta's defence, but also the possible source of an explosion equal in violence to one half of a Hiroshima bomb right in the centre of the dockyard. *Triumph*'s duty watch became firefighters. Harry Hague was among them but failed to return. At the age of thirty-five, Harry was *Triumph*'s first loss,[12] and an unwelcome reminder to her ship's company that the Mediterranean was a deadly place to fight the Axis.

Triumph and her sisters quickly fell into an operating routine that prevailed for most of the war. A patrol would be planned to last from fourteen to twenty-one days. The first two or three days were spent sailing fast, and largely surfaced, day and night at twelve to fourteen knots, to reach the patrol area quickly, usually close to the shores of Axis territory. Here she would find concentrations of merchant traffic leaving or arriving at known major ports. Hunting targets in the open sea was generally considered pointless – too much sea and too few ships made for a thin time. These surface dashes were made with constant, frequent zig-zagging to prevent a lurking Axis submarine from getting an accurate target lock for its torpedoes, and with four men permanently and intensely watching both skies and the sea surface for dangers. With good lookouts, aircraft were a manageable threat – during the day *Triumph*'s lookouts could see an enemy aircraft at seven miles, at least two minutes' flight time away and more usually four, allowing ample time for her to dive out of sight in less than thirty seconds.

On arrival in the patrol area – known as her 'billet' – the routine changed. Daylight was spent dived at three knots, searching for targets with her powerful binocular telescope and her sensitive hydrophones. The officer of the watch would bring her to periscope depth every twenty minutes for an all-round look for a target, and then dive to eighty feet, where she blended into the darkening depths of the Mediterranean.[13] At these times just ten men were on watch to drive the boat. Everyone else was either asleep or in their mess playing cards or uckers.[14]

Triumph was a daytime predator but largely a nocturnal creature. Once darkness had properly fallen, she spent her nights surfaced and running on her diesels at ten knots to recharge empty batteries and refresh her air. During these nighttime sessions, she usually used her speed to relocate to a new billet to keep the Axis guessing where she might be. Over the ten front-line days of an average patrol, *Triumph* could easily cover 1,000 miles of sea. Having no radar, a night attack was almost impossible, and if a contact was found at night, *Triumph*'s usual reaction was to move away as quickly and quietly as she could to avoid revealing her presence.

Triumph's crew reversed day and night. Breakfast was served shortly after surfacing, and the main meal of the day, dinner, each side of the watch change at midnight. Dinner was preceded by the sacred ritual of the daily rum issue to all sailors and NCOs. Officers did not receive rum, but usually enjoyed a single glass of duty-free sherry from the wardroom bar cupboard. The rum was issued to *Triumph* at fifty per cent alcohol, but the ration (called the tot, of seventy-one millilitres) was diluted four to one with water and was usually issued at 2300 every day. As the only alcohol allowed to non-officers on board, it was both welcome and sacred, and its issue, marked with the loudspeaker broadcast[15] of 'Up Spirits', marked the passing of each of the ten to twenty days of a patrol.

Boats spent the front-line part of their patrols in enemy waters in this day-night routine searching for Axis merchant traffic. Occasionally a signal would come out from Alexandria, via the powerful long wave transmitter at Rugby in the UK, directing a boat to a specific task – usually generated from an Ultra decrypt, though the source of the order was the deepest and darkest of secrets – or to a new billet, prompting a nighttime rush to the new job. *Triumph* almost never signalled back to her flotilla, for to do so risked compromising her location.

With Italy's major warships reluctant to put to sea, *Triumph*'s primary purpose in the Mediterranean became attacks on Axis merchant ships. Axis forces in Africa needed some 80,000 tonnes of stores per month; the average merchant ship size at the time meant one ship per day crossed one way or the other from Italy to Libya, and back. A similar traffic ran across the narrows from Italy to Albania, and at longer intervals a tanker would sail to or from the Black Sea oil fields. In addition to this heavy traffic, the Mediterranean was an ants' nest of smaller coasting traffic moving goods and men along the shores of Italy and Libya. Fishing vessels were exempt from attack (by agreement with the Axis in all theatres), and while Italian destroyers were fair game, they were considered too fast, too agile and too alert to be worth attacking, except in unusual circumstances.

The original intention of the Admiralty was that the T-class submarines would attack major enemy surface warships. Since these would be heavily escorted by a screen of destroyers, and would be moving at about twenty knots, attacks were expected to take place at long range (two to three miles, up to 6,000 yards). Long ranges meant that the torpedoes would take four minutes to reach their targets; in turn, that meant calculations of the target's predicted position would be necessarily imprecise, with estimates compounding on guesses multiplied by uncertainties. Even the use of a mechanical targeting computer did not guarantee an accurate prediction of where the target would be four minutes in the future, and to obtain a hit required predicting that point to within half the length of the target, about 150 yards for a cruiser.

With all these uncertainties, to obtain a reasonable chance of a hit, it was planned that the T-class submarines would fire a salvo of up to ten torpedoes in succession, at intervals of about ten seconds, to increase the allowable error by a factor of ten to nearly a mile. A well-practised team should be able to predict the target's position that accurately.

The salvo was a 'hosepipe' affair, each torpedo being fired on exactly the same track as the one ahead of it.[16] The T-class was therefore designed with ten forward-facing torpedo tubes. Six were built into the pressure hull. Two were placed outside the pressure hull in a large bulbous bulge over the bows, and the final two, also outside the pressure hull, sat alongside the bridge structure. *Triumph* had been given her full ten tubes at build, but when Sammy Woods looked over his bows his view lacked the bulbous hump containing the two external bow tubes that had been installed in *Triumph* just two years before. With a slight shudder he would have recalled that in December 1939, on one of her first patrols close to the coast of Germany, *Triumph* had run head-on into a floating German mine which had blown her bows clean off. By an extraordinary slice of luck (or good design, if her architect had been asked) the explosion failed to crack her pressure hull or to detonate any of the eight torpedo warheads a few feet away. Missing eighteen feet of her bows, *Triumph* stayed afloat and managed to get home alive.

The dockyard, in a great hurry to get her back to sea, decided to sacrifice her two external bow tubes for a quick turnaround and sent her back to the fleet without them. Sammy's forward view was now of a slightly ugly, truncated bow. He never had cause to regret the loss of the two extra torpedoes, but he did appreciate that *Triumph*'s smaller bows cut through heavy seas more elegantly, and added a knot to her top speed.

In the Mediterranean in 1941, *Triumph* expected little opportunity to make the dashing attack on an enemy battlefleet that her designers had anticipated. Half of Italy's battleships lay disabled in Taranto. The other half rarely put to sea since they had no aircraft carrier to provide air cover, limited fuel supplies, and a sanguine view of their chances against the Mediterranean Fleet's battleships, which their spies told them were waiting for them in Alexandria. *Triumph*'s war would be very different to what her builders had intended. Her targets would be merchant ships and tankers carrying fuel, food, men and ammunition from Italy to Libya and Albania, and fuel from the Black Sea to Italy. These usually sailed alone or in convoys of two or three ships. Each convoy was heavily escorted, usually with two or three corvettes or destroyers, one or two smaller fast patrol vessels, and constant air patrol above and ahead of the convoy.[17] The escorts weaved to and fro at about a mile and a half from the merchants, right in the position from which *Triumph* wanted to fire her torpedoes. A torpedo fired from outside the escort screen would almost certainly miss, so *Triumph* had to penetrate the screen undetected, snatching periscope sights at intervals of a few minutes to generate a reasonably accurate predicted position for the target.

Running at forty knots, a torpedo fired at one and a half miles would reach its target in 135 seconds. The target, usually about 100 yards in length, occupied just one degree of arc from *Triumph* and allowed a maximum aiming error of just fifty yards left or right. On firing, Woods therefore had to predict the position of the centre of the target 135 seconds ahead. Merchant ships in convoy in the Mediterranean usually sailed at about twelve knots, or six yards per second. So, between firing and arrival, the target might move 800 yards. The target's speed had to be estimated using visual clues – principally the size and location of her bow wave. If Woods guessed the target speed incorrectly by a single knot, his aim would be off by seventy yards either way, generating a near miss ahead or astern.

It was also necessary to guess the target's heading. If Woods' guess was wrong by just fifteen degrees (easily done) the target would be 200 yards nearer or further than calculated, changing the torpedo run time by ten seconds, during which the target would have moved either sixty yards more or less, again, a near miss ahead or astern.

The exact features of every attack, all its observations, numbers and comments, were recorded in detail in real time during the attack by an Able Seaman tucked into a corner of the crowded control room, writing everything down in pencil in a notebook. These notes were used to recreate the attack in the airy comfort of the Flotilla staff office to detect patterns of error, or success, that could be used to improve the captain's aim next time and be shared with other captains. If a submarine captain was a consistently bad shot, he might be sacked and replaced. There was nowhere to hide – the flotilla commander, Captain Sydney Raw in Alexandria – added his own detailed commentary to the report of the patrol to the analysis of each attack, and the whole package was flown as soon as possible to the head of the submarine service in London, Admiral Sir Max Horton, whose own staff would again pore over the attack making their own judgements and disseminating advice to submarine captains generally. Horton was no armchair admiral. During the previous war, he had become one of the Royal Navy's most successful submarine captains. When he was crouched at the attack periscope carrying out an attack, at the back of Woods' mind was the knowledge that every detail of his actions would be examined and judged by his Admiral, who he knew personally. This was not an example of the 'long screwdriver' in action, but an attempt, largely successful, to make the submarine service learn from collective experience as quickly as possible. Admiral Horton had been badly shaken by the devastation inflicted on his command during 1940, and by the loss of officers and men who were his personal friends, for the submarine service was a small tribe.[18] Now, in 1941, he was desperate to preserve his men and boats, and to ensure that the lethal risks they had to take at least paid back in enemy ships sunk and lessons learned. A submarine that was lost on patrol took all of the tactical knowledge it had gained to the seabed with it, so it was essential to spread the knowledge that survived as quickly as possible.

In an attack, a submarine captain covered the inevitable errors by firing multiple torpedoes in a 'hosepipe' stream, spaced so that each torpedo's aiming point overlapped the target by less than a ship's length. In practice, that usually meant firing at ten-second intervals or less. Torpedoes were not 100 per cent reliable. They might leave the tube and dive immediately to the deeps. On occasions, they would explode shortly after starting their run (possibly because their sensitive triggers hit some drifting marine debris). At worst, their steering gyro would freeze, locking the rudder into a hard turn, and they would circle back towards their parent submarine. There is no record of a boat actually sinking herself with a circling torpedo, not least because if it had happened, there would be no survivors to record it, but several submarine memoirs from the war mention circling torpedoes. *Urge*'s patrol reports record not one but two circlers on different patrols, which detonated beneath the boat. There are nineteen lost boats whose fates are unknown because their wrecks have yet to be found, and it is entirely possible that one or more of these sank herself.

If *Triumph*'s periscope or the tracks of her torpedoes were seen during her attack, or her dark shadow just twenty feet below the surface was detected by one of the escorting aircraft, it would take only thirty or forty seconds for the enemy unit to close the range and attack with depth charges. Detection was not the only risk. If Woods misjudged his approach, he could easily find himself under the bows of an escort. Ramming was invariably fatal to the submarine and all aboard. One blessing was that, in 1941 at least, Italian warships had only passive sonar, which worked best when the listening ship was moving slowly or stopped in the water. Before she declared her presence with a torpedo, *Triumph* could expect the escorts to be moving too fast to hear much on their sonars, but a sharp lookout would easily see her periscope if he looked in the right direction at the right time.

Triumph's attack routine, therefore, was to loiter at periscope depth across likely merchant ship routes, waiting for a target to appear. An attack was only possible if she found herself ahead of the target's track, because she lacked the speed and the battery power to chase after a distant target while dived. Using the small monocular attack periscope to snatch glances at the target and escorts in four-second 'looks', Woods would try to manoeuvre *Triumph* between the escorts to within a mile of the merchant ship. Here he would have just 120 seconds to take a last look to confirm his calculations, point his submarine on the firing track, and wait for the target to come 'on' to the calculated firing bearing. Any longer and the target would be past *Triumph* and moving away from her at a relative speed of nine knots, taking her out of range completely within ten minutes. In this position a submarine might fire a 'chasing' shot, because her torpedoes, moving at forty knots, could easily catch up with a merchantman, but firing at a ship's stern gave an angle so fine that a miss was almost guaranteed, as was the Admiral's displeasure at the waste of a precious torpedo.

As the bearing came 'on', and assuming that the target had not 'zigged' or 'zagged' off her previous track, Woods would order his torpedoes away. 'Fire One.' A second later, his order would be relayed to the man sitting at the torpedo tube doors, who would push the firing lever. A muffled thump from the fore ends was audible throughout the silent boat. A popping of the ears as the compressed air, used to push the torpedo out of the tube, vented back into the pressure hull ... perhaps a ten-second interval ...'fire two'... and so on until the required number of torpedoes had gone. The usual number was three or four for a larger or more valuable or distant ship, and two or three for a smaller or nearer target.

The calculations of *Triumph*'s firing angle were carried out by gunnery officer Lieutenant Robert Douglas-Don, on an electromechanical calculator in the control room, known as the 'fruit machine'. This had settings for the target's estimated speed, range, course and length, and outputted the angle ahead of the target at which *Triumph* had to aim. It also generated the predicted torpedo run time. At forty knots and a firing range of one mile, that was about forty seconds. Douglas-Don, a career officer of slim diminutive build but already the veteran of a major surface action in which he had won a Distinguished Service Cross,[19] held a stopwatch whose hand ticked off the seconds of the torpedo's run. If the attack was a success, everyone in the boat would hear the sound of the distant 'clang' of a torpedo detonation. Occasionally, the vagaries of sound transmission in water would prevent the sound of a hit reaching *Triumph*, but a quick look through the periscope would fill the gap. Failing that, belated congratulations on return to harbour would confirm the kill.

As soon as the first torpedo of a salvo left *Triumph* her life became endangered. The process of expelling a ton and a half of torpedo from its tube created a ten-metre-wide splash mark on the surface above the boat, which was immediately obvious to the lookouts and pilots of the escorting ships and aircraft. Being little more than a mile away, sometimes much less, *Triumph* could expect a counterattack to arrive within thirty or forty seconds of the launch of her first torpedo. To avoid it, Woods had two choices: speed up and evade, or slow down and hide. Speed increased the swish-swish-swish noise from *Triumph*'s propellers whose bearing (but not range) could be easily tracked by an escorting destroyer, but took *Triumph* away from the revealing datum point of her torpedo splashes.

Stealth was a better tactic. Diving hard and turning away from the target took *Triumph* out of sight of attacking aircraft and increased the vertical distance and thus the time that incoming depth charges would have to sink before detonating, which substantially muddied the destroyer's timing and reduced the chance of a fatal hit. On the debit side, diving took *Triumph* closer to her crush depth, eliminating a margin of safety if she was hit by a depth charge or sent out of control by a near miss. Increasing water pressure also added to the danger; her pressure hull's ability to absorb shock from a depth charge was effectively the sum of the external pressure plus the explosive shock. As water pressure increased, it took less explosive shock to crack her hull. The risk was compounded further because deeper denser water transmits shock more effectively.

Diving created a sonic problem as well. As a submarine dives, her hull compresses and she becomes denser. Without an adjustment, her higher density would cause her to sink. To counteract this, she must pump hundreds of litres of water from her internal ballast tanks out to sea, overcoming the external sea pressure to do so. The powerful pumps used inevitably make a noise, sometimes lots of noise, clearly audible on the sensitive passive sonar sets of the escorts. In the aftermath of an attack, with escorts and aircraft bearing down on her, intent on her death, the survival of *Triumph* and her sixty crew depended entirely on the second-to-second decisions made by Sammy Woods.

A hunt might pass in a few minutes, or it might continue for an hour if sonar conditions allowed the hunters to stay in contact. The Axis might drop just a few depth charges, or as many as a hundred. The propeller noises of a destroyer overhead are clearly audible inside a submarine, as loud as the noise of an express diesel train passing a platform at speed. A long counterattack meant repeatedly hearing the hunter's propellers approach, peak, and pass, followed by the detonation of large explosive charges perhaps just yards from the boat. The thirty minutes after making an attack were always the most dangerous moments in *Triumph*'s life. Twenty-six of the seventy-eight British submarines lost during the war were sunk by escorts after attacks, the great majority of them by Italian escorts in the Mediterranean, whose crews became experts in submarine hunting.

If she could survive the half hour after an attack, a submarine could usually sneak away, relying on the fact that once contact with a submarine is lost, it is almost impossible for an escort with only passive sonar to reacquire it. The sea is big, and a submarine is small.

Attacks were a rare event in *Triumph*'s life, most of which was spent waiting for a target to appear. At periscope depth, the officer on the large search periscope spent his watch searching for the masts of targets appearing over the horizon. He was also searching for aircraft. If a passing aircraft even looked as if it might be heading *Triumph*'s way, she would dive to a hundred feet for a while. So long as her officer of the watch was paying close attention to his air search, *Triumph* was at little risk from air attack while dived. But not always. In 1942, one Mediterranean submarine, HMS *Thrasher*, was spotted by a patrolling aircraft at periscope depth during an attack. The aircraft dropped four bombs. One exploded harmlessly near the boat. Two more hit her without exploding but penetrated her deck casing to lodge themselves in the crawl space between her pressure hull and the outer structure of her deck casing. No one in the boat knew anything about these two unexploded bombs until they made their presence known by rattling around in the water flow over her hull. On the surface, two men volunteered to wriggle under the casing to remove the unexploded bombs and drop them into the sea, in full daylight and in full knowledge that if another Axis aircraft arrived on the scene, *Thrasher* would be forced to dive and they would drown under the casing. Luckily, they managed to remove the bombs without detonating them.[20]

Surfaced at night (and in daylight on passage to a patrol area), *Triumph* was as vulnerable to torpedo attack from another dived submarine as any ship. The threat was real, Italy began the war with over 100 submarines of which at least thirty were always on patrol somewhere, and was made worse by the fact that *Triumph*'s lookouts' eyes were only about eighteen feet above sea level, limiting their visual horizon to four miles. To spot a periscope popping above the surface for ten seconds in a rough sea was far from guaranteed by day and impossible at night. *Salpa*'s lookouts failed and paid with their lives.

The remedy against a torpedo attack was to zigzag constantly and to maintain a brisk speed, to make the calculation of a future position nearly impossible, but even zig-zag would be ineffective against a torpedo launched at a very close range. At all times, day, night, surfaced or dived, perhaps the worst danger, because they were ever present, instantly lethal and completely silent, was the sea mine. The mines used in the Mediterranean were very simple but very dangerous. A canister of high explosive about the size of an oil barrel was fitted inside a round or oval watertight shell designed to be marginally buoyant. The outside of the shell was fitted with a choice of trigger device, the simplest being a soft metal horn containing a glass vial of electrically conductive liquid, and the most complex having electrical cables hanging in the water column like the stings of a particularly nasty jellyfish. The mine, generally floating at a pre-set depth of either ten feet (aimed at surface ships and surfaced submarines) or thirty feet (aimed at submarines at periscope depth), could wait for years for a victim. By August 1940, the Italian navy had laid 10,000 mines and would carry on laying them by the thousands each month for the rest of the war.

Because a mine had to support the full weight of its mooring cable, it could not be laid in water much deeper than 1,600 feet,[21] which meant that *Triumph*'s crew could only stop thinking about the threat of mines on the rare occasions they were sailing in very deep water. Ninety per cent of their time was spent in waters capable of holding an unseen minefield. When hit, clicked, or just touched by a passing submarine, the mine's trigger set off its main charge. Since this was usually touching the submarine's pressure hull, and since the charges could be very large (up to 1,100 pounds of high explosive), detonation was almost invariably lethal, cracking the pressure hull and causing a catastrophic instant flood from which few submarines could recover. *Triumph* had the rare distinction of being one of those few, from her 1939 encounter with a mine in the Heligoland Bight. In that incident, she was surfaced and was extremely lucky. Here, in the Mediterranean, her crew knew that a mine strike would almost certainly be fatal and would come completely without warning. The risk of mine strike arose as soon as *Triumph* left her berth (the Axis were not above laying mines by aircraft inside the harbours of Malta and Alexandria) and persisted until she was back alongside twenty days later.

Thanks to Bletchley Park, *Triumph*'s flotilla commander, Captain Sydney Raw in Alexandria, knew where many of the Italian mine fields had been laid – at least those whose laying had been ordered or reported by radio using the Enigma code machine, but many minefields closer to Axis shores were not ordered by radio and were therefore completely unknown to the flotilla crew. Even where a field was revealed by code-breaking, there was an inevitable delay between the decryption at Bletchley Park and the arrival of a signal describing the field in *Triumph*. Later in 1941, this delay would cause a major tragedy with the loss of the cruiser HMS *Neptune*, which sailed into a newly laid minefield off the coast of Tripoli and hit four mines in a single hour before drifting off into the dark and sinking with the loss of all 845 hands but one. The staff at Alexandria knew about the Tripoli field when *Neptune* had sailed, but news of it had not reached *Neptune* in time.

Triumph was fitted with a small mine-detecting sonar set, which in theory should have allowed her to detect and steer clear of minefields. In practice, it appears to have spent much of its time providing false echoes of things that were not mines, including rough water and overfalls, or just reflective anomalies in the water column. In the words of the gunnery officer Lieutenant Douglas-Don: '… mines are such an unknown quantity, and as most of the Mediterranean is a declared minefield, we take little or no notice of them; if we did we would all have been invalided with anxiety neurosis long ago'.[22]

The Italian navy also laid acoustic mines, which were set off by the noise of a passing submarine. It was suggested early on that these might be 'swept' by a boat herself by firing her bridge-mounted Lewis machine guns into the sea surface just ahead of her own track. The experiment worked.[23] Magnetic mines were present too, laid on the approaches to harbours and even inside them by Axis aircraft and fast attack boats. In 1941, Malta lacked a minesweeper with a magnetic sweeping loop, so men were assigned to plot the fall of likely magnetic mines inside Valletta's two harbours so that they could be avoided. When a suitably equipped minesweeper did arrive (the *Gloxinia*), she swiftly swept a dozen mines inside Valletta and more outside.

Most of the time, *Triumph* attacked targets which did not know she was there. Sometimes they could shoot back. If a target was too small to justify the £3,000 cost of a torpedo, or too small and agile to be hit with one, *Triumph* could ambush it with her deck gun, which could also be used to attack targets ashore. In Italy, the main rail lines often ran along the flat and accessible coast, placing steam engines and bridges within range of a submarine's deck gun. If the target could shoot back, or was covered by a shore battery, the risks inherent in an attack rose, for almost every part of a submarine's hull and superstructure was vital to her ability to dive, and a slight hit on the boat in a gun duel presented the serious risk of enough damage to leave her stuck on the surface, there to be sunk in short order.

An operating environment this dangerous was intensely wearing on submariners. Unlike their counterparts ashore or in the air, who might run frightening risks for short periods but then find rest and recuperation in some safety behind the front line, when on patrol, everyone in a submarine knew that they were in literally mortal danger at all times, and that disaster could strike without prelude or warning. They also knew how many of their shipmates had died in submarines in 1940, and that when disaster struck, their chances of escape and rescue were very nearly zero. It is hard to imagine how exhausting and corrosive that experience of permanent risk must have been, but it is possible to see how their leaders managed around it. A large submarine like *Triumph* operated on a roughly six-week cycle. A patrol of two, or at most three, weeks was followed by a period alongside of three or four weeks, to allow the crew to decompress. During these periods, there was much to do to prepare the boat for her next patrol, repairing kit that had broken, or maintaining kit that might break, but there was also much help from the staff at the submarine depot.

In Malta, the depot was an old Venetian quarantine hospital on Manoel Island in Valletta harbour called the Lazaretto.[24] The Lazaretto might have been built as a submarine depot. Three large stone buildings were wrapped around the southern edge of Manoel Island. Along the front of these ran a stone quay, long and deep enough to berth two or three submarines alongside. Outboard of the quay, the navy installed additional moorings, or 'trots', linked to the Lazaretto by narrow gangways. Behind the quay, three airy courtyards housed workshops for refurbishing torpedoes, mess decks, a dining hall and galley. Later in 1941, the depot's commanding officer, Commander George 'Shrimp' Simpson, had caverns dug into the sandstone cliffs behind the Lazaretto to protect men and workshops from bombing. The Lazaretto's walls were covered in ancient graffiti from past residents, including one Lord

Byron who wrote in 1811, 'Adieu thou damned'st quarantine, that gave me fever and the spleen'.[25]

On the Lazaretto's first floor, an airy gallery ran the length of the buildings which became the wardroom's open space. The wardroom lay inboard of this, next to Shrimp Simpson's office. Aged thirty-nine, Simpson was short, almost rotund, with a square, open, uncomplicated face, his eyes perhaps a touch too close together. Simpson was a veteran submariner, aptly sized for his profession at five feet nothing, and nicknamed by all 'Shrimp' from his days as a midshipman on his first battleship. Shrimp had arrived from London to run the Lazaretto just a few days before *Triumph* arrived in January 1941, via an exotic route. First, he crossed the Atlantic by fast troopship, then across the US by train to California, where he took a Pan Am flying boat to Hawaii, then Singapore, and then to Alexandria, and finally Malta. Apart from running the Lazaretto base, Shrimp's job was to act as operational commander for any submarines based at Malta. He quickly received three small 600-tonne U-class boats. These were half the size of *Triumph* and therefore capable of much shorter patrols, but looked ideal for the short-hop missions from Malta north to Sicily, south to Libya, and east to the convoy routes that linked the two.

But the staff in Malta had bigger ideas, and were happy to find *Triumph* resting alongside, fresh and eager for the fight.

Chapter 3

Special Operations – A New Form of Submarine Warfare

When he arrived at the Lazaretto on 8 January, Shrimp found no submarines alongside at all – his three U-class submaries were already at sea and *Triumph* was still a couple of days away. What he did find, two days later, was a half company of exotic newly created commandos under a Captain Taylor. Taylor's letter of appointment referred to a schedule detailing the tasks he was to undertake, but he found that this had been left out of the envelope, so he placed himself under Shrimp's command and moved into the Lazaretto with a collection of collapsible canoes, small arms and 1,000 pounds of high explosive. That same day, *Triumph*, en route to Alexandria, arrived alongside the Lazaretto. Admiral Cunningham's orders allowed Shrimp to task *Triumph* as he saw fit, for a week or two at least. Captain Taylor's men presented an ideal opportunity to do just that, and he asked Sammy Woods to join him in his office to tell him about an entirely new form of submarine warfare.

When the Royal Navy commissioned its first submarine, HMS *Holland 1*, in 1901, the idea of offensive submarine operations was still many years away. *Holland 1* was bought as a training boat to give surface ships a submarine target to practice on. At that time, the operational capabilities of these new submersible boats were tiny, and the idea of offensive operations at all was considered impossible. Possibilities grew as submarines grew in size, armament and operational range, and the navy experimented widely with different tactical ideas. One whole class of large boats was built with steam turbines and heavy guns to serve as part of the battle fleet.[1] Another class was fitted with its own aircraft in a pressure-tight hangar. Early in the war, submarines were used as convoy escorts. These experiments were all failures in their own ways, some of them disastrously so, and by the end of 1940, the tactical use of submarines had narrowed to offensive patrols to sink enemy warships and merchant ships, and to the covert laying of mines in enemy waters.

Shrimp Simpson was one of nature's natural rebels, never accepting a lazy consensus or the obvious answer to a problem. He had joined the submarine service at twenty, as soon as he could, to escape the surface fleet where rebels rarely prospered. Once underwater, he had longed for the freedom to practise the dark arts of the submariner to the fullest potential, but peacetime rules laid down by the battleship-trained naval staff were highly obstructive. Submarines were forbidden to dive after dark to reduce the risk of being run down by surface ships. Worse, on exercise, they were required to burn navigation lights at night, and their practice attacks on the fleet were constrained by caution and risk aversion. After one major pre-war exercise against the Home Fleet, Shrimp had attended the post-exercise conference as one of the submarine commanding officers and reported that he had in fact sunk half the Mediterranean fleet's battleships. The report was unwelcome. Shrimp was told, not too politely, to shut up and sit down.[2] His career survived his impetuosity, probably because his selection for promotion to commander at the young age of thirty-four depended on the opinion of his Flag Officer, Admiral Max Horton, who lived firmly in a world of reality, not illusion. When he arrived in Malta in January 1941, Shrimp came with orders to conduct offensive operations as he saw fit, with no written boundaries.

Shrimp's fertile and rebellious mind had been set to work by the arrival of his commandos, of *Triumph*, and of a handful of exotic folding canvas-and-wood canoes which were apparently called Folbots. The name originated in Austria, where the canoes had been developed just before the war for leisure boating, and remained in use throughout. The name was sometimes anglicised to Folboat. Shrimp and his staff had already worked out that these would just fit through the large hatch on the foredeck, which all his submarines used to load and unload torpedoes, and could be broken down into smaller packages while on passage. What if these Folboats were used to land and pick up agents, saboteurs and (why not) commandos on enemy beaches? A few well-trained and well-equipped men inserted ashore at night might do extraordinary damage. Even the risk of such landings would force the enemy to patrol every beach, bay and inlet of his shoreline, of which

Italy had thousands. A single submarine could tie down many thousands of troops in unproductive guard duties and still strike hard at sensitive points.

A mile southeast of the Lazaretto, in the Malta command bunker underneath the Venetian bastion of the Barraka, equally fertile if less rebellious minds were also at work. Inspired by the successes of Hitler's paratroopers in the attack on France, Churchill had ordered the creation of a British paratrooper force. This had been done with the speed that characteristically followed Churchill's demands. Searching for a suitable target on which to try out this new arm, the general staff had alighted on an aqueduct in southern Italy that supplied the whole of Apulia with fresh water. The aqueduct was located just two and a half hours' flight time northeast of Malta. On 7 February, a small detachment of thirty-eight men and three Italian translators from Unit Number 11 Special Air Service Battalion was formed into X Detachment and flew directly to Malta from England (remarkably overflying occupied France on the way) in their specially adapted Whitley bombers. Their job would be to attack the aqueduct.

Getting to the target was one thing. Extraction of the force after the raid was quite another. Shrimp and Captain Taylor brought their innovative minds to bear. They suggested that the raiders could be picked up by a submarine (using Folboats) off a long beach on Italy's west coast. The beach was fifty miles from the aqueduct, giving the raiding party two night marches of twenty-five miles each, well within the capabilities of the ultra-fit paratroopers. The operation was named Colossus. The extraction needed a large submarine, to provide physical internal space for the crowd of men and to provide enough breathable air for her to stay dived during the short winter days. By chance, Shrimp had *Triumph* on hand, and he requested and received permission to hold her back for a week to use for Colossus. This gave him and Woods an additional bonus: two weeks in which to practise working with Folboats and commandos in daylight and darkness. *Triumph* was to become the first boat in the war to conduct a special operation with commandos, paratroopers, and a beach recovery.

Triumph was much more suitable for the operation than her small U-class sisters. Assuming all forty-one men reached the pickup beach, the waiting submarine would need enough internal space to fit that many men with their weapons and kit inside her pressure hull, as well as enough internal air to allow just over 100 men to breathe during the daylight (and dived) part of her passage home. The U-class submarines had neither, *Triumph* had both.

Once she was out of dock on 18 January, handsome in her new dark blue paint to reduce her visibility from the air, and with her crew reassembled from their short leave in the Malta rest camp, *Triumph* spent days and nights in Sliema Creek working with Shrimp's commando force and the new Folboats, practising assembling them, launching them from the fore planes which were used as small jetties, recovering them and striking them down into the fore ends through the large torpedo hatch. The practice session was not without risk. The three-foot wide torpedo hatch through which torpedoes were loaded and unloaded lay just a few feet above the waterline. A submarine is designed to sink. The level of her waterline was set by the actions of the First Lieutenant and the Leading Stoker working the complex collection of valves that fed air into the ballast tanks – the 'blowing panel'. A small mistake on the blowing panel could bring the waterline down by just a few feet, which might accidentally submerge the open torpedo hatch, sinking the boat.

Just a mile away to the south, Stukas of Fliegerkorps X were continuing their daily bombing assault on the Malta dockyard and the aircraft carrier *Illustrious,* which was desperately trying to repair the damage from six 1,000-pound bombs received during the Malta convoy a few days before. If an aircraft decided to break away from the main raid and investigate the small submarine floating about in Sliema Creek, surrounded by soldiers in canoes, there was little *Triumph* could do about it, but happily, the Luftwaffe paid no attention to either the Lazaretto or to *Triumph*.

There was much else to prepare. This was the first beach recovery operation that the submarine service had ever carried out. How would the beach party communicate with the submarine, lurking out of sight in the darkness somewhere along the beach? Moreover, how would the submarine find her way to the precise part of the twenty-five-mile-long beach anyway? In the days before Google Earth, the charts of the Italian coastline were large-scale and not entirely helpful or accurate. How would the submarine check that the pickup beach had not accidentally become an armed camp, or been fortified with a shore battery? What would happen if the paratroopers were delayed by a day, or two? Would the boat wait around off the beach, or return at a set day and time later, and if so for how many days? What would be the radio schedule for the operation? Would the raiding party have a communications plan to contact *Triumph* directly by radio, and if it did would that risk compromising the whole mission and lead *Triumph* into an ambush in her most vulnerable state – surfaced, hatches open, and in shallow water unable to dive? If *Triumph* failed to show up, because of her own loss, or breakdown, or some other unsolvable problem, what would the men on the beach do? Finally, if the landing party was captured and forced to reveal the rendezvous, how would *Triumph* know that the beach rendezvous had become an Italian ambush?

At the pickup *Triumph* would have to creep towards the beach at night on the surface. Her surfaced draft of about twelve feet, plus a safety margin of (usually) a fathom more, defined how close to the beach she could come, generally no closer than 200 yards. A Folboat could carry a single passenger. With four Folboats and forty-one people to pick up, the canoes would have to make ten round trips each, paddling two miles, over ninety minutes of intense physical work. Sailors in 1941 were not noted for their physical fitness, and submariners particularly so – in a submarine a man's workspace was only ten yards or less away from his bunk or hammock.[3] Shrimp must have quickly realized that even the fittest sailors in the Lazaretto would be unable to row Folboats for that long. Fortunately, he had several dozen ultra-fit commandos under his command, some of whom could be detailed to join *Triumph* as Folboat paddlers.[4]

Colossus was set for the night of 10 February, the start of five days of almost full moon to provide light for the raid, for the march to the sea and for the beach pickup. The pickup was set for five days after the drop to give the paratroopers, now named X Detachment, ample time to reach the coast. The location for the pickup was a beach on the southern bank of the mouth of the Sele River, fifteen miles southeast of Salerno, and thirty-five miles as the crow flies southwest of the aqueduct. The location was probably chosen to fit within the navigational difficulties of the time, since it would be relatively easy to find the mouth of the river at night. After its attack, X Detachment had to march about nine miles southwest from the aqueduct, skirting the hills on their right, until they hit the Sele river somewhere near the hamlet of Calabritto. They would then follow the river down to the sea, bypassing villages and towns along the way, aiming at the south bank of its mouth. Conveniently, this part of the beach was backed by a large reedy marsh, which would provide cover for the hiding paratroopers and obstruct Italian beach patrols. The nearest town likely to have troops in residence was a dozen miles away.

Coming in from the open sea, *Triumph* would have little problem navigating her way to the river mouth at the centre of the twenty-five-mile-long beach of Salerno. It was agreed that *Triumph* would arrive in daylight, to spend the day before the rendezvous patrolling up and down the beach, inspecting it closely through the periscope. In so doing, she may well detect any unwelcome enemy activity or positions, while also plotting a detailed chart of the seabed for use later that day. The risk of mines was necessarily accepted. In any case, with no obvious military use, it was unlikely the Italians would have mined every beach in Italy.

Colossus was the first British paratrooper raid of the war, so it is hardly a surprise that almost everything went wrong. The paratroopers, led by Major Pritchard, left on time the night before *Triumph* was due to sail from Malta. Four aircraft made their drops exactly on target, within 250 yards of the aqueduct, but two couldn't drop their equipment containers because the release mechanisms had iced shut. One, the Whitley, carrying most of the high explosives and the engineers trained to use them, missed the drop zone by two miles and failed to make the rendezvous at all. Pritchard had brought a small quantity of explosives in his own kit as a backup, but on the ground, he found that the aqueduct was supported not by easily demolished brick piers but by reinforced concrete ones. Nevertheless, he used what he had and managed to drop the aqueduct pipe, which broke. Dividing his force into three groups and leaving the lost sappers to fend for themselves, Pritchard's force set off towards the rendezvous at the Sele River. Local Italian troops had been alerted by the explosion and by local farmers and police, and all three X Detachment groups were prisoners of war by dawn, along with the missing sappers.

There was yet more to go wrong. Two Whitleys of the Colossus force had been tasked with making a small bombing raid at Foggia, forty miles beyond the aqueduct, to cover the approach and departure of the drop aircraft. One of these suffered critical engine trouble, and its pilot radioed Malta in a low-grade cypher that he planned to ditch near the mouth of the River Sele 'at the rendezvous point'. When he heard that the rendezvous had been compromised, Shrimp Simpson first hit the roof, and then signalled

Triumph to abandon the pickup. Paratroopers were valuable, but nowhere near as valuable as a fully operational submarine. *Triumph* returned to Malta three days later, making two unsuccessful attacks on convoys on her way back. This time, there was no time for rest and recuperation, and in any case, *Triumph* had only been out for five days. Under orders to join her own flotilla, Sammy Woods turned his bows east for the last 1,000-mile run to Alexandria.

Alexandria was a different world to Malta. Air raids in Malta arrived in strength two or three times each day. In Alexandria, air raids were regular, even nightly at times, but were smaller and generally much less accurate attacks by aircraft at high level rather than the accurate dive-bombing attacks that felt quite personal to the men on the ground in Malta. The main targets were the Suez Canal, Alexandria's docks and its large harbour, all regularly attacked by Fleigerkorps X aircraft from Benghazi.[5] A Commando officer leading a docks' guard detachment at the time recalled later: '… a German machine came over at about 3,000 feet and was caught in the searchlights. Everything fired at her – the entire Alex Ack Ack defence, the Mediterranean Fleet, my own Bren guns, and I can even remember an excited Egyptian policeman firing his rifle at her. Finally, to our great excitement, three parachutes opened out and we thought that the plane would crash at any moment but she carried on seemingly unhit out to sea and away. The next day a ship blew up on a mine (which of course were the parachutes we had seen)'.[6] *Triumph*'s crew had grown used to air raids in Malta,[7] and probably thought that Axis action in Alexandria was little more than an annoyance. The main contrast with Malta was that Alexandria was a place of abundant food and drink without rationing or shortages.

Their principal source of joy was the presence of *Triumph*'s new depot ship, HMS *Medway*. *Medway* was a converted liner of some 18,000 tonnes fitted out with large cool mess decks, ample fresh hot and cold water, baths, a laundry, a barber's shop, a dentist, a NAAFI shop for everyday essentials, spacious decks for off-watch lounging and deck sports and even an onboard cinema. The staff of the First Submarine Flotilla were on hand to support *Triumph* in any way she needed with fully equipped workshops. *Medway* was just a short picket-boat ride from Alexandria's waterfront. As soon as 'leave' was piped at the end of the working day, *Triumph*'s off-watch men caught the picket boat to the Alexandria Corniche, where they could drink their fill of ice-cold beers at the bars in Sister Street. Alexandria's house of ill repute, Mary's, doubtless also drew a few of the more adventurous into its welcoming arms. It was Nelson who said that south of Gibraltar, all men are bachelors. *Triumph*'s officers were required to look for more respectable entertainment. Lieutenant Douglas-Don wrote home, '… in this place we look forward to a social life, and I will step ashore with introductions to the reputedly lovely Armenians who are called Contamiculas, and another to an Egyptian semi-millionaire … A submarine is always a social asset with the uninitiated and, when played carefully, a trump card for the scrounger'.[8]

Medway was home to Captain Sydney Raw, commander of the First Submarine Flotilla, to which *Triumph* belonged. Acutely aware of the need to decompress his boats' crews between patrols, Raw had secured the use of a Nile houseboat in Cairo, the *Puritan*, which lay opposite Cairo's country club. Here, his ratings (junior and senior) could relax in complete comfort, waited on hand and foot by Egyptian stewards in flowing white *djellabas* and away from the oversight of their officers. Men could visit Cairo's ancient monuments, and were given permission to use the outdoor facilities of the Cairo Country Club across the Nile, where they could swim and ride the club's horses.

But in February 1941, *Triumph*'s ship's company had too little time to enjoy these delights, for a new and innovative special operation was already being suggested by the General Staff in London and Cairo. In 1941, Italy owned the Dodecanese Islands, located at the southeast corner of the Aegean, which it had taken from the Ottoman Empire during its war over Libya in 1912. Centred on the large island of Rhodes, this archipelago of a dozen small islands (*Dodeka* means 'twelve' in Greek) had little strategic significance before 1940 but was now an easy 300-mile flight from Alexandria. Rhodes had ample space and harbours for Italian naval and Axis air forces and was the base for half of the air raids on Egypt.

In February 1941, flushed with success against the Italian army in the deserts of Libya, and ignorant of the fact that a German army corps under General Rommel was already on its way to Tripoli, London ordered General Wavell in Cairo to make preparations for an invasion of Rhodes by a single reinforced division, to take place at some time in June 1941. The operation was christened Cordite. Naturally, Cordite's attacking division would have to land on Rhodes over its beaches in what would be the first large amphibious operation of the war. Knowledge of the beaches was rudimentary. The staff in Cairo had worked out that it needed a much better understanding of where and how to land tanks and men. The only practical way of obtaining that information was to send someone to have a look, and the only way to do that was with a submarine. *Triumph* had just arrived and was having a maintenance inspection in drydock, so Captain Raw initially gave the job to the large minelaying submarine HMS *Rorqual*. The first attempt was designed to be a close inspection by periscope from a dived submarine.

On 26 February, *Rorqual* embarked the thirty-year-old Lieutenant Commander Nigel Willmott to serve as the observing officer. Willmott was probably chosen partly because of his career specialization as a Navigating Officer, partly because he had visited Rhodes before the war, and partly because he had served as Beach Master for landings at Narvik in 1940.[9] In 1941 he had found his way to the staff of the Sixth Division, tasked with planning Cordite. With recent and painful experience of a beach landing in Norway, Willmott had concluded that a successful landing depended heavily on having a detailed and accurate survey of the target beach beforehand. Well before he dumped his small bag of kit in the wardroom of *Rorqual* that day, he had been preparing himself for the job of gathering beach intelligence by swimming laps of the Cairo Club pool, 'practising sliding silently through the water as if approaching a beach watched by sentries'.[10]

Cordite included a deception plan, Operation Cascade, designed to persuade the Italians that the target of the invasion would be Karpathos, a much smaller island forty miles southwest of Rhodes. Perhaps as part of this plan, or perhaps as a practice mission for a later survey of Rhodes itself, *Rorqual* was ordered to spend three days at periscope depth sailing close aboard the 120-mile-long coastlines of Karpathos and its neighbour Kasos at a slow walking pace. At the same time, Willmott repeatedly raised and lowered the search periscope for thirty-second looks followed by frantic map drawing and note taking on her chart table. Willmott could rest from the intense concentration required at night, when *Rorqual* surfaced and sailed to sea to recharge her batteries and refresh her air.

The task was deeply unrewarding. The foreshores of both islands were mostly rock, relieved occasionally by cliffs. Only one beach of any size provided a possible landing place – a mile-long stretch of sandy shingle reaching north from Karpathos' main town. The record does not relate, but it is likely that *Rorqual* deliberately revealed something of her position and movements with radio transmissions to reinforce the Cascade deception plan. The operation generated one clear conclusion: it was all very well to plot the defences of a beach from a periscope 300 yards offshore, but that could not reveal whether the beach was actually suitable for landing thousands of men and hundreds of heavy trucks and tanks. The landing beach had to be inspected and surveyed beforehand to discover the angle of the seabed at its threshold, whether sand bars would strand approaching landing craft, and the physical nature of the beach – sand or pebbles, firm or soft, steep or shallow. The last question was to discover how, or if, vehicles could leave the beach and move inland.[11] Willmott's three days at *Rorqual*'s periscope had 'convinced him of only one thing: somebody would have to explore those beaches more closely than from a reconnaissance plane – or even from a periscope'.[12]

The new Folboats appeared to offer an answer. Willmott suggested that a small group of strong fit men – commandos were the obvious choice – might paddle ashore at night from a submarine to spend the hours of darkness personally measuring and testing a beach. While one man stayed in the Folboat, the other would slip into the water and swim silently ashore. Here, the swimmer could take samples of beach sand or shingle, and measure and record the gradient of the beach and its underwater foreshore by using his own body as the measuring tape. Swimming further out, he could test for the presence of sand bars or rocks. Emerging from the water onto the beach, the swimmer could measure the distance from the beach to its hinterland and check for exit points and barriers, natural or man-made.

This work would have to be repeated at intervals along each beach. After his survey, the exhausted swimmer would return to the Folboat, which would keep track of his movements as best as it could in the pitch dark. The exhausted swimmer would climb aboard and be paddled back to the waiting submarine. Willmott proposed his plan to the commander of Cordite's naval element, Admiral Baillie-Grohman. His initial reaction was a refusal, because if the men were captured, their presence would reveal the intended landing beach, and in any case, Willmott knew far too much about the Cordite plan to risk him anywhere near any Italians. But a day later, Cordite's Army staff decided it had to land tanks close to Rhodes, and 'no' became 'yes'. Willmott's plan was approved, and the two-man Folboat team was given a new name – a Combined Operations Pilotage Party, or COPP. Willmott probably had only a glimmering idea of the significance of COPP parties in later years of the war. The landings on Sicily, Italy and ultimately Normandy itself depended on COPP reconnaissance beforehand.

Triumph, with her recent and innovative experience of working with Folboats, was assigned to the mission. Willmott needed a Folboat and a man to paddle it. *Triumph* had left her Folboats in Malta, but Willmott knew that only a few hours' drive southeast of Alexandria, a small group of commandos was practising with a collection of Folboats on the Great Bitter Lake, part of the Suez Canal, under the command of a rogue in uniform, Captain Roger Courtney.

Courtney, known to his friends as Jumbo, had already lived several lives. He started as a bank clerk in Leeds and a subaltern in the Territorial Army but had left to become a professional hunter and gold prospector in Kenya. He then decided to travel north from East Africa partly by paddling down the Nile in a canoe, armed only with a spear.[13] Arriving in Egypt in 1937 penniless and unemployed, he travelled to Palestine to take a job in the Palestinian Police Force. In 1938, Courtney married and spent his honeymoon paddling down the Danube in a new collapsible canoe invented in Austria – the first British encounter with the Folboat that later arrived in Malta with Captain Taylor's commandos. Before the war broke out, he had already returned to England to join the King's Royal Rifle Corps as a rifleman. Quickly promoted to corporal, he was commissioned in November 1939.

After Dunkirk, the army found itself safely in Britain but lacking opportunities for bringing the war to the enemy. Winston Churchill, newly appointed Prime Minister in May 1940 and an enthusiast for offensive action, ordered the formation of a small, elite, mobile force which could carry out raids against the Axis in occupied Europe on the principle of 'butcher and bolt'. Remembering the Afrikaner commandos in the Boer War he had encountered as a war correspondent, Churchill suggested that the new Special Service Brigades be called commandos. Volunteers were sought from units within Britain, and Courtney naturally stepped forward.

Twelve commandos were formed, of 500 men each, and a commando training centre was set up in Scotland. Courtney wanted to put his kayaking experience to work, pointing out that a canoe allowed a man to approach and escape his target in complete silence. His commanding officer was unreceptive, so Courtney bet him that he could board a ship by canoe at night and escape, even if the ship's company had been forewarned. A few nights later, Courtney raided the resident amphibious landing ship HMS *Glengyle*, marked her hull with chalk crosses to represent the limpet mines he might have laid, climbed aboard undetected, stole the breech block and gun cover of one of her anti-aircraft guns and then paddled ashore.

Here, naked except for a pair of trunks, he presented his trophies to *Glengyle*'s captain, who was hosting a drinks party in the local hotel. He'd won his argument, but to prove it beyond doubt, he was invited to repeat the exercise against HMS *Forth*, the submarine depot ship at anchor in the Holy Loch. Having done so successfully, he was given a section of twelve men to train in the use of Folboats – the Folboat Troop – which he quickly renamed Number 1 Special Boat Section. It was this unit that Willmott sought out on the Bitter Lake in the first week of March 1941.

Courtney immediately volunteered to be the Folboat paddler himself – this was too good an opportunity to pass on to one of his sections, and in any case, they would expect him to lead from the front. Courtney nominated one of his men to join him to help with the Folboat aboard the submarine, and to act as a backup in case of illness or accident. The choice fell on Corporal Jimmy Sherwood, who would become one of *Triumph*'s regular Folboat operators. The COPP operation needed to be carried out in complete darkness since Willmott might be working only feet from a patrolling Italian guard, which meant that Willmott, Courtney and Sherwood had almost a fortnight in which to practise while they waited for a moonless night. Courtney practised silently paddling up to beaches manned with men of his section and found that he could usually get almost ashore before being spotted. That meant that off Rhodes, he could safely drop Willmott less than a hundred yards from a beach. Willmott, in turn, practised coming ashore from the water and silently trying to get behind a searching Courtney, something he managed to do two times out of three. A commando history later said, 'The two officers also spent hours in games of hide and seek'. 'Generally speaking, it's surprising what one can do at night if one keeps low to the ground or water and quiet', Willmott wrote afterwards. They also found that as long as Willmott remained motionless in the sea, a torch shone on him would dazzle Courtney rather than illuminate Willmott'.[14]

A new difficulty arose. The COPP party would be dropped from *Triumph* a few hundred yards from the beach on a pitch-black night and then paddle off into the darkness for a couple of hours. How would Folboat and submarine find each other at the end of the reconnaissance without betraying the presence of either to men patrolling the beach? The answer lay in a new and unfamiliar piece of equipment, an infra-red transmitter and receiver. This depended on two uncertainties – the man holding the infra-red transmitter on *Triumph*'s bridge (Corporal Sherwood) had to be pointing his equipment roughly at the Folboat, and the man in the Folboat had to be pointing his receiver roughly in the direction of *Triumph*, but the men at both ends of the invisible lifeline of infra-red light had only a vague idea of where the other might be. Sherwood and Courtney practised techniques off the darkened lighthouse at the end of the Alexandria breakwater[15] and reached a level of proficiency that seemed to offer a chance of success. On 24 March 1941, *Triumph* sailed from Alexandria with Willmott, Courtney, Sherwood and a Folboat to carry out the world's first beach reconnaissance by submarine.

In the middle of a Greek summer, the Aegean is warm. In March, it is not. A hundred yards off the beach, Willmott had to slip over the side of the Folboat into the ice-cold sea with a torch waterproofed inside a condom and swim ashore to measure the beach. Wetsuits had not been invented in 1941. Willmott improvized protection against the cold and camouflage for the dark by smearing a thick white submariner's jersey and long socks in thick black grease. For buoyancy, he used a Gieves and Hawkes inflatable waistcoat. Midnight of 30 March saw *Triumph* creeping towards the two-mile-long Kritika beach that lines the northwest tip of Rhodes, a mile or so behind the town of Rhodes itself. Courtney's Folboat was brought up onto the casing and launched from *Triumph*'s forward hydroplanes. Willmott brought with him a thermos flask of hot coffee and the cumbersome infra-red detector, with which he hoped he might be able to find *Triumph* hiding in the moonless night at the end of his mission. The party was armed with a Thompson sub-machine gun and a Webley .38 revolver, though both men knew that if they had to use these, their chances of escape would be small.

The beach lay nearly a mile away. After paddling in, Willmott slipped into the water a hundred yards out and swam silently towards the shore. The cold took his breath away. In front of him lay the massive dark bulk of the Hotel de Roses, built in 1927 as a destination hotel and now the headquarters of

Axis forces on Rhodes.[16] As he swam silently along the beach, measuring its gradient and water depth (it was immediately obvious that it was too steep for tanks), he saw the dark forms of two sentries walking to and fro just behind the low wall at the head of the beach. Willmott left the water, timing his moves with the wavelets of surf that broke over him, and silently crawled up the shingle. Here he could see the silhouettes of the two guards against the background of clear stars. One silhouette periodically glowed from the light of an illicit cigarette. '[Willmott] had got halfway to the wall when he saw one of the soldiers looking at him. He froze. The hours of practice with Courtney had taught him that if he stayed absolutely still, he resembled nothing more unusual than a rock in the dark. Through his wet clothes, he felt a breeze coming from the sea, and he clamped his teeth together to stop them from chattering. The sentry turned his head again and moved away. Peering over the wall, Willmott realized that the Germans[17] were no more than ten yards from him. A truck passed between them, and the headlights revealed two others stationed further up the road. His limbs felt tired and numb, and he did not relish going back into the water. Digging deep into his reserves of willpower, he dragged himself back down to the sea and began methodically to explore the shallows'.[18]

Satisfied that there were no gun emplacements or machine-gun nests, Willmott stowed a few pebbles of shingle and sand in his pocket as beach samples. Beginning to pass out with the first stages of hypothermia, he held his condom-wrapped torch and signalled a Morse 'R' into the dark where he thought, hoped, that Courtney was waiting. He had lost sensation in his legs and was on the point of passing out when the Folboat crunched softly onto the shingle. The infra-red rendezvous worked, and four hours after their departure, Willmott was back in *Triumph*'s wardroom warming up with chef Cornelius O'Brien's soup and First Lieutenant Michael Janvrin's whisky.

The following night, Courtney and Willmott repeated the mission, this time on the long beach west of Rhodes. Willmott penetrated the barbed wire at the edge of the beach and reached the esplanade of Rhodes town itself, narrowly escaping capture for, as he swam back out to the Folboat, he could see German sentries with torches closely searching the area he had inspected. Willmott was thoroughly exhausted. The two men agreed that the next night Courtney would act as the swimmer and Willmott as the paddler. Willmott dropped Courtney, probably with a shudder of gratitude that this time he would be warm and safe in the Folboat while Courtney suffered and paddled up the beach to take soundings. Returning at the agreed time, a few hours later, there was no sign of Courtney. Waiting in the silent dark, his Folboat rising and falling with the slight swell, and with growing alarm, Willmott wondered if Courtney had been captured. Was a party of Germans or Italians waiting in the dark with loaded rifles aimed at him? What would happen to Cordite if he was captured? Willmott felt acutely exposed, sitting in his tiny canoe less than a hundred yards off an enemy beach.

The silence was broken not by a spurt of a German machine gun fire and the whipping of bullets but by an angry dog, followed by a long, muted whistle. Skin crawling, for the whistle might be a deliberate lure designed to make him reveal his position to a waiting Italian machine gunner, Willmott nosed towards the beach, one hand working his paddle, the other on the pistol grip of his Tommy gun cradled across the crook of his paddling arm. When he was almost aground on the beach, the large, dark form of Courtney came floundering through the low surf to clamber aboard the Folboat. The cold had given Courtney a cramp so severe that he could not swim out to the canoe.

Four days later, *Triumph* came alongside *Medway* and Courtney and Willmott dashed ashore to report their findings to the Sixth Division's staff. Arriving in Cairo too late that day to do more than give the briefest summary of their findings, they arranged to have a more detailed conference the next morning. Their intelligence was swept aside by the first item of business that day – news that 150,000 German troops had started crossing the northern borders of Greece a few hours earlier. Operation Cordite was forgotten. Operation Marita had begun.

Chapter 4

Operation Marita, the Invasion of Greece

While Willmott and Courtney were dressing and shaving for their meeting at the General Staff in Cairo on the morning of 7 April 1941, hundreds of thousands of German troops were leaving their start lines on the northern border of Greece to head south and west into Greece and Yugoslavia. *Triumph*'s crew, recently alongside *Medway* and enjoying fresh food and hot baths for the first time in ten days, heard the news but had no idea that they would soon find themselves drawn into the chaotic aftermath of that operation.

At this point in our story, we need to leave *Triumph*'s people recuperating in *Medway* and dive into the messy and complex story of 1941 Greece. This diversion is necessary because, while none of Sydney Raw's submarines played a part in the defence of Greece, the story of the second half of *Triumph*'s year in the Mediterranean became intimately connected with its aftermath, and that story makes little sense unless placed within the context of the invasion itself.

When we think about the invasion of Greece and the Allies' attempt to stop it, we must ask why the Allies intervened at all. Without the benefit of hindsight, intervention is not the obvious choice. The idea of intervention arose in the War Cabinet in London in January 1941, but just six months earlier, the British army had been overwhelmed at Dunkirk, even though it was fighting alongside millions of French troops. A last-minute attempt to defend Norway had done no better. The Cabinet knew that most of the German army was in the Balkans, just north of Greece. A cool observer might have advised that any attempt to prevent Germany from taking Greece was futile. But the attempt was made, nevertheless. Why?

Planning for the German invasion of Greece, Operation Marita, had been launched two months earlier, on 4 November 1940, in response to the failure of Italy's invasion. On 3 November, Greek forces counterattacked Mussolini's army, stalled in the deep snow in the mountains of northwest

Greece and were already making rapid progress. The Italian units were crowded into the narrow valleys of the Pindus, pinned to roads for their tanks and supply trucks. The Greek infantry was on the ridges above them, supplied by pack animals rather than wheeled vehicles, advancing into their rear to sweep down on the roads from above. Far from being occupied by Italian forces, Greece was advancing into Albania, and the Italian invasion was falling apart. This was probably the first piece of the Allied intervention puzzle – if Greek forces could halt, and even turn back, a large Italian army, then perhaps they could do the same to a German one, with a little help.

Marita and Operation Barbarossa have closely linked timelines, with their directives issues within days of each other. Barbarossa's start date had been set as 15 May, but planning revealed an uncomfortable vulnerability: complete dependence on a secure supply of fuel for tanks, aircraft and trucks. Practically all of Germany's fuel came from the oilfields at Ploesti in southern Romania, and from its associated refinery a few miles away. Ploesti was a completely unreachable 1,250 miles from Bomber Command's airfields in Yorkshire and Lincolnshire, but a very reachable 300 miles from a bomber based on an airfield in northern Greece. If Greece joined the Allied camp, the oilfields of Ploesti would be vulnerable, and that made Barbarossa vulnerable as well. Oil was not the only German problem. Greece's 370-mile northern land border with Bulgaria, Albania and Yugoslavia was an open door to a flanking attack by the Allies, a repeat of what had happened in 1916. While Greece was neither a British ally nor at war with Germany, its conflict with Italy might push it into the Allied camp sooner or later. Barbarossa was too important, and too difficult, for the Ober Kommando der Wehrmacht (OKW) to live with either risk. Marita was conceived to mitigate that risk before Barbarossa began.

Churchill, who knew about Barbarossa from Ultra decrypts, could see both risks just as clearly, and always keen for action pushed for intervention, to repeat the success of the Balkan front in 1918. While the cost of defending Greece might be high, the prize was large. Another part of the prize would be to keep Greece from becoming an active German ally – something that was all too likely given the political stance of its dictator, for at the end of 1940 Greece was hovering in a state of partial neutrality towards Germany under the fascist leadership and control of an aged army general, Ioannis Metaxas. Short, fat and unprepossessing, Metaxas was at sixty-nine a veteran of Greek politics. He looked an unlikely dictator, right up until the day he seized power and declared martial law in August 1936. The background to his self-elevation lay in a decade of chaos and failure in the Greek political sphere, which had led to a collective decision to recall and re-enthrone the exiled King George of Greece[1] in 1935.

Metaxas was a royalist; he had served the king's father who had been the Kaiser's brother-in-law. He was deeply pro-German and had been trained by the German army, attempting to remain neutral in 1914 in the great contest between France, Britain and Germany that resulted in outright war. In August 1936, Metaxas declared martial law. Greece joined Germany, Italy and Spain in the ranks of fascist dictatorships, and declared a 'Third Greek Civilization' to mirror the Third Reich and the Third Rome. But Metaxas differed from the other two dictators in one important respect – he had no territorial ambitions. Indeed, the reverse was the case, his main foreign policy agenda was to protect 'our dear little Greece'[2] from its aggressive and hungry neighbours to the north and west. Knowing full well how vulnerable Greece was, after Italy's occupation of Albania, Metaxas had sought reassurance from Germany that it would prevent Mussolini from invading Greece. The reply came back that it would, if Greece joined the Axis. For Metaxas, this was a step too far. A neutralist at heart and aware of how much Greece's economy depended on the sea and on shipping, Metaxas demurred. Up until the Italian invasion in October 1940, he would probably have been happy with an informal neutrality towards the Axis, acting as their supportive little brother. His warmth towards the dictatorships, however, chilled on 28 October 1940. That autumn evening in Athens had seen a brilliant party at the Italian embassy. The Italian ambassador, Count Grazzi, hosted a glittering dinner for the leading lights in Greek politics and business. At the head of the room, Italian and Greek flags were intertwined in a symbolic demonstration of fellowship and neighbourly love, and beneath them, the party drank toasts and 'pledged eternal friendship to Greece'.[3]

At three the next morning, a few hours after the party had broken up, Count Grazzi was driven to the house of General Metaxas and demanded an interview. Metaxas eventually appeared in his dressing gown, heavy with interrupted sleep. Grazzi presented an ultimatum demanding free passage for

Italian troops through Greece and the occupation by Italy of key points on the mainland and islands. 'To all the demands [Metaxas] gave a simple "no".'[4]

'Then this means war' said Grazzi.

'Sir, it does', replied Metaxas.

Two hours later Italian troops began flooding across the Albanian border into Greece's Pindus Mountains.

After that day, immortalized now in Greece as Ohi Day,[5] Metaxas had no choice but to abandon his neutralist yet pro-Axis stance and accept that the solution to Greece's geopolitical problems was an alliance with Britain. This was not an entirely new strategy. Two years earlier he had sought an alliance with Britain, to the point of begging. Then the Foreign Office in London refused the invitation, concluding privately that Britain would receive everything it needed from Greece in due course anyway without the burdens of a formal alliance. A few months later, among rumours that Italy planned to occupy the island of Corfu, Britain's Foreign Secretary Lord Halifax had made a speech in the House of Lords in which he declared that '[His Majesty's Government has] come to the conclusion that in the event of any action being taken which clearly threatened the independence of Greece … and which the Greek … Government … considered it vital to resist with their national forces, His Majesty's Government would feel themselves bound at once to lend the Greek … Government … all support in their power'.[6]

Metaxas called on this pledge after 28 October 1940. Churchill, newly in post as Prime Minister and fully engaged in worrying about the war in Europe and the Atlantic, sent reassurances but no commitments, though a few RAF bombers were deployed to Greece to give substance to Lord Halifax's declaration.

With this background, it is easy to see why Hitler expected Greece to eventually align with Britain and the Allies, and why he decided that Greece must be neutralized before Barbarossa could start. Hitler's first concept was to use just ten divisions to take the northern strip of northeast Greece between Corfu in the west and the Turkish border in the east, coming to rest on the north coast of the Aegean at Salonika. This would relieve pressure on the Italians in Albania, who would then, presumably, finish the job and defeat the Greek army[7] for him. Success would move potential Allied bomber bases at least 100 miles further south, away from Ploesti. The original version of the plan, also christened Operation Marita, would not delay Barbarossa's start date since it required the use of only seven per cent of the forces allocated to the invasion of Russia and only a couple of weeks of swift action.

Since there seemed to be little reason to hurry, the start of formal planning for this partial invasion of Greece, Marita 1.0, was delayed to 13 December 1940. Perhaps Hitler entertained some residual hopes that Metaxas would settle the Italian war by joining the Axis, or that Italy would win and force the same result. German forces were not even standing on Greece's border because neutral Bulgaria lay in their way, so Marita's starting point would be the southern border of Romania, informally allied to the Axis and willing to allow passage for the invasion force to the Bulgarian border. Only then would Bulgaria be given an offer it could not refuse – passage of the force through Bulgaria to its borders with Greece in the east and Yugoslavia to the west.

When they arrived on the Greek–Bulgarian border, German forces would face a line of newly built forts (the Metaxas Line) along the 4,000-foot-high range of the Rodope Mountains. To the invaders camped in the Struma Valley to its north, the Metaxas Line looked 'like a wall, inhospitable and forbidding. The mountain peaks were covered in snow … into the rough gorge and rugged rocks, the Greeks had cut out a huge number of bunkers, and gun positions and dug trenches, MG nests and casemates … not even the most reckless of assault troops would be able to come anywhere close to the bunkers'.[8]

The existence of the Metaxas Line was another reason for the Allied decision to intervene. While France's Maginot Line may have been outflanked, here, neutral Yugoslavia blocked such a move. London thought that Greece simply needed a little 'shoring up' to hold its fortified Bulgarian frontier. Moreover, if the Metaxas Line fell, then a second line could be established on a range of mountains running north from the Aegean to the Bulgarian border – the Aliakhmon Mountains. It would not take much additional force to keep the Germans at bay.

There was another reason why Churchill wanted Greece to remain outside the Axis: Turkey. In early 1941, Turkey was neutral – a reversal of its 1914 policy. The earlier decision to fight the Allies had cost it dearly, losing over a million square miles of territory (an area about the size of Western Europe), and nearly the western half of Turkey itself, as well as 100,000 lives. But the territorial losses and the humiliations of the Treaty of Sevres that settled

Turkey's borders after the Great War continued to rankle, and Germany had sympathizers in positions of power in both Turkey and Iraq. If Ankara threw its hand in with Germany, General Wavell in Egypt would find his entire rear under threat, not just from Turkey but also from hostile Vichy French forces in Syria.[9] Anything that tipped the balance of power in the Eastern Mediterranean against Britain could tip Turkey into the war and lead to defeat in the desert and the loss of Egypt. If Greece fell to an Axis occupation, British prestige would be damaged, and Greece would be able to blackmail Ankara to throw its lot in with the Axis by obstructing Turkish sea trade. It was thus desirable that Greece not fall to the Axis.

MI6's Major Pirie in Athens reported that the Greek army fighting in the Pindus Mountains and, reliant on arms from France and Czechoslovakia, was running out of ammunition. With both suppliers under Axis control, resupply was impossible, threatening Greek resistance to Italy.

Faced with these risks and opportunities at the beginning of 1941, the Cabinet decided to instruct the General Staff to draw up proposals for the reinforcement of Greece. General Wavell was sent to Athens on 13 January to make plans with the Greek General Staff. 'It was a piercing cold day as we stood on the airfield and waited for the single plane to appear in the southern sky. There was a certain tension, for a single plane can be so easily shot down by a stray marauder, but all was well and the short sturdy figure of [Wavell] alighted from a graceful aircraft that made a perfect landing.'[10]

At the staff conference that followed, General Papagos, commander in chief of the Greek forces, expressed his firm opinion that Yugoslavia would remain neutral, protecting the western part of Greece's northern border and thus confining a German attack to the defensible Metaxas Line. He requested an Allied force of nine divisions to reinforce that line and to hold the Bulgarian border against a German assault; he wanted it in place before the German forces left Romania for the assault. But with the Italians in Africa still not quite beaten, and just three suitable landing ships to carry his forces, the most that Wavell would offer was two-and-a-half divisions with minimal air support. Metaxas demurred, fearing that minor reinforcement would trigger precisely the invasion he feared – he did not know that plans were already well in hand at OKW. There the matter rested, but his objections dissolved when he unexpectedly died on 29 January. Foreign Secretary Anthony Eden and Wavell reacted swiftly, recommending that one of each of the New Zealand and Australian divisions in reserve in Egypt be moved to Greece, along with another half-division of British infantry, a tank brigade, and half a division of logistics forces from the Royal Army Service Corps. The ships to carry them had prudently been sent from Scotland to Egypt in advance and had just arrived in Suez, and on 7 March, they began to move 58,000 men across the Mediterranean to Greece. The operation's troops were christened Lustre Force.

The Italian Navy, swiftly informed by agents in Alexandria, knew very well what was happening. A battleship and supporting cruisers were ordered to sail east to the Aegean to intercept and sink the reinforcements. Equally well informed, Cunningham sailed his three battleships of the Mediterranean Fleet[11] to ambush the ambushers. The groundswell of Marita reached *Triumph*, lurking off Rhodes with Courtney and Willmott about to step into their Folboat for their reconnaissance. She received a signal to sail west 'with all possible despatch' to join the ambush off Cape Matapan. *Triumph* thundered west at her best speed for two days, but was too late – her arrival was imminent when Cunningham's ships detected the Italian cruisers on radar at night and closed to a range of two miles. On command, they switched on their searchlights to pick out the Italian cruisers in the night. Two seconds after the lights dazzled the Italian lookouts, twenty-four half-tonne shells from the three battleships crashed into the cruisers *Fiume* and *Zara* at point-blank range. The Italians' gun turrets were seen to fly a hundred feet into the air.[12] The threat to Lustre Force sank with them, allowing *Triumph* to dash back to Rhodes to carry on with her interrupted special operation. Roger Courtney and Willmott were probably grateful for the rest.

At first glance, the decision to oppose a large part of the German army with just 58,000 men (for most, this would have been their first battle) looks rash. Australian historians today excoriate the decision to launch Lustre Force as a second Gallipoli, conceived by the same impetuous man who had ordered the first Gallipoli – Winston Churchill.[13] Their adverse conclusion is probably fatally influenced by their pain at its outcome rather than by an objective analysis of decisions taken at the time. The result was nothing like as painful as Gallipoli. There, 50,000 Australians landed, of whom 8,709 were killed. In Greece, 18,000 Australians landed, of whom 594 were killed. Perhaps what scars Australian memories more is the number of prisoners taken from their Sixth Division – 5,132.[14] What may also scar that memory is the painful fact that so many of these Australian prisoners surrendered. Antipodean historians blame British command decisions. Other historians look to the Australians themselves and other circumstances. The issue remains a painfully live one in the Australian narrative of the war.

But today's criticism rests on a great deal of hindsight and some misunderstood data. Central to the question is exactly how many Germans the Allies believed would take part in Marita. The deployment of Lustre Force rested on a (reasonable) assumption that Yugoslavia would be neutral or friendly. It also rested on an assumption that two additional divisions would follow from Egypt, and that the main battle would be fought first along the strong Metaxas Line and then fall back to the defensible Aliakhmon Range. Experience in the Pindus Mountains had shown how difficult it was for an invader to penetrate well-defended Greek mountains.

Australian criticism of the British intervention in Greece contrasts the presence of just 58,000 Allied troops with a total invasion force of 500,000, but the latter number is a gross exaggeration. In fact, most of the German invasion force that eventually took part in the campaign was aimed at Yugoslavia, not Greece. When the detail of force allocation is examined more carefully, those taking part in Marita were considerably smaller than the lazy consensus (and especially the Australian consensus) suggests.[15] The German invasion force aimed at Greece alone was about one third of the number that is generally accepted in the Marita narrative (150,000 against 500,000, or 600,000, depending on what source is used). The Allies' original plan was that two additional divisions would be added to the 58,000 men who arrived in March 1941. This plan had to be abandoned when Wavell found himself facing a new German armoured corps in the western desert, Rommel's Afrika Korps, lifted secretly from Italy in late March.

The decision to intervene looks even more rational when it is remembered that General Papagos had committed to move the Greek divisions stationed further east along the Bulgarian border, plus three divisions from the Italian front, back to the Aliakhmon line to join Lustre Force. With these commitments, Marita's 150,000 men would meet an approximately equal number of defenders situated in strongly defended prepared positions – no Hail Mary there. However, when the invasion arrived the Papagos commitment melted. One of his divisions was deployed elsewhere, and the two that did arrive comprised just one third and one half of a division respectively, whose men had been in uniform for mere months and arrived with no transport and almost no artillery.[16] Finally, the Allies had no idea that Yugoslavia would collapse as spectacularly quickly as it did, allowing the OKW to outflank the Allied defence lines completely.

Marita's start date was 6 April 1941. Athens fell on day seventeen – an advance of fifteen miles per day, a fraction of the rate seen in France, and later in Russia. The southern end of the Peloponnese fell a week later. A week's rest and recuperation would precede an invasion of Crete by a combined sea and paratrooper invasion, finishing on day forty-five, 21 May. It would then take Marita's forces a week to move by rail back to Barbarossa's start lines. Even on this optimistic timetable OKW accepted that Marita required Barbarossa's start date to be set back by half a month, for it was clear early on that the Axis could not run Barbarossa and two invasions (Greece and Yugoslavia) in parallel. Marita and the invasion of Yugoslavia would occupy fully one quarter of the forces allocated to Barbarossa. The development of Marita and its effect on Barbarossa, and therefore the outcome of the war as a whole, remains the subject of angry controversy among historians, not least those from Australia, over whether Marita fatally delayed Barbarossa or not, and whether the 'disasters' that befell the Australian and New Zealand divisions deployed to Greece to oppose it were therefore pointless, or not. The Australian consensus is that Marita did not delay Barbarossa, and was pointless.

The single historical work that begins to address this question was published in 1947 by a soldier rather than a historian, and lacks the benefit of decades of subsequent disclosures and declassifications, as well as the knowledge Bletchley Park's insights now provide. It is today difficult to see how the delay caused by Marita did not affect Barbarossa: Marita occupied one quarter of the German army for some forty spring and summer days, time during which Barbarossa could have covered many hundreds of additional miles of Russian steppe. Events in Russia corroborate the thesis that the delay fatally damaged Barbarossa. German forces reached the village of Krasnaya Polyana (Red Glade), less than twenty miles from the Kremlin, on 30 November 1941. From here, German motorcycle reconnaissance units could see the gilded domes of central Moscow on the horizon. In Moscow, both the government and people were in panic, packing and fleeing as fast as they could. Just five days later, Russian forces brought from the east counterattacked. If Barbarossa had started on time, on 15 May instead of 22 June, German units would have arrived at Moscow six weeks earlier, Moscow may well have fallen, and Stalin would have fled to his emergency headquarters in Kuibyshev with a loss of credibility both inside and outside Russia that might have been fatal to Russia's war effort. While it is not certain that Marita sowed the seeds of Barbarossa's failure, it does seem very likely. What is also not clear is whether Churchill, who knew about Barbarossa from Bletchley Park code-breaking, deliberately promoted the defence of Greece as a way of distracting and delaying Barbarossa's start date. With the collapse of Yugoslavia, Marita 1.0 quickly mutated into Marita 1.1 – the capture of the whole of Greece, not just its northern quarter. Marita would not stop until Allied forces had either been destroyed completely or driven out of Greece.

Two men who became part of *Triumph*'s story sailed to Greece in Lustre Force convoys in March 1941. In the 22nd Battalion of the New Zealand Division Lieutenant Jim Craig was a young platoon commander, apprehensive about his first experience under fire. In the support troops of the Royal Army Service Corps (RASC), the newly-minted 2nd Lieutenant John Atkinson also landed, as second-in-command of his transport platoon. He, too, had yet to see action. Both men's fates became tied to that of *Triumph*.

Chapter 5

Atkinson, Craig and the Fall of Greece

John George Paterson Atkinson's story before 1941 is sadly lost to the record. Born in 1911, he appears to have had no military experience before the start of the war. He likely joined the RASC instead of a line regiment because, in 1939 and early 1940, regular army units were not actively recruiting at all. Before Dunkirk, losses in action had been minimal. Existing Territorial Army members were the first men called on to fill additional battalions. Conscription was brought in as soon as the war began, but was staged by age group. Atkinson, at twenty-eight going on twenty-nine, would have had to wait until June or July of 1940 before even being eligible for call-up registration.[1] The social observer Richard Titmuss wrote that the call-up seemed to progress with 'the speed of an elephant trying to compete in the Derby'.

In any case Atkinson hardly looked like the model modern army officer. Shorter than average, perhaps five feet four or five, he had a round almost chubby head with a small button-like nose, below which he essayed a thin moustache. Heavy-lidded eyes gave him a slightly dreamy look. But later events reveal that Atkinson was not a man to wait around peacefully for a slow-time summons to arms. One formation that was actively recruiting in the spring of 1940 was the Royal Army Service Corps. An RASC veteran later recalled 'in September, 1939 there were six of us standing on the corner opposite the Duke of York Barracks on the Kings Road. We had been to all the [infantry] recruiting centres between Putney and Chelsea and received the same reply; there would be no recruiting until they had re-organised to accommodate a massive intake. However, as we stood talking, an army lorry came along with a banner, which read: "Join the RASC". We waved the driver down. He stopped, and we asked him if they were recruiting today. "Oh yes," he said, "Jump in the back and I'll take you to Woolwich".'[2]

Atkinson must have applied to join the RASC early in 1940 for by 26 October that year he was commissioned as a second lieutenant. Volunteers were being sought for service in the Middle East, and it seems likely that Atkinson broke the soldiers' dictum of never volunteer for anything, volunteered for service in Egypt, and found himself sailing to North Africa the long way round aboard a troopship to arrive early in 1941.

The New Zealand accountant Jim Craig was almost the same age as Atkinson. As soon as the war began, New Zealand raised an infantry division to commit to the Empire's forces, and one of its new battalions was the 22nd,[3] formed in January 1940 under the leadership of Colonel Andrew, a First World War veteran with a Victoria Cross (VC) who was quickly nicknamed 'Old February' because of his fondness for twenty-eight day detentions for minor infractions. The battalion sailed for Europe in the late spring of 1940 and arrived in Gourock on 17 June 1940, just as Paris was falling. It spent the rest of the year in the south of England practising its military skills (mostly route marching) while waiting for a German invasion that did not come. In early January 1941 22nd Battalion was ordered to Egypt aboard the converted merchant ship *Duchess of Bedford*. Craig arrived with his battalion just outside Cairo on 6 March.[4]

After three weeks of acclimatization and kit issues Craig's battalion was embarked for Greece on 26 March in the steamer *Hellas*. Lieutenant Ed McAra, one of Craig's fellow platoon commanders wrote home en route, 'If events go well the little foothold we can find in Europe in the Mediterranean may prove as disastrous in the end to Hitler as Wellington's foothold in remote Portugal proved to a scornful Napoleon. On the other hand, it may just as easily lead to another Dunkirk – who knows, or cares, so long as we have the chance of a smack at them at last? The whole camp is as cheerful and a-whistle as though we were embarking for home. We're as fit as men can be and only ask a fair chance'.[5]

Hellas was slow and the sea rough so it was not until 30 March that Craig's battalion disembarked at Piraeus. Allied[6] troops had been arriving in Greece for a fortnight, making Craig a latecomer to the party. As soon as they arrived, units were despatched on a slow road trip 250 miles north to create a defensible line against the anticipated attack along the eastern slopes of the Aliakhmon Mountains. With too few men to protect everywhere, the commander of Lustre Force, General 'Jumbo' Wilson,[7] decided to dig defensive positions on the forward slopes of this ridge of steep high hills that runs for sixty miles north from the Aegean sea to the Yugoslav border and cuts off the rolling farmland of Thrace from the heartland of Greece. His choice meant that defence of the northeastern parts of Greece, those bordering the Aegean that include the major port of Salonika, would have to depend on the Metaxas Line and Greek troops. So long as Yugoslavia remained neutral, Wilson's left flank would rest on its border, forcing the German army to assault a well-defended mountainous position in order to enter Greece.

Wilson was also banking on General Papagos' promise to pull three of his divisions back from the Bulgarian border to the Aliakhmon Line, and on receiving two more divisions from the reserve in Egypt. These would give Wilson seven entrenched divisions to defend sixty miles of steep mountain.[8] This promised Greek withdrawal was an effective surrender of northeast Greece and its city Salonika, which it had acquired at great cost from Bulgaria only thirty years before. However, though the order was given in Athens, it was not actioned, leaving Wilson with just two divisions to face the German assault: the Australians in the north and the New Zealanders in the south. Craig's battalion was allocated a position at the southern end of the line on the foothill slopes of Mount Olympus, facing north and east between the mountain and the Aegean Sea.

At four on the morning of 6 April 1941, Jim Craig was lying in his bedding roll contemplating another spring day of digging trenches and fire pits, and the morning cup of tea which his batman would shortly be bringing him. A hundred miles to his northeast Corporal Sepp di Giampietro of the Brandenburger Regiment was already up and turned-to to go to war for the first time: 'zero hour was here … we got ready to decamp. Nothing but absolute essentials was to be packed into our rucksacks: toiletries and one change of clothing. The rest of the kit was stuffed into our laundry bags and thrown onto the baggage vehicle. We checked our ammunition, oiled our MG belts, filled our rifle magazines with new bullets to prevent anything from getting stuck, and cleaned our hand grenades. Finally we filled our flasks with hot tea'.[9]

Born in Tyrol to a family with an Italian name but a fanatically Austrian and Germanic heritage, di Giampietro's name concealed a passionate devotion to Germany and Germanism that only a true exile can feel. Tyrolean hopes of reunification with the Reich had been dashed when Hitler and Mussolini had formally accepted the borders agreed at Versailles in 1919, so di Giampietro decided to make a personal unilateral reunification by smuggling himself across the border and joining the Wehrmacht. As a mountain dweller and a proficient linguist, he had been allocated to a company of Gebirgsjager – German mountain troops. In November 1940, his company's second-in-command, Lieutenant Grabert, had assembled his men and briefed them, under dire threats of court martial if they breathed a word outside the company, that they were now a company of the Brandenburgers.[10]

Neither di Giampietro nor his comrades had any idea what was special about Brandenburgers. Grabert quickly enlightened them. The Brandenburgers' task was to act as the tip of the German Army spear; dressing in enemy uniforms to infiltrate his front before the main assault started, they would sow confusion, misdirect and, where possible, kill. The Brandenburgers were allocated to Marita. On 6 April 1941, di Giampietro's company, Number Eight, would be part of the flanking movement moving west into Yugoslavia. Once the campaign had begun, Greek prisoners quickly began to trickle through, where they were relieved of their coats and helmets and searched for identity papers, which proved useful to the Brandenburgers later in the attack. On 8 April, di Giampietro and his section were aboard a captured Greek truck, dressed in a motley assortment of Greek and Serb overcoats, driving through the collapsing front line to a bridge over the river Vardar at Polykastro.[11] Even this early in Marita, day two, the Greek front was chaotic. Greek soldiers, mistaking the Brandenburgers for Serbs, hitched a ride on the southbound truck, helpfully aiding its cover. 'They … wanted to climb up onto our truck. They handed us up their rifles, which we of course gratefully accepted. Some soldiers actually managed to climb into the truck … others simply stood on the footboard … everyone seemed to be happy',[12] the Greeks because they were moving away from the front, and the Brandenburgers because their camouflage was being enhanced by a crowd of Greek hangers-on.

General Wilson's defence plan also dissolved on day one of Marita, when half of the 150,000 German invasion force simply crossed the border with Yugoslavia and drove west for fifty miles before turning south along the thirty-mile-wide valley of the Strimon River, to appear in his rear. By day four, a German panzer division was advancing up the Strimon Valley towards the district town of Kozani. Wilson, threatened with rapid envelopment from his rear, immediately started to pull his troops back from the Aliakhmon

Mountains, to begin a rapid fighting withdrawal. No Greek divisions had come to his aid. His rear was being enveloped, and he was outnumbered three to one. Another part of Wilson's problem was that he had almost no air force. A small handful of RAF fighters had been sent to Greece, where they found themselves pitted against some 400 Luftwaffe fighters and bombers supporting Marita. One of the Hurricanes deployed to Greece was flown by Pilot Officer Roald Dahl of 33 Squadron: 'for once our entire force of Hurricanes in Greece, all twelve of us … took off and headed for Athens, which was no more than four minutes' flying time away … suddenly the whole sky around us seemed to explode with German fighters. They came down on us from high above, not only 109s but also the twin-engined 110s … wherever I looked I saw an endless blur of enemy fighters whizzing towards me from every side … I threw my Hurricane around as best I could and whenever a Hun came into my sights, I pressed the button. It was truly the most breathless and in a way the most exhilarating time I have ever had in my life. The sky was so full of aircraft that half my time was spent in actually avoiding collisions.'[13]

Dahl was fighting over Athens. Wilson, 200 miles to the north, had no air cover at all. The handful of bad roads connecting his supply base at Piraeus with his front were under constant air attack, as were any formations that tried to withdraw along them. His position quickly grew even worse. Wilson was in part depending on Greek divisions on his flanks to stand their ground. These quickly melted away. On 15 April (day nine of Marita), General Tsolakoglou, commanding the Greek army in Epirus and the Pindus Mountains facing the Italian army, ordered his men to leave their weapons behind and withdraw about forty miles southeast, where new weapons were waiting for them. Australian memoirs of that day record that no new weapons were waiting, and that the men just carried on past their mustering points and headed home. One Australian Brigadier recalled seeing 'a convoy of magnificent cars and charabancs, filled with Greek officers, [drive] past to cross the bridge. In the second or third car was General Tsolakoglou who leant out of the window and waved farewell to me with a broad smile on his face'.[14] It appeared that General Metaxas was not the only senior Greek officer to favour the Axis. On the same day, in Athens, the minister for the army and the Greek General Headquarters (GHQ) were issuing an order for two months' leave for most of the Greek army, effective immediately.

The fascist members of the Greek dictatorship were deliberately sabotaging their own defence.

Even with a Greek army beside it, Lustre Force had been outnumbered. Now, effectively fighting a force three times larger than his own, which was enjoying air superiority verging on air dominance, Wilson's only option was to retire and evacuate as fast as possible. Lieutenant Ed McAra's prediction of another Dunkirk was about to come true. To cover the retreat, Wilson had to leave a handful of battalions to fight delaying actions in the gorges and valleys leading out of the Aliakhmon Hills. Craig's 22nd Battalion was one of these. By day ten of Marita, Allied forces were already boarding ships at Volos on Greece's east coast, fifty miles behind the Aliakhmon Line, and at Piraeus. On the same day, 16 April, the new Prime Minister of Greece, Alexander Koryzis (appointed in February after the death of Metaxas), shot himself. Six days later, the Greek government informed the German ambassador in Athens that it was surrendering, and had ordered Greek forces to return home on indefinite leave.

In a nod to the classics, which would have pleased British public-school-educated officers, a delaying stand was made at Thermopylae, buying a few more days for retreat and evacuation. Forces in retreat can usually move faster than forces in pursuit because they can demolish bridges and roads behind them and leave dumps of stores and fuel in flames. This, and delaying actions north of Athens, allowed General Wilson to get the great majority of Lustre Force embarked on one ship or another, first at Volos, then at Piraeus and Porto Rafti east of Athens, and finally, when German forces entered Athens on day twenty-one, from the old Venetian port of Nafplion.

Jim Craig's battalion was lifted from Rafti beach east of Athens on day eighteen of the invasion by HMS *Glengyle*, just three weeks after he had landed. Evacuations were highly dangerous. Everywhere, the Luftwaffe's Stuka dive-bombers were attacking ships, while fighter aircraft were attacking columns of men and machines on the few roads to the beaches. *Glengyle* fought off a dive-bombing attack with a rifle barrage from the 5,000 men crammed onto her decks. Other ships were less lucky. Only a few days were left in which it would be possible to bring ships of any kind, merchant or military, close to the beaches. Day twenty-one of Marita saw the Greek spring bursting into gorgeous bright sunshine. Road verges were a riot of wildflowers, where they weren't a drift of wrecked or abandoned vehicles.

Sepp di Giampietro's section had reached Thebes (modern Thiva) with two Opel Blitz light trucks and was just thirty miles, as the crow flies, from Athens. The main road southeast to Athens had been rendered unusable by the retreating Lustre Force. Di Giampietro was ordered to find any route possible to Athens at the fastest speed possible. A road to the east was open, which led after just fifteen miles to the Evripos Strait at Chalkis and the island of Evvia. Here, the Brandenburgers met the reconnaissance unit of an SS Panzer division. They quickly decided that they were in a race to Athens, so they abandoned the main road, which went south before turning towards Athens. Instead, di Giampietro took the direct line southwest towards the capital along back tracks and even, for several miles, along the tracks and sleepers of a rail line.

The Brandenburgers won the race. A few hours later, di Giampietro and his comrades dumped their Opels at the threshold of the Acropolis. Grabbing their Swastika flag from under a seat, the young men ran enthusiastically up the Acropolis hill, sparks flying off their hobnailed boots. 'We sprinted as we could see the [SS] motorcyclists driving up the hill behind us, and we certainly didn't want to have them beating us to it. We reached the flagpole on the northern flank of the Acropolis … and quickly fastened to the mast our creased and crumpled flag … Lieutenant Grabert issued the order: "hoist the flag".'[15] The Swastika fluttered out in the late afternoon sun. Greece had fallen.

Or more correctly, the mainland of Greece had fallen precipitately, but a Greek tragedy needs two acts. Thanks largely to the delaying actions fought by Australians and New Zealanders, General Wilson had managed to extricate some eighty-five per cent of his men from the mainland in a variety of ships. Most of the evacuees went straight back to Egypt, but a large number, some 20,000, were dropped off at Souda Bay on the north side of Crete to form a new garrison against a new invasion which GHQ in Cairo knew was coming, for Ultra decrypts had delivered the entire operational plan. Operation Marita was finished, and Operation Mercury was about to begin.

Marita's operational plan had allowed just seven days for rest and resupply before its divisions returned north for Barbarossa. Marita was already running late – its original timetable had been for Athens to fall on 21 April rather than 27 April, with its forces rushing north for Barbarossa within a week.

An invasion of Crete was not originally a part of Marita. One man set out to change that, as much for his own satisfaction as for any strategic gain.

General Kurt Student had started his military career in the army, but during the Great War had transferred to the Luftwaffe, where he achieved considerable success and a close friendship with his fellow flyer Hermann Goering. The Treaty of Versailles deprived Germany of an air force, leaving this hardened, ascetic, dedicated warrior with time on his hands. This he filled by developing ideas to use air-dropped troops, which he had seen developed in Russia, which had carried out its first paratrooper exercises in 1935. To men whose early experience had been slogging towards enemy lines through mud and artillery barrages, the idea of being dropped in force behind those lines to envelop them from the rear was immensely appealing. Russia's pioneering work on the use of paratroopers ended on the same day that its proponent, Marshal Tukhachevsky, was arrested in a Stalin purge in 1937, but Germany's interest had taken root and its paratrooper arm was formally born in 1936 as a unit of the army. Student inveigled his way to command of the new unit in 1938, in the process wresting its control from the army to the Luftwaffe. During the Sudeten crisis in 1938, Student carried out a demonstration drop from 250 Junkers 52 aircraft. By the end of 1939, the Luftwaffe had two Flieger (flyer) regiments of about 4,000 men each (a German regiment was roughly equivalent to a British brigade).

These were no ordinary men, but the pick of German youth: tall, educated and fanatically dedicated to Germany and National Socialism. Student's paratroopers took part in the invasions of Norway and Belgium, with considerable success, and were also central to the capture of the Corinth isthmus and canal in Greece just after the fall of Athens in April 1941. Student's reputation was assured, but he wasn't finished. He wanted to show that his elite force could go beyond supporting the army and win a victory of its own, and in Crete, he saw an opportunity to show exactly what his force could do. Student's idea had originally been rejected as part of Marita. In April 1941, he therefore boarded his personal aircraft and flew to Austria to see if he could change Marita's second act.

Marita's operational command was being conducted some 600 miles behind the fighting, from the Austrian town of Semmering. Here, on 20 April, Student presented himself and traded on his relationship with Goering to win an audience. Goering listened and acknowledged one of Student's key points – that an Allied occupation of Crete was an asset to the control of the shipping route for Romanian oil and might provide a base for air attacks on the oilfields themselves, and would anyway become a source of permanent irritation to Axis forces in the Eastern Mediterranean. Goering also agreed to sponsor a meeting with Hitler himself. Aboard Hitler's private train (ironically named the *Amerika*), Hitler agreed with Student's points and overruled the OKW, with an order to occupy Crete expressed in Leader Directive number 28, released on 25 April. Operation Mercury was on.

Student had probably not expected to win the argument. Only one-fifth of his paratroopers were actually in Greece. The rest, three regiments of some 4,000 men each, had to be rushed south from their barracks, along with their gliders, past the flood of infantry and panzer divisions repositioning north to Barbarossa's start line. Student had to plan Mercury in detail – where to land, and whether to land in a single set of drops or in sequential drops. Hitler complicated the planning by insisting that the attack include two battalions of ground troops and heavy equipment sent by sea, in case the airborne assault faltered. Whatever the plan, nothing could happen until Student had enough aviation fuel. Each round trip from Athens to Crete by a Junkers 52 would consume a tonne and a half of fuel. With the necessary follow-on supply trips and fuel for supporting fighters and dive-bombers, Mercury needed a stock of 12,000 tonnes of fuel on hand before it could start. Some stocks of aviation fuel had been captured in Greece, but not enough. More would have to come from Italy, and the fastest way to get it to Greece was through the Corinth Canal. But Lieutenant Mike Cumberlege, of the Royal Naval Volunteer Reserve (RNVR), had other ideas.

The idea of blocking the Corinth Canal had been drifting around both Cairo and London for over a year. The canal was not, and is still not, a vital strategic route, for it cuts just 150 miles and half a day's sailing from the route connecting the Romanian oil fields to Italy. However, in a Mediterranean patrolled by the Royal Navy, it had the advantage of moving Axis merchant traffic a welcome distance northwards, away from detection and attack. It also helped Italy protect the flow of fuel and ammunition to its Dodecanese Islands. Without the canal, supplies bound for Rhodes would have to sail close by Crete, where British aircraft and ships were waiting. The Corinth Canal became an early Allied target, in theory at least. In September 1940, a month before Italy's invasion of Greece, Admiral Godfrey, in charge of naval Intelligence in London, ordered Special Operations Executive (SOE) to prepare to block it by acquiring one or more suitable small ships which could be used either as a blockship or to lay mines. No actual action was to be taken before Greece became a belligerent with one or other of the Axis powers. A small flotilla of old merchantmen and caiques was bought and assembled at Alexandria in preparation.[16] Destruction of the canal was easy to order but less easy to deliver. The canal runs for just three miles through a deep, steep cut in the sandstone of the Corinth isthmus. From the water level, its sides rise some 150 feet almost vertically, rendering them inaccessible to high-level bombing.

Because the canal was both shallow and short, a blockship sunk anywhere along it would block the canal only for as long as it took to blow the wreck apart with explosives and drag the pieces away. If the canal were mined, it would be a simple task to search its bottom and remove or countermine the charge. With only three miles to guard anyway, it would be difficult, if not impossible, to lay a mine from a transiting boat unobserved. A detailed study revealed that the only permanent way to block the canal was to undercut one of its precipitous sides with a large explosive charge detonated at the base of the canal in the hope of dropping a landslide of rock into the waterway. However, an attack on the canal sides would need many tons of high explosive and leisurely access to the canal to plant them.

The coming of Marita changed the requirement, if not the mechanics. On 21 April, leading German units were less than 100 miles from Athens and moving south fast. The naval attaché in Athens, Admiral Richard Turle, delegated the blockage of the canal to a naval reservist who had sailed extensively in Greece before the war, Lieutenant Mike Cumberlege. Cumberlege had spent his secondary school years in the nautically orientated Pangbourne College, which acted as a feeder school for young naval officers. From there, he had instead joined the Merchant rather than the Royal Navy. After winning his second mate's certificate, Cumberlege more or less retired from full-time seagoing, married and settled down in a rented cottage at Cap d'Antibes from where he took on jobs working in and around the world of luxury yachts. In 1939, Cumberlege did a favour for his family friend, Admiral Godfrey, by closely inspecting the Italian coast for possible landing spots in his American employer's yacht *Landfall*,[17] before sailing her through the Corinth Canal to the Aegean. Cumberlege was called up in 1940, and in February 1941, he arrived in Alexandria to work with the odd flotilla of small ships being collected there by SOE. Three days before Marita he took command of the ketch *Dolphin II* in Athens. *Dolphin II* was supplied with eight depth charges, a 1,650-pound magnetic mine and a set of limpet mines with time fuses. On 24 April, when it had become clear that Greece would fall (and that the canal would be of no more use to Allied forces), Cumberlege sailed his yacht 'innocently' along it under the cover of rescuing Allied troops from the Gulf of Corinth.

The depth charges, hidden in a dinghy towed astern, were sunk by the simple means of sinking the dinghy itself, with an axe. A few yards further on, the mine, slung under a canvas cover over *Dolphin II*'s side, was also cut free. All the charges were fitted with limpet mines set to a seven-day delay. If all went according to plan, they would detonate on 1 May,[18] and their tonne of high explosive would hopefully collapse the steep side of the canal. After this, *Dolphin II*'s charges disappear from sight. History does not relate what happened to them. The most likely outcomes were either that they were found and disarmed by an Axis sweep of the canal or that they detonated but did no damage to the canal's walls. Either way, the canal remained open.

Cumberlege was not the only man tasked with damaging the canal. SOE had also been working on sinking a barge at its entrance and successfully did so at the end of April. Thirdly, during the battle in which the canal was captured by Student's paratroopers, the road bridge over it had fallen into the waterway after a last desperate demolition charge was detonated by a Hail Mary rifle shot. Work to clear the canal took until 16 May, and the delay meant that the shipload of aviation fuel ordered from Italy for Operation Mercury did not arrive until 19 May.

The final plan for the invasion of Crete, Operation Mercury, was for one large drop of 4,000 men onto the airfield at Maleme at the western end of Crete by a force of 500 Junkers 52s, with a second drop several hours later on the eastern airfields of Rethymno and Heraklion. A mountain division would land at Maleme in a third wave of Junkers 52s, with the seaborne force arriving at more or less the same time. Operation Mercury would be the largest paratrooper operation of the war, until Operation Market Garden dropped some 65,000 men into Holland in 1944. What was obviously an operation with a very high risk of disaster would be made less risky with the intensive use of close air support. As a first step, the Luftwaffe began the systematic destruction of Crete's small RAF presence on 14 May, taking just five days to establish effective air superiority. On the warmer than average 19 May, with plenty of fuel on hand, and with dusk turning into a velvet night, the first wave of Student's men boarded their aircraft. Loading took most of the short summer night. 'It was a few minutes after 4am when my aircraft taxied onto the runway. The first light of dawn scarcely penetrated the red dust raised by the machines during the night [testing their engines] which hung like a dense fog over the airfield.'[19]

General Freyberg, the New Zealander in command of Crete's garrison, knew perfectly well the invasion was coming. Ultra decrypts had revealed a plan to attack Crete as early as 1 May (less than a week after Hitler's Directive Number 28), and had also revealed the start date as 17 May, not that the date was delayed by the blockage of the Corinth Canal. Freyberg had been initiated into Ultra when he was appointed to the command of Crete. A decrypt of 13 May revealed Mercury's plan in outline, with the numbers of troops involved and how they would arrive on Crete, but the exact detail of who, where and when was either not clear or, if it was known, was not passed on. Freyberg, a veteran of the First World War, was unaware of the size and power of Student's airborne division. He was, however, aware that islands usually fell to a seaborne invasion. He therefore spread his forces, 35,000 Allied troops and 10,000 Cretans, thinly along the whole eighty miles of coast from Maleme to Heraklion, averaging just 550 men per mile. Jim Craig found himself and the 612 men of 22nd Battalion, who had managed to escape from Greece unhurt at the very western end of Freyberg's thin khaki line, guarding the four-mile perimeter of the airfield at Maleme. Two thousand more New Zealanders were positioned seven miles to the east. None of the forces around Maleme had any heavy weapons, because these had been abandoned in Greece. They also lacked radios, but they were amply equipped with ammunition and had had some three weeks in which to rest and recuperate after their hasty departure from Porto Rafti. Jim Craig was not privy to Ultra, and had no idea that on the next day a brigade of Germany's most elite troops would literally descend on his head.

A visitor to Maleme today finds little to commemorate the battle which lost Crete to German occupation, and which resulted in the deaths of many thousands of Cretans who ferociously resisted both the invasion and the occupation that followed. The runway is still in use for small private planes. A hundred yards to the north, the Mediterranean flops gently onto a beach. A thousand yards south, the ground rises slightly to a 350-foot high pimple, grandly named Hill 107. Now, as it was in 1941, the hill is a stony landscape of hard earth and scrubby olive trees that obscure the view north from ground level. On a staff map, it may have looked possible that a battalion placed around Hill 107 could 'cover' the open landing ground of the airfield. In practice, the view was then, as now, obscured by the olive groves that fill the ground between the hill and the airstrip. Five hundred yards north of the hill, about halfway between it and the runway, one comes across a two-acre cemetery where the bodies of 4,500 German soldiers lie. Most of these were General Student's paratroopers, and most died on the first day of the invasion.

Dawn on 20 May found Craig bivouacked on the western slope of Hill 107, a few hundred yards south of the airstrip. The rest of his battalion was thinly spread on a 650 yard perimeter encircling the airfield, with one detachment on the field itself. Craig's battalion was the westernmost unit of a line that stretched all the way east to Heraklion and beyond, and Craig was almost the westernmost man in that line, overlooking the dry riverbed of the Tavronitis River, which formed the western boundary of Maleme Airfield. A few minutes after dawn, the German attack was announced by a wave of bombers, dropping some 3,000 bombs on 22nd Battalion's positions. The New Zealand Official History of the war, written in 1958, described this attack: 'Dust and smoke billowed up; the earth shook with explosions; trees splintered; slit trenches caved in (in one substantial five-man trench only [one man] survived); men, dazed and numb with the fury of the assault, bled from ears and mouths'.[20] Sergeant Sargeson wrote later, 'the silence after the blitz was eerie, acrid and ominous'.[21] The blitz killed few men but cut all of the telephone lines connecting Craig to Battalion headquarters on Hill 107.

Three-hundred-and-twenty miles north of Craig, on the outskirts of Athens, the paratrooper force of 500 Junkers 52 aircraft carrying some 3,500 men, towing forty gliders with 400 more, had taken off as dawn pinked the spring Aegean sky. By 5.30 am the force was assembled and organized and on its way. The gliders arrived first at 7.45 am, not on the airfield but on the empty ground west of Craig's position. Craig's comrade, Captain Campbell, later wrote: 'I still have vivid recollections of the gliders coming down with their quiet swish, swish, dipping down and swishing in'.[22]

Wherever they landed, they met with immediate, intense fire. Many of the men in the gliders were shot while still airborne, and if they managed to land were shot before they had escaped the aircraft's fuselage. Craig's D company was in the middle of a line of three depleted companies, each of about twenty men, occupying 150 yards of front overlooking the Tavronitis riverbed and the flat ground beyond. Seventeen gliders landed here and disgorged 150 paratroopers. Craig engaged them as they left the gliders, killing a third and wounding another third. A sharp firefight ensued between roughly equal numbers of survivors – about sixty on each side.

A few minutes after the gliders came half of the Junkers 52s, dropping three battalions of paratroopers. Two of these landed a mile west of the Tavronitis riverbed, where they could extract their weapons from their cargo containers and assemble into an effective fighting order safe from New Zealander fire. Craig's company now had some 1,800 of Germany's best-trained, most highly motivated soldiers advancing towards his sixty men dug in along the east bank of the Tavronitis river. On Craig's right lay the 100 men of C Company, in trenches between him and the airfield. North of Craig and slightly behind him, a third German assault battalion had landed by parachute on the airfield, where it was being slaughtered by the rest of 22nd Battalion and other units. Here, the German mortality rate reached sixty per cent, with almost all the survivors receiving wounds. Men were shot while still aboard their aircraft. Men were shot as they floated earthwards. Men were shot as they struggled out of their harnesses, and men were shot while they searched for their weapons containers. Almost no one among the paratroopers survived.

The slaughter was prodigious, but the men facing Craig had suffered no such depredations. The Germans who landed west of the Tavronitis River focussed their assault on the platoons to Craig's right, between him and the sea, leaving just a small handful of paratroopers to engage Craig's Company directly from a distance. In Jim Craig's own words, 'No. 17 Platoon had a fairly easy time of it most of the day'. Craig must have listened to the sounds of intense small-arms fire crackling to his right and away to the north for most of that day with an uneasy sense of uncertainty as to what was happening, while occasionally engaging the paratroopers to his front. Runners were sent to and from Craig's platoon but failed to arrive, either dead, wounded, captured or lost. Late in the afternoon, the firefights around Maleme died away, as the Germans reformed and called their rolls. At the end of the first day, resistance over the airfield had faded, and German paratroopers were in occupation, though in the most tenuous way.

In the evening twilight, the survivors of D company, about fifty men unhurt and out of ammunition, decided to retire towards their battalion headquarters on Hill 107. There, they found the position empty. With no orders or information beyond what they had already seen, including an earlier agreement that if Maleme was taken, the battalion would withdraw and reform to the south, at 3.00 am on 21 May, D Company started a weary slog southwards and eastwards.

22nd Battalion was part of the 5th New Zealand Brigade. Craig's brigadier, Hargest, seemed not to realize how serious the position was, for he had retired to bed in his pyjamas. Shortly afterwards, a messenger arrived to tell him that 22nd Battalion's defence of the airfield had been almost overcome. While Hargest slept, Craig, threading the dark olive groves southwards, did not know that ahead of him the ground was already occupied by paratroopers who had landed more or less unopposed and worked around his southern flank. As the black Cretan night gave way to a rosy dawn, Craig found himself surrounded. His men had fired off all their ammunition the day before, with just two rounds per man left. After Craig had taken cover, a German officer appeared under a white flag and politely pointed out that he knew they had no ammunition left since they were not firing at his men, and that in those circumstances the most sensible course of action was to surrender. Craig agreed.[23]

On that disastrous first day, when the paratroopers were at their most vulnerable, Hargest made no moves to order his three fresh battalions forward to retake the airfield. By the time they did counterattack (between 3.00 and 7.00 am on 22 May, twenty-four hours later), 1,000 more Germans had landed on Maleme and were ready for action. The counterattack, weakly coordinated, disorganized and delayed until daylight revealed it to the ever-present Luftwaffe, was broken up. Maleme had fallen, and Crete would soon follow. It took ten more days for the survivors of Student's force to drive the Island's defenders south into the White Mountains and to Crete's south coast, where the Royal Navy waited to pick them up. 22nd Battalion started the battle with 612 men. Just 200 of them made it back to Egypt, leaving 100 dead and the rest captured, including Jim Craig.

With little time and few spare men, Student's paratroopers were none too fussy about the Geneva Conventions. Hundreds of Allied troops and thousands of Cretans were shot out of hand after capture.[24] One cause of this systematic war crime was doubtless an impulse to avenge the appalling mortality rate experienced by the paratroopers themselves (in many cases more than half, in some seventy-five per cent). Other factors were a belief that Cretan irregular forces should not have resisted at all, being civilians, and that a civilian who fought was not entitled to any rights after capture. And finally, the sheer number of prisoners threatened to overwhelm the small number of men available to guard them. The survivors of German retribution found themselves behind barbed wire in a temporary, highly unsanitary camp at Galatas. Jim Craig was one of these. Somewhere else in the Galatas camp, which held thousands of men, both fit and wounded, was Lieutenant John Atkinson. Atkinson had been in command of a detachment guarding a transport pool somewhere behind Hargest's New Zealand Brigade, but close enough to have been fighting off glider-borne troops. Atkinson had been part of the retreat across the White Mountains but had missed the chance of a ship home from Sphakia on Crete's south coast and ended up in Galatas.

By the end of May, the Cretan summer was in full swing. Galatas became a petri dish for the diseases of neglect and poor sanitation, compounded by malaria. We have no detailed records, but Atkinson and Craig must both have fallen badly ill, for within days of their capture, they were on Junkers flights from Maleme to Athens. From the dusty landing ground outside Athens, they were trucked a few miles to Kokkinia, where a prisoner of war hospital had been hurriedly set up in an old barracks between Athens and Piraeus. At Kokkinia, both men would have had some time to reflect and recover from the shock of their experiences. The fall of Crete will have left them reeling. Just 10,000 Germans had managed to cross 150 miles of water, which was under enemy control and set a force of 45,000 running in chaos verging on panic. The defenders lacked heavy weapons because of their hurried departure from Greece, but the paratroopers, too, had few guns and no tanks. Some 8,500 Allied troops had been captured. As with Dunkirk just a year before, the Allied narrative focussed on the heroic rescue of 35,000 men rather than the humiliating defeat that preceded it, but Craig and Atkinson knew the reality and must have felt its pain acutely. Their pain was probably worsened by the fact that for both men, this was their second rout in a month. As their health returned Craig and Atkinson, who were acquainted but evidently not friends, independently made plans to escape from Kokkinia and return to the war as quickly as they could. Neither man knew that they would do so in HMS *Triumph*, with tragic consequences.

Chapter 6

The Bardia Raid

Marita's start day, 6 April, was a Sunday. In His Majesty's ships, Sunday routine was a welcome break from the six-day working week. On the very second of half past seven *Medway*'s quartermaster, the Leading Seaman who had been guarding the ship's gangway for three and a half hours in his small caboose, clicked the main broadcast tannoy microphone, gripped his silver bosun's call between his front teeth and blew into it the call-the-hands pipe at full pitch. The piercing notes of his whistling shocked *Medway*'s ship's company from sleep, and were immediately followed by a cheery, slightly gloating, shout of 'call the hands call the hands call the hands. Lash up and stow'. In *Medway* messdecks jerked into wakefulness, while her officers were more gently roused by the knock of a steward on their cabin doors with 'tea sir?'.

There was nothing to do between call-the-hands and divine service on the quarterdeck (attendance compulsory) except make sure that tropical white uniforms were clean and pressed, so *Triumph*'s ship's company enjoyed a leisurely breakfast with fresh fruit and newly baked bread for the first time in a fortnight. The German invasion of Greece that morning was not much more than the news of the day. Their week ahead contained the usual routine of swapping their torpedoes for freshly maintained ones from *Medway*'s torpedo workshop, replenishing fuel, water and food, greasing every external valve and hinge on their boat, getting the flotilla staff to work on minor defects that had appeared off Rhodes and, most important, evening runs ashore to the fleshpots of Alexandria. Domestic concerns were never far from their minds. Telegraphist Billy White wrote home that week, 'I may increase my allotment [of pay sent home to help his parents] as I might as well give up trying to save money, for from what I can gather we are paying [fifty per cent] income tax. Some of the single Petty Officers are paying nearly a pound a week. If the war lasts much longer we'll be getting paid in IOUs'[1]. In Alexandria, beer and female company were abundant, but not cheap.

During the hour-long gap that divided breakfast and church, Woods and his first lieutenant, Michael Janvrin, presented themselves in the airy office of their Flotilla Commander, Captain Sydney Raw, with their patrol report to discuss the Rhodes beach survey and to hear what might be in store for *Triumph*'s next patrol. Both officers had swapped their seagoing 'pirate rig' for a set of freshly laundered crisp white tropical uniforms which they'd found waiting for them in their cabins in *Medway*, for their Commander in Chief, Admiral Cunningham, was a stickler for keeping the men in his command smartly turned out in the rig of the day. Raw told Woods and Janvrin that Cordite was cancelled, but that the success of *Triumph*'s cooperation off Rhodes with her three commandos meant that he had promised her to the General Staff for another commando mission – a raid in force on Axis supply lines along the coast of Libya.

The situation in the Western Desert had turned swiftly from excellent to awful. Just two months earlier, on 7 February, the war against the Italians looked almost as good as won. Nine Italian divisions (130,000 men) had surrendered at El Agheila, 620 miles west of Cairo. Another 150,000 men still barred the remaining 400 miles to Tripoli, but the Italian threat to Egypt and the Persian Gulf oil fields had effectively been neutralized. On 9 February, Churchill had ordered the rest of the army to stop, catch its breath, and concentrate on its long supply line back to Egypt. But while Wavell's army was resting in Africa, Hitler had been working hard to bail out his Italian ally. A month before the Italian defeat, on 11 January, Hitler issued Leader Directive Number 22, which began: 'Tripolitania must be held…'[2] and went on to direct that 'Commander In Chief Army will provide covering forces sufficient to render valuable service to our allies in the defence of Tripolitania, particularly against British armoured divisions. Special orders for the composition of this force will follow'.[3]

The operation that ensued was christened Sunflower,[4] and saw the arrival in Libya of a force equivalent to an armoured division and an infantry division, a month later, more or less at the same time as the Italian surrender. The arrival of Sunflower's forces, quickly named the Afrika Korps under General Erwin Rommel, has to be seen as a major strategic defeat for the British. Rommel's men could only arrive in Libya by ship and had to pass Malta en route. They should have been sunk at sea by a combination of Malta's submarines, surface ships and aircraft. Shrimp Simpson had six newly arrived small U-class boats under his command, and he could reliably have at least two, and sometimes three, on patrol across the Axis convoy route. He also had the intelligence product of Bletchley Park, though it was unlikely that he knew where his intelligence came from. Simpson's submarines did try to engage Rommel's transports. During February 1941, they fired thirty-five torpedoes, but thirty-four either missed or failed to run true.[5] The single hit made little difference. It was characteristic of submarine commanders in 1941 that they took two or three patrols to refine their targeting skills, and Simpson's little flotilla had just arrived and was still firmly in its learning phase. Malta had little in the way of surface fleet in early 1941, and its aircraft were hard pressed defending the island against bombing raids, with little time to spare for attacks on shipping. The Afrika Korps arrived without losing a man.

Rommel himself reached Africa on 12 February. He quickly got to work organising his new command, to which had been added two Italian armoured divisions. Within a fortnight, Rommel's forces were seen by reconnaissance aircraft nearing El Agheila, and in March, the Afrika Korps was engaging and pushing back Allied forces 100 miles east and turning north to reach the port of Benghazi. The porous line of contact between the two forces continued to move north and east at about twenty-five miles per day as the Germans pressed forward and the Allies retired, usually in some confusion. At this pace, Cairo was theoretically now only three weeks away from the leading units of the Afrika Korps. With its defensive front creaking, if not actually collapsing, the General Staff in Cairo was looking furiously for a way of disrupting, distracting, or at least slowing Rommel's charge towards Egypt. It was obvious that both sides were suffering from acute supply problems. Units depended entirely on bulky supplies of fuel and water arriving by truck from supply bases hundreds of miles away. Rommel's supplies had to come from Tripoli, along a coastal road 800 miles long. If that road could be threatened from the sea, Rommel would be forced to move substantial forces, perhaps as much as half a division, from his front to his rear to guard it. But how could a force be projected ashore that far from Alexandria? What was needed was a unit trained and prepared for raiding operations from the sea, sufficiently large to pose a real threat. By chance, or perhaps foresight, just such a force was on hand a few miles from Cairo, in the form of the commandos.

In the second half of 1940, the new commandos, ten units of 500 men each, had begun to present something of a problem back home in England. Formed in quick time after Dunkirk and made up of volunteers from throughout the British Army, two early commando raids on the coasts of France and the Channel Islands had been farcical failures which only escaped becoming disasters through extreme good luck and some flexible thinking by the commanding officer of one of the destroyers that had carried it. Operation Colossus (the raid on the Calibri aqueduct that we saw in Chapter Three)[6] had turned out to be an actual disaster, with the entire force captured and its interpreters shot as traitors.

The army was growing jealous of the special status and somewhat eccentric and non-military approach to discipline enjoyed by the commandos, as well as of the fact that they had sucked the army's best and brightest men and officers out of line battalions while leaving them on their parent unit's payroll. If pinprick raids on Hitler's Fortress Europe were not going to work, why should this brigade-sized unit continue to exist? The only theatre in which significant operations against the Axis were in train was Egypt. Perhaps the commandos could make their mark there? The head of the Special Service Brigade, Charles Haydon, had decided to despatch three commandos (1,500 men) to the desert in the three Glen-class landing ships at the start of the year.[7] Roger Courtney, who was one of *Triumph*'s COPP party at Rhodes, reached Egypt in 8 Commando.

In command of this force was a man whose name became synonymous with the commandos after the war, Colonel Robert Laycock.[8] For some reason, General Wavell's staff enjoyed giving eponymous names to ad hoc units and groups of units, usually derived from the names or initials of their commanders. Laycock's force left the United Kingdom on 31 January 1941 as Force Z, but in its encampment in Egypt, it became Layforce. Among Laycock's command team was a young and eccentric author who would later use Laycock and Layforce as the inspiration for an autobiographical novel – Evelyn Waugh.

Whatever its name, at first no one on the staff had any idea how to use these 1,500 highly aggressive trained killers who came with no transport, artillery, mortars or logistic resources. They certainly would not fit into a normal infantry division and were too small and too lightly equipped to use as an independent unit anywhere else in the desert. However, lightness, speed and aggression might work very well in a surprise raid from the sea – exactly the kind of 'butcher and bolt' mission that Winston Churchill had in mind when he ordered the creation of the commando force nine months before. Under acute pressure from Rommel, General Wavell quickly saw the opportunity and ordered Laycock to prepare a raid on Rommel's supply line for the third week of April. The mission would be to land one commando (7 Commando) from the landing ships *Glenearn* and *Glengyle* with a cruiser and two destroyer escorts. Once ashore, they would kill, destroy, disrupt, and then depart within a few hours.

The operation would have to take place in darkness because a force of ships loitering off the beach of Bardia in daylight would likely be sunk by air attack. The commandos were used to working at night but finding the target beach in complete darkness was a different sort of challenge. What the raiding force needed was a lighthouse to show them where the beach was. Captain Raw suggested that one of his submarines could serve as the lighthouse, arriving in daylight at precisely the right spot then loitering until dark to surface and show an agreed light signal. He had a submarine on hand, fresh back from a patrol and ready for a new task – *Triumph*.

On 15 April, advance units of the Afrika Korps had already reached Sollum, just inside the border of Egypt and only 360 miles from Cairo. Behind the front, a dozen miles north of Sollum, their supplies travelled along the coast road just two miles from the sea outside the village of Bardia. This was chosen as the target of Layforce's first raid. Ideally the strike would have been aimed further west, away from Rommel's frontline units, but that would have demanded that Layforce's ships spend two days off Libya's coast, in plain sight, going and coming back, and would also have added a three- or four-day delay to the start of the operation.

Triumph sailed after lunch on 15 April, risking a departure in full daylight because she was in a tearing hurry. At full speed of about fourteen knots, Woods had 250 miles to cover. He expected to dive off the target beach shortly before dawn on 16 April and then carry out a slow survey of the area by periscope. Hunkered down on piles of tinned food in her fore ends were Roger Courtney and Corporal Sherwood, by now quite familiar with their temporary home, and Sergeant Major George Barnes, whose first trip in a submarine was probably noisier and rougher than he had expected. Woods had two tasks at Bardia. The first was to land the commando party by Folboat on a small rock at the southern end of the target beach, where they would put up a temporary navigation light to identify the exact landing beach. The second was to place *Triumph* two miles off the beach, where she would show a light out to sea to guide the landing ships in.

Everything was going according to plan, until the RAF interfered. On passage, on the surface and in daylight, off the Egyptian coast, *Triumph* was attacked by an RAF bomber.[9] In 1941, RAF aircrew were often poorly trained in ship recognition and many found navigation over a featureless sea a challenge. No matter how many briefings they might receive about the whereabouts of friendly forces, when they came across submarines on the surface they tended to attack without hesitation. Of the seventy-eight British submarines sunk during the war, two were sunk by the RAF.[10] A third was sunk by a USAF Liberator. Fully one third of the RN submarines sunk by aircraft in the war were sunk by the RAF. At least one submarine captain admitted in his memoirs that attack by the RAF was one of his chief worries on approaching his home base after a patrol. In addition to these actual sinkings, submariner memoirs contain many near misses. One submarine commanding officer returned to his base at Beirut having narrowly survived an attack by the RAF to find the aircrew who had nearly killed him and his men celebrating their supposed success in their mess.

On *Triumph*'s bridge that day, the lookouts would have seen the bomber well before it arrived over them. Able Seaman White, one of the boat's signallers, was probably furiously flashing the day's recognition signal skywards, but to no avail. Happily, the bomber's aim was as bad as its ship recognition. *Triumph* survived the attack, but it was a near miss, and one man was badly injured. With his life hanging in the balance, Woods turned around and headed back to Alexandria to land him and pick up a replacement from the Flotilla spare crew. Details are fuzzy because Woods' formal patrol report for the trip never made it to the archives in Kew – *Triumph*'s file records a single cryptic paragraph: '15th to 21st April – Special Operation' – and the attack is only referred to elsewhere in the record twice by inference.

While *Triumph* dashed to and fro, the landing force also returned briefly to Alexandria. *Triumph* reached Alexandria on the afternoon of 18 April and was under way again a few hours later. Racing back to Bardia at full speed she was just able to reach the beach in daylight, allowing her to make sure she was in the right place. Surfacing after dark on 19 April, her Folboat was passed up through the large torpedo loading hatch onto her casing, where Courtney, Sherwood and Barnes were waiting. The wood-and-wire stand for the light and its batteries were stowed in the canoe. The landing force was just over the horizon heading towards them at twenty knots. *Triumph* lay just a few hundred yards off a hostile shore, and everyone on board was tense.

As *Triumph* pitched and rolled in the heavy northerly swell, Courtney attempted to launch his Folboat off the fore planes. As soon as the canoe was in the water the swell lifted *Triumph* and dropped her onto the Folboat, smashing it to matchwood. There would be no beach light for the landing craft, though Courtney and Sherwood managed to climb back aboard. *Triumph* herself would have to serve as the sole beach lighthouse. An hour later most of 7 Commando and a troop of tanks had been landed, but when they moved inland, they found that there was very little to attack. An Italian supply dump was blown up, and an artillery battery destroyed. One man was lost to friendly fire as nervous men blundered around in the dark on their first actual operation. A troop of commandos got lost and returned to the wrong beach to find no landing craft waiting for them. They were captured the next day. The rest of the force successfully re-embarked and was well over the horizon by dawn, with *Triumph* in their rear, now thankfully running at periscope depth to keep the RAF at bay.

The raid did little actual damage, but it succeeded in its strategic aim of convincing Rommel that his supply line was vulnerable to a raid from the sea anywhere along its 800-mile length. A panzer brigade was taken out of the line to guard it, much to the relief of Wavell in Cairo. Laycock had conducted the Commandos' first successful operation, which had depended for its navigation on one of His Majesty's submarines. But while *Triumph* and her crew rested at eighty feet on their way back to Alexandria, Greece was falling. In Cairo, staff minds were already turning to the question of how to react to the coming fall, though in a state of chaotic confusion that would have painful consequences for *Triumph* and the exotic collection of spies, agents and special forces that she was to collect around her.

Triumph under way in 1938 in her pre-war paint.

Torpedo damage to *Triumph*'s bows, 1939. Undetonated torpedoes can still be seen in their tubes. (*The National Archives*)

The control room of a T-class submarine. (*IWM*)

Triumph leaving Malta on patrol.

Wilfrid (Sammy) Woods in November 1941 after his promotion to commander.

The view from the bridge of a T-class submarine while under way on the surface. (*IWM*)

Michael Janvrin, *Triumph*'s first lieutenant, in 1940.

The junior ratings' mess in a T-class submarine, home to twenty men. The junior engineering ratings had a similar mess. (*IWM*)

The torpedo stowage compartment (or fore ends). Spare torpedoes are lashed to the sides. (*IWM*)

A torpedo being loaded into its rack through the large torpedo hatch. (*IWM*)

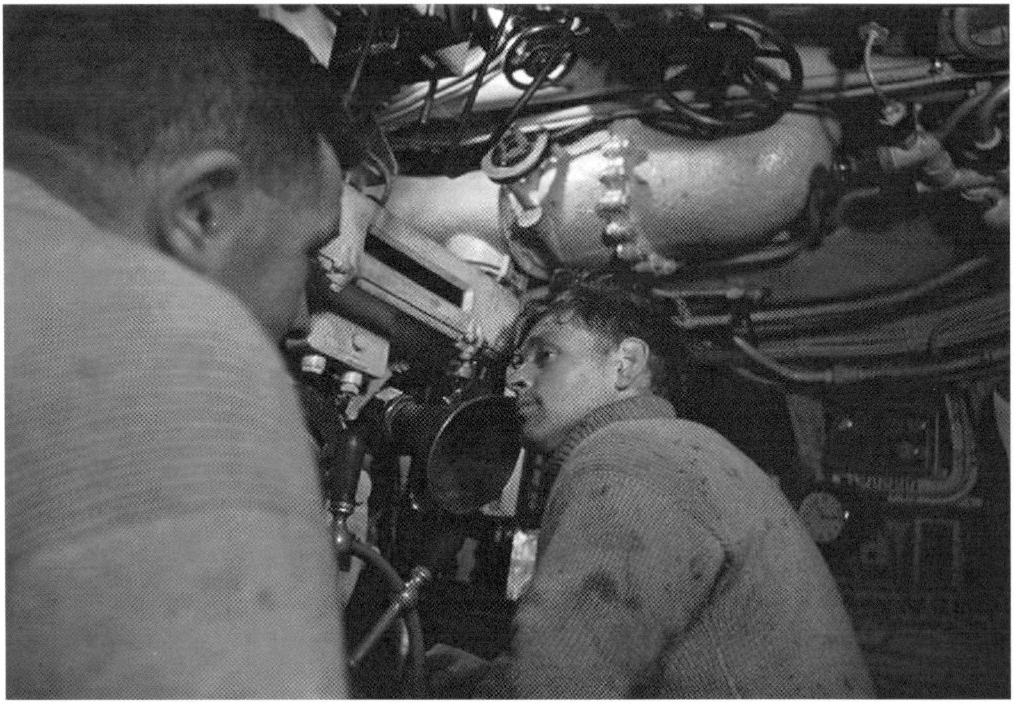

A man at the helm in the control room. Cleanliness was not a priority. (*IWM*)

Junior ratings playing cards in their mess. Patrols were ninety-nine per cent waiting around. (*IWM*)

The engine room of a T-class submarine. (*IWM*)

The duty watch alongside HMS *Medway* in Alexandria. (*Waye Family Collection*)

A leave party from *Triumph* at the pyramids in Egypt. The man in RAF uniform on the left was the party's driver. (*Wilkinson Family Archive*)

The Atkinson escape party at Cairo. Atkinson is on the left and Craig is seated on the right. (*NA Kew and Molloy Family Archive*)

Atkinson in the garden at 9 Patission Street. (*The Ioannou Family*)

Petty Officer Frank Collison, in charge of *Triumph*'s torpedoes. (*Frances Impey*)

Stoker Bert Gates. (*David Maclellan*)

Petty Officer Colin Duffay as a junior rate. (*Stuart Morrissey*)

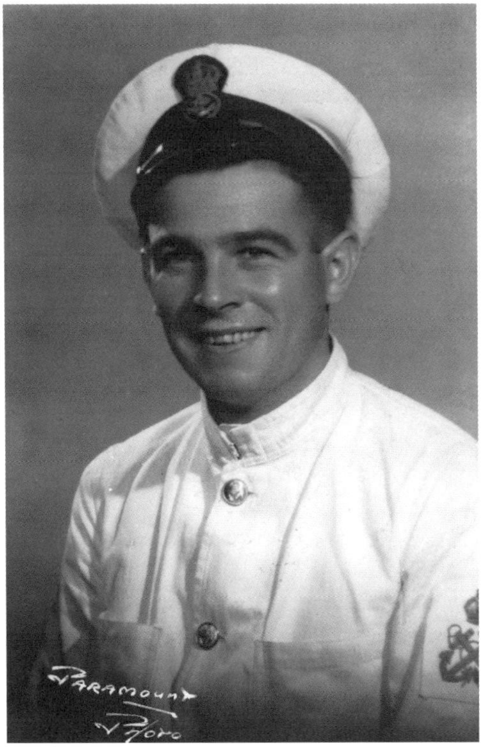

Artificer Bill Dempster. (*Rob Dempster*)

Leading Seaman John Hinds. (*Denise Rutherford*)

Able Seaman Richard Howard. (*Ann Carrington*)

Stoker Arthur Robinson. (*Harvey Taylor*)

Stoker Claude Baxter. (*Alun Baxter*)

Midshipman George Waterall. (*George May*)

Petty Officer Walter Wickham as a leading seaman. (*Wally Wickham*)

Lieutenant Robert Douglas-Don. (*Author's collection*)

A Mark VIII warhead, 600 pounds of high explosive. (*Author's collection*)

Harry Grammatikakis. (*The National Archives*)

Gun action. (*IWM*)

An Italian minelayer embarking mines. (*La Guerra di Mine*)

A two-man Folbot of the type used by *Triumph*. (*RNSMM*)

Wreaths laid by the Triumph Association above her wreck at Cape Sounio, 2024. (*Author's collection*)

Admiral Lord Boyce presents a memorial board of *Triumph*'s medals to the nuclear submarine HMS *Triumph*'s Junior Rates Mess. (*Author's photograph*)

The author in the control room of HMS *Alliance*. (*Pix*)

Triumph's wreck today. (*Kostas Thoctarides PlanetBlue*)

The descendants of *Triumph*'s crew gather to lay wreaths off the coast of Sounio.

Chapter 7

Secret House, Cairo

The commandos were not the only special operations organization conceived during Churchill's first month as Prime Minister. Two other secret entities, that were to play a major part in *Triumph*'s war, were formed at about the same time – the Special Operations Executive (SOE) and MI9.

SOE's birth was the culmination of an elephantine gestation. Its conception can be roughly dated to 1938, when a Royal Engineers major, Jo Holland, was appointed to a new 'desk' in the War Office with the obscure name of General Staff (Research), or GS(R). As Hitler was annexing parts of Czechoslovakia and Austria, Major Holland's brief was to study and analyze examples of guerilla warfare from recent wars, including the Boer War, the Russian Civil War, the wars in Spain and China, the Jewish insurrection in Palestine, and the war in Ireland – in which he had been wounded in 1919.

In a happy coincidence, so common in the history of the war, one of Holland's cadet classmates, Major Lawrence Grand, had more or less simultaneously been seconded from the Royal Engineers to the Secret Intelligence Service (MI6) to create a new section 'D', for demolition. Grand and Holland were essentially researching the same subjects – irregular warfare, the art of sabotage, how to stir up labour unrest and so on. The two men disliked each other personally: 'Holland thought Grand rash and careless of detail, while Grand thought Holland a stick-in-the-mud',[1] but because they knew each other well, and shared a history, they cooperated well enough to agree that Holland, in the War Office, would concentrate on tactics for men in uniform, while Grand, in MI6, would think about tactics for men in civilian clothing – unavowed operatives. By March 1939, Grand was actively arranging for sabotage and the dissemination of leaflets in Bohemia and Austria, and a year later their secret crew, which had grown to around 150 officers, was working on plans to block the River Danube, blow up a key part of the Ploesti oil refinery, and disrupt telephone networks on the Siegfried line, among other ideas. Meanwhile they had prepared detailed manuals on sabotage, irregular warfare and explosives, and had invented plastic explosive.

In the summer of 1940, Major Holland came up with the idea of forming independent companies of ultra-high-quality light infantry which was the seed bed for the commandos, and had also recruited a school acquaintance[2] to form a new organization (MI9) to facilitate escape and evasion. Holland and Grand may have worked closely together for most of the first half of 1940, but they kept in mind that they ran separate, and to an extent competing, organizations. After the fall of France their differences became acute when they fell out over the creation of a 'stay-behind' force to resist a German invasion of England. The aftermath of Dunkirk left no room for departmental bickering and Churchill, as always pressing for 'action this day', asked the veteran Whitehall warrior, Lord Hankey, to take charge. Hankey, although recently sacked from the cabinet by Churchill himself, set to work. On 13 June 1940, he brought Holland and Grand together in a meeting and obtained their agreement to work together under a single minister. A month later, on 19 July 1940, this minister, the Labour MP Hugh Dalton, was appointed and was placed in executive charge of a new, unified organization which 'shall be established forthwith to co-ordinate all action, by way of subversion and sabotage, against the enemy overseas … This organisation will be known as the Special Operations Executive'.[3] Dalton was given power to co-opt anyone he needed into SOE (whether in uniform or in government), and to lay whatever plans he saw fit, while merely keeping the General Staff informed. Among the people he coopted was MI6's burgeoning Section D. On 22 July 1940, the Cabinet met and formally approved SOE's formation. The first enemy the SOE took on was the War Office itself, and it was not until October 1940 that it had finally wrested operational control over MI(R)'s personnel. A new secret army had effectively come to life.

This army hid in the shadows from the outset, not even having a single office or address, though by the end of 1940 it had more or less taken over 64 Baker Street in London.[4] Even its name was secret, and it appeared in correspondence with other departments in a variety of obscure codenames and acronyms. Two of these, the Inter Services Research Bureau and Force 133, were the ones that would come to be used in Cairo. Its personnel too sought anonymity. Following the example of MI6 and its head, 'C', Dalton christened himself 'CD', and SOE officers signed their signals with personal code-letters[5] which were derived in descending order of seniority and ascending length from their leader's 'CD', with letters and numbers being added as personnel became more junior. SOE had no central file registry (and therefore no chance of being comprehensively 'blown' by a single spy), no single secretary, and a multiplicity of sections under two- or three-letter acronyms whose names and responsibilities chopped and changed as circumstances required. A Cairo desk was set up under James Stewart Abercrombie Pearson, at twenty-nine a very young lieutenant colonel; he adopted the code name DHV.

As 1940 drew to a close, SOE now existed with staff, offices and a charter, but no assets outside the United Kingdom and no clear plans of how to acquire them, or to use them once acquired. In Cairo, before SOE was born, both the War Office and MI6 had small covert operations. MI6 called its office in Cairo MO4, a name invented in 1914 and re-used in the hope that some of the Lawrentian glamour of the Arab Revolt, and the Seven Pillars of Wisdom, would rub off. The War Office set up a Cairene version of MI(R) under the British equivalent's name of G(R). These two competing offices refused to amalgamate under the new SOE flag until they were forced to do so in 1942. An SOE veteran wrote after the war: 'Nobody who did not experience it can possibly imagine the atmosphere of jealousy, suspicion and intrigue which embittered the relations between the various secret and semi-secret departments in Cairo during the summer of 1941'.[6] The competition in Cairo flowed from personal jealousies, from men competing for the promotions that would flow to the leaders of secret organizations, from the delights of access to unaccountable secret funds in large amounts, and the inevitable competition for reputation and credit. Members of the secret community dressed in uniforms made from gaberdene. Cairene observers, well-informed about who was who and what was what, nicknamed them the Gaberdene Swine.

Concealed under its cover names of Force 101 and Force 133, and with its people under obscure codenames, Pearson might have imagined that SOE's role was effectively covert, but it was rather less covert than he wished, for the Cairene taxi drivers knew SOE's office building at Rustum Buildings in Salamlik Street as 'Secret Building',[7] and Cairo's gossiping and connected society knew his plans almost as soon as he did. At his desk in Secret

Building, with Greece now under occupation (and Crete soon to follow), Pearson found himself responsible for SOE operations in Greece. But how and where was he to begin?

The experience of the campaign to eject the Italians from Abyssinia had taught the staff in Cairo that when operating in occupied enemy territory, with a disorganized population, what seemed to work well was the insertion of small groups of officers and NCOs trained in sabotage and aggressive action.[8] These needed support from local patriots to obtain food, intelligence and help to move around on the ground. Pearson's challenge was that Greece had been evacuated in such a tearing hurry that there had been no time to set up any sort of stay-behind forces or covert Greek support network. Subversion would have to pull itself up by its own bootstraps. When the dust of the evacuation settled, Pearson knew that SOE's assets in Greece amounted to a single radio set in Athens in the hands of a Colonel Bakirzis, and a few British officers lurking in the mountains of western Crete. The codes and communications plan for the Athens radio set had left Greece on 28 April in the caique *Irene* in company with Ian Pirie (MI6's man in Athens), but *Irene* had been sunk, taking the signals plan with her. There was no way to communicate into or out of Greece other than to land men who could communicate in person. We don't know if Pearson had read Evelyn Waugh's recent novel *Scoop*, but if he had he would have given a rueful smile at the thought of messages travelling back and forth in the fork of a cleft stick.

As great a challenge was the political situation in Greece. With the death of General Metaxas, the suicide of his successor Koryzis, and the exile of the king of Greece to Cairo, it was far from clear who Pearson should seek as an ally. Greek social, economic and military leaders hated each other almost as much as they hated the Axis. The Royalists hated the liberal democratic republican Venizelists, who hated the fascist supporters of Metaxas, who hated the recently established communists. The army, now disbanded, was factionalized into royalists, republicans and fascists. These were not low-key hatreds: over the past two generations Greek factionalism had caused opponents to be exiled to barren dry islets in the Aegean, far from Athens. Hundreds of army officers had, for example, been exiled to the isolated island of Skyros (where at least they had the tomb of Rupert Brooke for company), and others to Gavdos, where they had no company at all. Many had been put up in front of firing squads. In Greece, politics was a contact sport.

In an ideal world, Athens would have fallen with an effective network of British MI6 agents in place, ready to help, after the occupation. MI6 had begun to build just such a network in 1939 but with little progress, since Greece was then seen as an unimportant and neutral state. The British Minister[9] Sir Michael Palairet, flatly refused to allow his mission to have anything to do with spying, so MI6 was forced to recruit a group of prominent British businessmen, working in Athens and later christened the Apostles. In late 1940, these were joined and taken under charge, by Ian Pirie, under cover as general manager of a local power generating company.

Pirie set about making contacts with leading Greeks whose politics were varied but were unified through their opposition to the fascist regime of Metaxas, and by implication, to a future Axis occupation. When he fled Athens in *Irene* on 28 April, Pirie brought with him his girlfriend (the nightclub singer Nikki Demertzi),[10] leaving behind a dozen or so people in Athens and Salonika who could be relied on to carry out secret work against the Axis in future. It was these people who would feature large in the lives of Lieutenants John Atkinson and Jim Craig a few months later. SOE had learnt that survival in enemy-occupied territory was impossible without local contacts and support. In the urban environment, agents had to have current identity documents and cover stories, somewhere to plan operations, somewhere to sleep, somewhere to store equipment, and recent intelligence on what to hit and how to hit it. A key item of equipment was a radio, with which to report intelligence, receive tasking, and coordinate infiltrations and exfiltrations. A radio by itself was of little use without a dedicated cypher, a trained operator, and a communications plan laying out timings and frequencies of transmissions. Pearson had none of these.

Greece is a country approximately the size of England, largely comprised of mountains whose lower slopes and valleys provide its agricultural land.[11] Two areas of urban concentration provided large ports and effective railways: Salonika in the north (modern Thessaloniki), and Athens in the centre. As soon as they arrived, the Axis began to use these centres to collect and remove Greece's resources. Food stocks, factory equipment and the nation's considerable gold reserve, were loaded onto trains and shipped north to the Fatherland. Any shipping caught in Greek ports was co-opted into the service of the Axis. Pearson decided that his first target was to disrupt Greece's logistics system, while laying the foundations for a popular mass resistance movement, to be used in the distant future when the Axis finally retreated. Along the way, the more trouble SOE could cause, the more troops the Axis would have to allocate to the policing of Greece, and so remove them from active battlefronts.

Greece's geography was problematic. In flat open country it was possible, and indeed relatively easy, to drop men and equipment by parachute in darkness. However, men dropped in the mountains at night would almost certainly be injured on landing and would lose track of their equipment in what was effectively a wild and rocky wilderness. An air drop would be more successful if a reception party on the ground selected and prepared an open, flattish area and then signalled its location with fires or lanterns. However, in Greece, if an air drop was successful, then its men would still find themselves many days' journey from Athens or Salonika in a country with poor roads and few railways. The roads that did exist were relatively easy for the Axis to patrol and guard. Later in the war, air drops became the commonplace way of landing men and supplies, but in the early summer of 1941, there were no reception parties, and no spare aircraft. About a quarter of the population of Greece favoured the Axis anyway, at least in the early stages of the war before famine and brutal oppression had revealed the true nature of the Axis. Therefore, an air drop could easily have been betrayed in areas where the population knew precisely what everyone else was up to much of the time.

Insertion by a surface ship was also impractical; the voyage to Greece from Alexandria was too long to complete in a single night. A ship trying to make a surface insertion would be detected and attacked by patrolling aircraft or stopped and searched by an Axis patrol boat. The problem of access magnified when the challenge of picking up agents for rest and de-briefing was added. In France, SOE ran what amounted to an air-taxi service into wide, flat fields sheltered by huge oak forests, but Greece lacked the fields and the in-place agents on the ground to copy the French model. Pearson found himself forced, by distance and lack of people in place, to seek out the services of the only force capable of putting men and equipment ashore anywhere near Greece's major cities – the submarine service. Thus, he found himself relying on Captain Sydney Raw and his 1st Flotilla.

A submarine was the ideal machine for landing and picking up agents and supplies. The landing place could be approached invisibly in daylight while dived. At periscope depth a submarine was effectively undetectable, unless she revealed herself by making an attack, or had the bad luck to be overflown by a very observant aircraft; there was a firm rule that, when on special operations, the boat would make no attacks for twelve hours before a landing, so as not to alert local Axis forces. In the waning hours of daylight, the submarine would cruise slowly up and down off the landing beach, carefully inspecting it, through its search periscope, to detect enemy activity or installations. Later in the war, the Axis learnt what was happening under their noses and built guard bunkers above many beaches, but in 1941 this work lay in the future. If the beach was quiet, the submarine would surface an hour after dark, sail out to sea for two or three hours to charge its batteries and cook a hot meal, then return silently to the shore on electric motors in the small hours.

Lying 200 yards off a beach, invisible and inaudible in the black night, the landing party would climb into one or two Folboats, each rowed by a strong, fit man from Courtney's Special Boat Section, and paddle ashore. Men and kit were landed and walked off into the dark, at first alone, but later in the war accompanied by their local reception committee. Half an hour later, with Folboats struck down through the torpedo hatch and the ship's company enjoying its daily ration of diluted rum, the submarine crept back out to sea, started her diesels to complete her battery charge, and by an hour before dawn was safely back underwater to carry on her patrol. Pearson's request for underwater help was probably not a surprise to Raw. Nor was the answer. When it came to beach landings with special forces, one boat in his flotilla had a growing reputation – *Triumph*.

SOE's job was to land men in Greece. Its younger sibling's (MI9) job was to get them out. It will be recalled that during the fall of Greece and Crete some 16,000 men were taken prisoner. More, perhaps 2,500 Allied troops, mostly Australians, New Zealanders and British troops from the Royal Army Service Corps, were in hiding in Greece. MI9 was formed, not just to rescue escapers, but to prepare men for escape and evasion, under the oversight of the same Major Holland who took part in the creation of SOE. Sadly, despite their shared parentage, in Cairo MI9 and SOE came to regard each other as opponents rather than colleagues. Holland recommended an old friend of his as MI9's overall chief in London, Major N. R. Crockatt. Crockatt had served in the Royal Scots during the Great War where he had won a DSO (Distinguished Service Order) and an MC (Military Cross) and been badly wounded. After the war, taking the Staff Course in 1927 at the age of thirty-one, he realized the army bored him, and left to become a stockbroker in the City of London, which is where Holland found him in 1939. Crockatt was appointed head of MI9 in London, in December 1939.

Crockatt's focus was on training the British Army, that had escaped from Dunkirk, to prepare for future escape, on the assumption that they would, in due course, return to fight in Europe. Simultaneously, he worked on debriefing the steady stream of escapers that arrived in Britain after Dunkirk. Though extremely busy at home, Crockatt had not forgotten the Middle East. In August 1940 he sent Major Michael Harrison, an escape veteran from the Great War,[12] to Cairo to teach escape-mindedness – a determination to escape if captured by the enemy. Harrison found a home with another of Crockatt's friends, Colonel Dudley Clarke, who was working under Wavell on a massive deception campaign to convince the Italians that Wavell's forces were much larger than they were. Their office was located in part of a Cairo brothel near the popular nightclub Groppi's. Clarke politely allowed the ladies of the house to continue to ply their trade in the rooms he did not need.[13]

After the fall of Greece in April 1941, and Crete a month later, Harrison's briefings of young men heading for war began to bear fruit. For an escaper in Greece, two routes home were practical. One was southeast by sea across the 300 miles of water between Crete and Alexandria (500 miles if the escape started near Athens). The first 100 miles of this route was patrolled by the Luftwaffe, and by Axis patrol boats and submarines, and was highly dangerous. Alternatively, an escaper could try to reach neutral Turkey by sailing just 100 miles east across the Aegean. In Turkey, he would find two retired naval officers, turned consuls: Commander Wolfson in Istanbul and Lieutenant Commander Noel Rees in Smyrna (present day Izmir). Rees was closer, half-Greek, and rich enough to subsidize his escape route personally, so he set up an informal base for a flotilla of Aegean fishing and cargo caiques at Cesme, on the western tip of Aegean Turkey fifty miles west of Smyrna.

At first, with the occupation of Greece's islands and extremities only partially completed, escape parties succeeded in travelling both routes. A few days after the fall of Crete, a party of thirty-one Anzacs appeared at Port Said, having sailed in a caique bought in Skyros. A total of 302 men were recorded as arriving in Egypt in May 1941. The Axis quickly stemmed the supply of caiques. As the availability of surface craft dribbled away, the next solution, obvious to both escapers and MI9, was to use a submarine. The idea was simple in concept, but rather less so in execution. Captain Raw was certainly not going to allow his precious boats[14] to approach enemy coasts on the off chance that a group of escapers might be waiting on a beach. A mission to pick up escapers, therefore, required a pre-set rendezvous, the promise of a reasonably large party of escapers to make the prize worth the risk, the assurance that the escape party would maintain its own security and not become the bait for a trap, and an available submarine. One of Raw's informal conditions was that a boat would only try to pick up escapers at the end of a patrol, for to do so earlier would hazard the submarine. Twenty or thirty extra bodies in her fore ends generating carbon dioxide would reduce a boat's dived endurance by a third, forcing her to surface in daylight to breathe – tantamount to suicide. Escapers would also badly obstruct the crew's task of reloading torpedo tubes, would overload the boat's domestic capabilities (food, cooking, fresh water and the capacity of her heads)[15] and even her underwater stability. Finally, the reaction of soldiers to a depth-charge attack was uncertain and potentially extremely dangerous.

The many hundreds of escapers hiding in Greece and Crete had no radios, and therefore no means of arranging a rendezvous that fitted Sydney Raw's rules, so apart from some desperate rescues from Crete in May 1941, the idea of submarine rescue lay in abeyance for the whole of that summer. Crete was an exception. Just days after its collapse, Major Harrison and Sydney Raw knew that a very large number of men were flooding southwards over Crete's White Mountains, collecting in and around the handful of bays and beaches of Crete's south coast. There was a high probability that a submarine arriving at one of those beaches would find a group of men large enough to make the risk of just turning up worthwhile. On 27 July 1941 *Triumph*'s sister HMS *Thrasher* was tasked with landing an SOE agent, Lieutenant Commander Francis Pool, with a radio on southern Crete[16] and picking up as many escapers as she could. Pool went ashore and immediately found a large party of men. He arranged a rendezvous for the next night by radio, and at 2.00 am on 28 July *Thrasher* came in and picked up seventy-eight men. Heavily overloaded, she came straight home to Alexandria. While she was away, Pool was busy assembling more escapers in Crete. By the middle of

August, he had gathered nearly 150 men on Crete's south coast and requested a submarine lift home by radio. HMS *Torbay* was coming to the end of a sixteen-day patrol in the Aegean, and Raw diverted her to rendezvous with Pool on the night of 18 August. Two days later, *Torbay* delivered 131 men to Alexandria – the absolute maximum number a submarine could carry, since she had to leave fifteen Greeks on the beach.

While Crete was falling in May 1941, *Triumph* was patrolling the north coast of Libya to find and sink Rommel's supply ships. Woods and his men probably thought of this as a welcome return to normal submarine business, but orders for a special operation were already being coded in *Medway*'s signals office. If you stand today on the southern slopes of the White Mountains in Crete and look south, and if the day is clear, you will just see, on the far horizon, the tip of the small rocky island Gavdos. Ten miles long by four miles wide, Gavdos is an inhospitable place, mostly bare rock or scrub rising to 1,000 feet, without a river or a lake to refresh the traveller. Indeed, so inhospitable is it that between the wars Gavdos was used as an open prison for opponents of whatever regime was in power. 'Exile to an island' did not mean to the soft delights of Skiathos, but rather to the waterless heat of this bare rock regularly thrashed by the hot dry sandy Meltemi wind blowing off the Sahara a couple of hundred miles away to the south. Harrison told Raw that there were reports of men hiding on Gavdos. Could he arrange for their rescue?

Sydney Raw knew that *Triumph* was coming to the end of her patrol and that her route home would pass just eighty miles south of Gavdos. We don't know whether he was certain that some troops had escaped there from Crete, or whether the pressure from Cairo was enough for him to take a chance. We do know that his direct boss, Admiral Cunningham, ordered his surface ships to continue picking up troops at almost any cost. During the evacuation from Crete, Cunningham was losing two ships each day. Rather than withdraw, he told his fleet 'it takes three years to build a ship, but 300 years to build a reputation. We'll stay'. It was probably Cunningham's example that led Raw to order *Triumph* to head for Gavdos surfaced in daylight (for speed) to search for escapers hiding on the island. The voyage must have been acutely uncomfortable for Woods. Used to sheltering in daylight between periscope depth and the dark of the deep Mediterranean, he had to dash in clear sight just thirty minutes flying time away from the

Axis airfield at Maleme. When he arrived at Gavdos, in the setting sun, Woods used the last of the light to take a close look at possible beaches for a Folboat landing. He was probably also deliberately showing himself in the hope that men hiding on the island might get the message that rescue was in the offing. At 10.30 pm, *Triumph* nosed her way towards the beach where her resident commando, Corporal Bremner, paddled her gunnery officer, Robert Douglas-Don, ashore. Hauling their canoe above the gentle surf line, Douglas-Don and Bremner, armed with revolvers and Thompson sub-machineguns, set off into the dark to knock up islanders and ask if there were any Allied troops in hiding nearby. No one knew whether Gavdos had an Axis garrison, or if it did where it might be, or what guards it might have posted. It must have felt surreal for the two men, who had landed on beaches before but never gone inland, to be wandering the interior of an island in the Greek night with the scent of sage and olives sharp to noses accustomed to oil, cigarette smoke and week-old sweat.

They found no escapers. There had been some troops on the island the day before, or even two days before, but no one knew where they were. At 2.30 am the landing party returned to *Triumph* and reported back. A short conference on the bridge led to a decision to try something else. A spare union flag was tied to the partly raised periscope. In the morning, *Triumph* would sail around the island's coast at periscope depth and raise her flagged periscope above the sea surface. If there were any Allied troops ashore, they would probably see it and use their initiative to gather at one of Gavdos' half-dozen beaches. All of these were at most three miles from the centre of the Island. A gathering would be spotted by the man on periscope watch, and the boat would come in at night to pick them up. Dawn had broken when men were seen gathering on the first beach. Taking his courage in both hands, Woods ordered the boat to surface in daylight and again Douglas-Don and Bremner paddled ashore, now in some haste since at any moment an Axis aircraft or corvette might appear. Caught on the surface in daylight, in water too shallow to allow her to dive, *Triumph*'s chances of survival would be slim to nil. On the beach, the men turned out to be Greek locals, one of whom spoke enough French to communicate effectively with Douglas-Don. The news was not good. Eighteen Allied troops had been on the island but had been captured and flown off the previous day. A German patrol had been left ashore just three miles to the south and might even now be summoning an air strike. *Triumph* furled her flag and dived, thankful that her latest special operation had not ended in disaster. Two days later, she arrived back in Alexandria. Despite the strident requests for help in Greece from SOE and MI9, there was no way of setting up a mission that was both an efficient use of a submarine and offered a reasonable chance of survival. For now, *Triumph* would go back to her day job of attacking Rommel's supply line, but the pull of special operations was strong, and she would soon be back on the job, this time not in Greece but in Sicily.

Chapter 8

Return to Malta, and Another Special Operation

Triumph was in action almost as soon as she left Alexandria. On the second day of her patrol, she came across and sank the Italian submarine *Salpa*, indiscreetly loitering on the surface in daylight in the approaches to Alexandria.[1] A quiet week passed until 5 July, when Woods encountered two small merchant ships half a mile off the Libyan coast at night. Torpedoes were in short supply in the Mediterranean, so he decided to attack these with gunfire instead. *Triumph*'s gun crew were busy sinking the second ship when they ran out of flashless ammunition, used to conceal her own position. Having used up her small stock she was now firing standard ammunition, whose vivid propellant flashes clearly revealed her position to a nearby shore battery, as well as dazzling the aimer and trainer, and Lieutenant Douglas-Don on the bridge directing their fire. The vivid flashes of *Triumph*'s gun gave the crews of two Italian guns ashore a clear aiming point, and they opened fire. The Italian fire was accurate. Their first shell soaked the bridge crew with its splash. Woods, perhaps remembering the saying of Admiral Lord Nelson that 'a ship's a fool to fight a fort', melted into the night at high speed. The incoming shell had looked like a miss, but when safely out of range, Leading Stoker Claude Baxter was sent down onto the casing to see if it had caused any damage.

At forty-one, Baxter was one of the oldest men in the boat and was married with a young son. Claude was heavily built, with a stocky, square face and a determined jutting chin. He had joined *Triumph* from the Submarine School at Dolphin in November 1940 and had recently been promoted from Able to Leading rate. As a stoker, Claude's expertise was tanks, pumps and valves. This trip to the casing, with a summer Mediterranean swim included, was his first taste of fresh air since leaving Alexandria nine days before. *Triumph* gently rose and fell on the slight swell as Baxter slipped into the warm sea, a rope around his well-built middle. What he saw there must have made his heart miss a beat – his torch clearly showed a jagged hole in *Triumph*'s foremost ballast tank, just a few feet back from her bows. This tank was wrapped around the six torpedo tubes, each containing its armed torpedo with 660 pounds of high-explosive warhead just a couple of feet from where he was clinging. Had they been damaged as well? Were they about to detonate? Most alarming of all, with the sea sucking in and out of the hole, would *Triumph* be able to dive? If she was found on the surface in daylight, just a few miles off Libya, her life expectancy would be short.

On *Triumph*'s bridge Baxter made his report to Sammy Woods and his immediate boss, the boat's engineer officer, Lieutenant Denys Wright. Claude would not have been able to see their faces in the pitch dark, but he could probably hear the concern in their voices as they discussed what to do. The first order of business was to put as much sea between *Triumph* and the coast as they could before dawn.

'How fast do you think we can go, Engines?' Asked Woods.

Would the tank give way under the pressure of *Triumph*'s bow cutting through the Mediterranean at her best speed of fifteen knots? Thirty-one-year-old Wright was born in India in 1912 and was sent home to be educated at Haileybury at the age of thirteen. From there he began a career as a naval engineer at the navy's engineering school near Plymouth. For his first three appointments he was a big-ship engineer, but in 1939 he joined the submarine service and was appointed to *Triumph* in May 1940, probably making him the boat's longest-serving crew member. Wright, a thin, serious man, rarely smiled and always looked as if he was worrying that the cares of the world were about to descend on his head. As *Triumph*'s engineering officer they in fact did, at regular intervals, since every mechanical defect landed on his tiny desk in the Motor Room. Wright knew *Triumph* inside out, probably better than any man aboard.

'We might be alright, Sir. There's a large empty auxiliary tank just astern of Number One Ballast Tank. I can pressure test that to see if it's been damaged, but listening to Baxter's report I doubt that the damage reached that far astern, and in any case the aft side of the ballast tank is the pressure hull – nearly an inch thick – which can take quite a bit of a pounding.'

Wright looked into the dark night while he calculated the odds.

'If the Auxiliary tank holds pressure then we should be safe to dive, though I wouldn't want to go too deep in case I'm wrong. Surface speed shouldn't be a problem either – most of the pounding will be on the casing. And we can balance out the trim by flooding Zulu tank over the rudders. She'll be a bit less responsive at periscope depth, but we should make port alright. One thing I think we need to check is whether the shell did any damage to the torpedo tubes.'

Now it was Woods' turn to think. A signal had arrived that morning extending *Triumph*'s patrol by two days. When she got in, she would need a fully equipped dockyard to take the bows apart and fix the damage. Egypt had the dock but not the people[2] – it would probably have to be Malta, and that meant signalling Sydney Raw in *Medway*, which in turn meant getting some sea-room to hide *Triumph*'s position from Axis radio detection stations. 'Right chaps, here's what we're going to do. We'll make offing at twelve knots until 0300. We'll then do a test dive. If nothing goes wrong, we'll surface again to charge until 0500 and head back inshore. We'll spend the day on patrol, then head out again tomorrow night and, if the weather permits, we'll let you get a proper look at the damage, Denys. You might have to dive with an escape set. We'll then signal *Medway* with a report and let them decide what happens next. But it looks like we'll be back in Malta by the end of the week.'

The following night Woods took his boat twenty miles out to sea in darkness. Denys Wright stripped and put on a Davis escape breathing set with its small supply of compressed oxygen – designed to allow a man just enough time to float to the surface from a bottomed submarine. He slipped off *Triumph*'s fore planes into the warm Mediterranean with a waterproofed torch to inspect her starboard torpedo tubes. As the luminescent water glowed around his arms and chest Wright stuck his head and torch inside the jagged shell hole in the ballast tank, from where he could see the outboard sides of the three starboard torpedo tubes and the back of the tank where it joined the pressure hull. The pressure hull looked undamaged, but the delicate venting pipes attached to all three tubes had suffered from the detonation, and one of the tube doors was not working. The three tubes were unusable. Wright must have felt a shiver of combined relief and fear – if the German gunner had fired just one second later, his shell would have hit ten feet further aft and penetrated the pressure hull into the torpedo tube space.

Triumph would have been trapped on the surface thirty hours from home. She would have been unlikely to escape. If it had penetrated just two feet further into the tank, it might have set off one of the armed torpedoes in its tube, an instant catastrophe.

Next day the signal came back from Alexandria: proceed to Malta for repairs. Alexandria's fleshpots and fresh food were off the menu. Everyone aboard *Triumph* must have been apprehensive as she once more tied up alongside the Lazaretto at breakfast on Saturday 12 July but there was some cheering news in the mess. With Barbarossa in full swing the Luftwaffe was paying little attention to Malta. A small-scale Stuka attack was arriving once or twice a week, but focussed on the dockyard. The Italians were less active too. Two or three times a week three high-level Italian bombers overflew Valletta. Always one, sometimes two, were shot down, and bombs dropped from height rarely hit their intended targets. Food and alcohol might be in short supply in Malta, but at least men would be able to sleep a little more peacefully in their hammocks. After the war Shrimp Simpson wrote, 'It was exciting to stand at night on our front gallery [in the Lazaretto] with overhead protection from shrapnel, to watch what the Army's new radar controlled searchlights and the RAF's Beaufighters would lay on for our entertainment … at once two or three searchlight beams would lock onto the enemy and all other searchlights go out on that instant … suddenly from behind the enemy a Beaufighter would open up with a burst of cannon fire for perhaps three seconds … "there they go" would be the shout, "one, two, and there's three parachutes open now"… then another burst from the Beaufighter and suddenly the whole aircraft was a mass of flame cartwheeling to earth'.[3]

The Lazaretto and its submarines had continued to escape notice from the Axis air attacks. Shrimp Simpson had taken care to forbid the flying of any white ensigns by day, and to order all men in uniform to take shelter in Manoel Island's rock caves, behind the Lazaretto, as German aircraft overflew the island after each raid, close enough for men on the island to make out their faces and hands in their cockpits. Supplies were still short, especially in the matter of beer and gin, but the island was far from starvation. With five weeks of work to repair the damage and then prepare the boat for another patrol, *Triumph*'s crew may have been hungry and thirsty, but they at least had an opportunity for some relaxation. Shrimp Simpson had set up a camp at the Ghajn Tuffeia beach, about ten miles west of Valletta, where men could relax, away from the air raids on the city and dockyard. *Triumph*'s crew took it in turns to have a short beach holiday, though probably with less beer than they'd have liked. Back at the Lazaretto, Simpson's staff had been digging vigorously into the rock behind, with the help of a squad of twenty Maltese workmen. As well as workshops and messdecks, the Lazaretto now had a rock cavern cinema which was supplied with special copies of Hollywood's latest releases. *Triumph*'s men enjoyed *Dumbo*, and Ginger Rogers in *Roxy Hart*, an early version of the modern movie *Chicago*. Submariners in the Lazaretto enjoyed unlimited hot water, heated by a combination of sawdust from the dockyard timber shop and waste engine-lubricating oil. Rations were supplemented by pork and bacon from a family of pigs kept by the flotilla on Manoel Island, fed with food waste from the galleys. Many of Simpson's submariners kept rabbits in hutches, for entertainment as much as for eating. There was nothing for hens to eat, and therefore a dearth of eggs, but a single turkey stalked the yards and courts of the Lazaretto, perhaps eyeing the calendar with apprehension. For the wardroom officers, social life was busy, at least as far as petrol for cars permitted. Visits ashore were made on bicycles. One submarine commanding officer kept a pony and cart to extend his social range. Malta was full of retired naval officers who gathered at the Union Club in Valletta to drink and swap gossip. Each submarine was allocated a set of flats in Sliema, to reduce the risk of catastrophic loss of men if a bombing raid were to hit the Lazaretto, and to allow men to relax in plain clothes away from naval discipline. While sailors and their NCOs congregated at the Dun Cow pub to drink the execrable locally brewed siege beer, the Lazaretto's wardroom became a relaxed club for officers, where they could drink the island's remaining supply of gin and learn from each other how to survive the Mediterranean.

Lounging on beach towels in the sun, *Triumph*'s crew must have taken stock. Everyone knew that the usual commission for a submarine was a year, and that they were just over halfway through. It was also common knowledge that, during 1940, submarine warfare in the Mediterranean had been a near suicidal business. We know now that the average mortality rate for a Mediterranean submarine, heading on patrol in 1940, was eleven per cent for each departure, and that with an expected twelve patrols over the course of a year, only one boat in five was likely to survive her commission. But, by July 1941, it was looking as if something had changed. During the first half of 1941, Malta and Alexandria had sent out 106 patrols, but just two had resulted in lost boats – *Usk* and *Undaunted* – both to causes unknown then and now. *Triumph*'s men might have put their survival down to the combination of skill and caution on the part of their skipper, Sammy Woods, or down to sheer luck, but sunning themselves on the beach they must have begun to feel a glimmer of hope that they might survive the Mediterranean to return home at the end of the year.

In the middle of Triumph's mid-summer break more good news arrived. On 24 July, thirteen merchant ships of Convoy GM1 arrived in Valletta, with 59,000 tons of stores, ammunition and fuel. Business at the Dun Cow pub in Sliema was brisk next day. After the parties, there was still much work to be done. Malta's own flotilla of little U-Class submarines (about half the size of *Triumph*) had at last begun to sink substantial numbers of merchant ships carrying troops and supplies to Rommel. Ships were not the only targets. Shrimp Simpson, at the Lazaretto, still had his personal unit of commandos in residence, and these he aimed at the Italian railway networks, which mostly and conveniently ran along Italy's coastlines and were in easy reach of a commando raid delivered by submarine and Folboat. On 27 June, while *Triumph* was sinking the submarine *Salpa*, *Urge* was landing a demolition party of commandos to destroy the rail tunnel north of Taormina on Sicily. Simpson wrote of one raid: 'It was nearly two o'clock when an electric train, winding north from Catania to Messina, entered the tunnel. Then a vivid blue flash belched out of the north end of the tunnel followed by an uncanny silence … for the next three days and nights the tunnel was alight with arc cutting and demolition lights'.[4]

Shrimp Simpson wanted to scale up his railway-cutting operations to extend the time needed to repair the lines. An earlier periscope reconnaissance, by one of his boats, had discovered a long railway viaduct across the river Torrente Furiano, on Sicily's north coast. If this could be cut, it would take weeks to repair, during which the port of Palermo would be completely cut off from supplies, concentrating Rommel's supply line into fewer routes and making them easier to attack. The problem was that the viaduct's construction was substantial – the track was supported by six massive stone piers each of which would need hundreds of pounds each of high explosive. Those in turn would need many more commandos than could be squeezed into a U-class torpedo compartment. What was needed was a T-class boat. Happily, he had one on hand almost returned to service – *Triumph*. Shrimp's staff calculated that it would take about a quarter of a tonne of high explosive to bring one of the bridge supports down and drop the rail span into the riverbed.

The explosives would work best if wrapped around the pier, and to do this the commando section leader, Lieutenant Schofield (former Royal Fusiliers) planned to stuff close to 100 pounds of explosives into six two-yard-long fire hoses. These explosive sausages would be tied to the pier and detonated simultaneously. A single commando could carry just one explosive sausage from the landing beach to the river. Four men would be left on the beach to guard the Folboats while the demolition party was away, six would carry the explosives, and, with Schofield in command, the whole raid would need eleven men. After some practice, it was decided to add a twelfth man – Petty Officer Taffy Telfer from *Triumph*, whose seamanship skills would be used to tie the sausages to the bridge pier with ropes. A Folboat could not carry men as well as the heavy explosive sausages. Schofield worked out that the party would need nine Folboats to get his men and equipment ashore. Woods looked at the problem – eleven commandos, nine Folboats, six unwieldy explosive sausages, detonation cord, personal weapons plus ammunition and emergency rations, and suggested that the only way to get the landing party into his boat was to land all of his reload torpedoes and use the now-empty fore ends as an army mess for the commandos. The operation was authorized by the Commander in Chief Mediterranean and given the name Operation Walrus.

Before Walrus could go ahead, *Triumph* had to get out of the dockyard and spend some time at sea testing the repair for watertightness at diving depth, and test-firing torpedoes out of the repaired tubes. This meant it was not until dusk on 19 August that Woods slipped from *Triumph*'s berth alongside the Lazaretto and waved goodbye to Shrimp on his balcony above. The mission was marginal. The eleven extra men inside *Triumph* were adding twenty per cent to the amount of carbon dioxide in the boat, cutting her dived endurance by one fifth. In the short nights of the summer there was no margin for safety – Woods would have to surface as soon as twilight had ended, if not before, and dive well after the morning twilight was softening the night's welcome darkness. All of this, just a mile off the north coast of Sicily, in clear sight of sentries and only a few minutes' flight time from Fliegerkorps X's airstrips.

The landing beach on Sicily lay 250 miles north of Malta – forty-eight hours at *Triumph*'s normal dived/surfaced routine, so dawn on 22 August found Woods inspecting the viaduct and the planned landing beach half a mile north and east of it though *Triumph*'s periscope. By this time in 1941, covert beach landings had become commonplace among Mediterranean submarines and a safe routine had become well established. The submarine approached the beach dived shortly after dawn, when the light was coming in low and strong and the air was at its clearest to give the maximum possible contrast. Any fortifications or other defences would become more visible because they would throw strong shadows. The boat sailed at a slow walking pace to and fro along the beach several times, as close as she could while leaving some water in which to dive and escape if she was found. Multiple short, swift looks through the periscope, interrupted by all-round sweeps to check for attack from the air or surface, slowly revealed the state of the beach. Guarded? Patrolled? Wired? Covered by machine guns or artillery? Check, check and check again. In the middle of the day the sun rose to its zenith and detail flattened in the Mediterranean glare. With the sun right above, *Triumph* could easily be seen from the air as a large black object, outlined against the clear yellow seabed of Sicilian sand, so she retired a few miles to dive deep for the midday meal, a rum ration, and for the landing party to review its plans in light of the morning's reconnaissance.

Triumph's single chef, Leading Cook Cornelius O'Brien, was working double tides. A Kentish man, at well over six feet, Cornelius was uncomfortably tall for a submariner. A large head was joined to large shoulders by an unusually large neck, giving him the appearance of having been slightly stretched. Unlike many naval chefs, Cornelius usually had a broad smile on his face, though it may have slipped while he prepared lunch for seventy-five in *Triumph*'s minute galley. *Triumph*'s crew were used to having their main meal at midnight, but the commandos were not, and in any case were expecting to spend the night hard at work and under acute stress, so they needed a full load of calories well in advance.

As the afternoon sun began its long descent to the horizon, Woods brought his boat back inshore for another extended look; the Italians might mount a night guard at dusk or come down to the beach to swim or to party. All looked clear. Surfacing after dark a few miles offshore, *Triumph* carried out her normal night routine: breakfast, charge the batteries, allow fresh air to flood the boat, cigarettes, maintenance and cleaning, and listen for incoming morse messages transmitted by the powerful station at Rugby. In the comms office, just aft of the control room and by far the most comfortable working space in the boat, Leading Telegraphist Reg Waye, was reading morse traffic from Malta in case *Triumph*'s callsign came up. Waye had turned twenty-five two days before *Triumph* had sailed from Malta, and his most welcome presents had been sippers from the rum rations of his messmates. A sailor since a week after his sixteenth birthday, until he joined the submarine service in 1940, Waye had been a big ship man who had also spent a happy year in a shore billet in Bermuda. But here he was in a very small ship. He had grown a full beard and carefully shaped moustache, which meant that he didn't have to use his small ration of fresh water to shave on patrol.

At 7.30 pm *Triumph*'s call sign dotted its way over the ether. A few minutes later, Reg Waye was knocking at the door of the wardroom.

'Signal from SM10, Sir, marked Flash.'

Flash was the word for signals of the highest priority, reserved for enemy sighting reports or other extremely urgent business, and SM10 meant Shrimp Simpson in Malta, who had just been appointed captain in charge of the new 10th Submarine Flotilla. Lieutenant Michael Janvrin was *Triumph*'s signals officer (she was too small to carry a dedicated signals officer) and was responsible for decoding the jumble of letters on the flimsy page torn from a message pad that Waye handed to him with the code books from the comms office safe. Half an hour later, Woods was reading the decoded message sitting at the wardroom table with his officers around him, all curious to know what Shrimp had to tell them.

'On completion of special operation proceed at best possible speed to north entrance to strait of Messina. Enemy heavy units expected to transit Messina southbound from Sardinia in daylight on 26 August. Use best efforts to intercept and sink. Good hunting. SM10.'[5]

The three young junior officers in the wardroom had to suppress their excitement since their commanding officer was now a newly-promoted commander, a brass hat, and not to be trifled with by mere lieutenants, even in the family atmosphere of a submarine wardroom. But their excitement was intense even so. *Triumph* had been designed exactly to intercept and sink battleships and cruisers. This was why she had been given no less than ten forward-firing torpedo tubes (though two had been permanently lost to the mine strike off Germany in 1939). Shrimp's signal was the starting gun for a hunt that might cost the Italian navy one of its four operating battleships, or a cruiser at the least.

'Well, this is a turn-up for the books, chaps, but let's not get too excited too quickly. First, we've got the railway bridge to deal with.'

Turning to Lieutenant Alf Peterkin, who had just finished the second dog watch[6] on the bridge he asked, 'what's the weather like up top, Pilot? Are we going to get the raiding party ashore tonight?'

Woods had been concerned all day by the swell, which could be seen crashing onto the beach from the northwest in waves large enough to upset, or even wreck, a fragile Folboat. A few hours later, after dinner, the issue of the daily rum ration, and much checking by the commandos of their equipment, Woods nosed *Triumph* on her electric motors silently through the moonless dark towards the beach. Beneath his feet he could feel the familiar motion of his boat in the swell and hear the distant boom of surf on beach. There was no way he could get a dozen men and their explosives ashore without risking a disaster tonight, but a smaller reconnaissance party with just personal weapons should be able to land and come off, and this was ready on the casing – two Folboats and four men barely visible as darker lumps waiting by the fore planes. A thousand yards south the beach was just visible in the starlight, a dim line of fluorescence visible against the harder black of the shoreline.

'Casing there, reconnaissance party away.'

Schofield, with two sergeants and Petty Officer Telfer, paddled their Folboats swiftly into the night. There was no doubt about where to head, the beach was clearly audible, and as they rose and fell on the swell the surf line could also be clearly seen. Fast rhythmic paddling brought the men ashore within fifteen minutes. They knew they had just half an hour ashore to check the angle at which the beach entered the sea, search quickly around for sentries, wires or emplacements, and check that the beach had a clear exit to the hinterland behind it. If there were mines lurking in the sand well, too bad. In this case, hope was indeed a strategy. An hour later, the two Folboats were nestling back against Triumph's bows again and the four men were clambering onto the fore planes.

'Bridge, casing. Casing secured, fore hatch shut and clipped, Sir.'

Robert Douglas-Don was the last man to climb over the side of the bridge and disappear down the ladder to the control room below. Alf Peterkin stooped to the green brass voice pipe that led to the control room.

'Stop both motors. Out clutches. Start main engines. Revolutions two zero zero. Steer zero six zero.'

The orders were repeated back by a tinny voice. *Triumph*'s bridge shuddered gently as her large twin diesels coughed into life and began to thrust her northeast at twelve knots. There was just time to make the south end of Vulcano Island twenty-five miles away before diving for the dawn. From there, a slow creep east, all day on batteries, would bring her to the northern jaws of the strait of Messina. With just a mile between Italy and Sicily, the enemy battle squadron, if it arrived, would have to sail right past her, and her eight torpedoes were ready and waiting.

Waiting seemed to be the order of that day. From dawn to dusk, *Triumph* sailed a four-mile-long patrol line outside the entrance to Messina, waiting for her targets to appear. A succession of smaller craft – minesweeping trawlers, a single destroyer (the *Albatross*) busily fussing to and fro, a drifter, and a handful of aircraft – passed by but no battleship. To *Triumph*'s crew this was all in the normal run of business, for she spent most of her time waiting quietly for a target to appear over the horizon, but for her dozen commandos it must have been unpleasant, both boring and frightening, since an attack probably meant a counterattack, and no one in the commando party had experienced one of those.

That day and the following night passed quietly, until the middle of the first watch at 5.54 am, when *Triumph* had already been dived for an hour. The first sign of the approaching enemy fleet, was a succession of depth charges being dropped randomly in the west – a common practice among Italian destroyer escorts intended to disrupt and discourage an attacking submarine. It also served to herald the approach of a heavy ship under destroyer escort.

Six minutes later the Italian force came in sight. Woods, at the attack periscope, the larger search periscope had fogged up the night before, crisply briefed his control room team on the force. The Italian squadron had second-guessed him. Instead of approaching the strait from the north it was coming in fast from the west.

'I have one battleship and two heavy cruisers at two eight zero, range three miles. I am thirty degrees on their starboard bow. Eight, no, nine, no ten,

ten destroyer escorts. Two in line abreast ahead of the force, four on each beam. I estimate target speed at eighteen knots. Make ready tubes one, two, three, four, five, six, nine and ten. Down.'

At the final word Able Seaman John Underwood, operating the periscope hoist, lowered it smoothly into its housing in the control room deck. Robert Douglas-Don was setting the target data on the attack computer – the large electro-mechanical calculator that looked a little like a fruit machine and was generally called by that name. The battleship was 6,000 yards away and approaching *Triumph* at ten yards per second. Ideally, Woods would fire his torpedoes from 500 yards ahead of the battleship's track, which meant that *Triumph* had just nine minutes in which to manoeuvre into position at a walking pace, while avoiding detection by the destroyers or being hit by the rain of depth charges they were dropping ahead of the force. The nearest destroyer was stationed 1,500 yards abeam of the battleship, exactly where Woods would want to be to fire his torpedoes. The Regia Marina (Italian Royal Navy) could evidently do maths as competently as the Royal Navy.

'Pilot, come to port, increase speed to five knots, settle on southwest.'

Woods was creating a mental picture in his head of angles, ranges, relative speeds and an idea of where he wanted to be when he fired his torpedoes. With no time to get inside the destroyer screen, and in any case a high risk of being hit by a depth charge if he did try, he had already decided to fire from outside the screen, at an uncomfortably long range but at a good firing angle. His long, slow turn to port, almost a half-circle, should bring him to the target's starboard side at the right range. This is what *Triumph* had been designed for. An attack at maximum range, of perhaps three miles or 6,000 yards, using approximate target data, the uncertain maths balanced by using a spread of eight torpedoes, like a hunter bringing down a fast pheasant at range with a hail of shotgun pellets. Here the hunter had not one but three pheasants, and a miss of the leading ship might easily turn into a hit on one of her consorts in line astern.

Three hundred of the precious seconds had passed when Woods decided to take another look. He would ideally need at least three sighting looks to generate enough data for the fruit machine to provide a reliable aiming point.

'Blast', thought but not spoken.

As the sea smeared off the small lens of the periscope, Woods saw that while he had been turning north to get into position, the Italian squadron had turned sixty degrees to starboard, towards him, exactly to throw off the calculations of a stalking submarine. Where five minutes earlier *Triumph* had been on the squadron's starboard bow and racing for a shot from its starboard beam, she was now on its port bow, and almost exactly in the path of the four destroyers of the port wing escort. The leading destroyer's bow wave was just over a mile away and would be on him in something under three minutes. Woods had just seconds to decide what to do.

The first thought that might have flashed into his head was not to wait for target data but to fire a snap salvo after making a tight turn to starboard and firing one torpedo every ten seconds in a wide fan in the general direction of the three large ships just a mile away when they came in line with his bows. Maths suggested that, on average, two of his eight torpedoes would make hits, perhaps on different ships. A single hit was unlikely to sink the battleship but might sink a cruiser. But what if all eight happened to miss? Shrimp Simpson would not be happy at the waste of torpedoes in a wild, undisciplined attack. Discard. Another thought flashed up. A destroyer was coming towards him at eighteen knots, now maybe 150 seconds away. It would take eighty seconds to fire eight torpedoes in a fan. As it left its tube each torpedo would leave a thirty-foot wide splash circle on the calm sea surface above *Triumph* – eight bullseyes clearly visible from the bridge of the approaching destroyer and from any of the several aircraft he had already noticed above the squadron. The destroyer would increase speed quickly and be on top of *Triumph* perhaps thirty seconds after he fired the last torpedo. At three knots *Triumph*, moving at less than two yards per second, would be just sixty yards forward of the last splash and perhaps just eighty feet down, even if she dived. While diving she would have to run her ballast pumps hard, which the destroyer would clearly hear. The probability of her surviving the counterattack after a snapshot was low, almost certainly zero. No, a snapshot was not the way to go. Ten seconds of time lost in thought. Woods mentally turned to his other choices.

He could widen his right turn towards the squadron in the hope of slipping between the escort and the battleship. There would be little time to gather target data. With the target just 700 yards away and crossing ahead, at ten yards per second, its bearing would move left at high speed, taking just fifteen seconds to pass *Triumph*'s bows. *Triumph* was a big boat – nearly 100 yards long – and moving at walking pace. The turn would take at least sixty seconds.

By the time he was in the right place and pointing his torpedoes in the right direction, the battleship would be past and gone, and probably the leading cruiser too. If he did get a shot away, the torpedo's run time at 700 yards was thirty seconds. He would miss astern by at least a ship's length and have no chance of a second shot before the squadron was gone.

Finally, *Triumph* could continue in the direction she was already pointing, roughly southwest, crossing the battleship's track about half a mile and 100 seconds ahead of her, then make a long turn to port to swing her torpedo tubes towards her track from her starboard side. The disadvantage of this choice was that by the time he had crossed her track and swung to port, she would be past him, but his firing angle would be better – from her quarter instead of close aboard her beam. That would mean the rate at which her bearing changed would be slower, and from that angle she and her consorts would present an almost complete line of grey steel for him to aim at. If he missed the battleship, he would have a reasonable chance of hitting one of her followers.

Another fifteen seconds had passed in thought as Woods calculated angles, speeds and times. All eyes in the control room were on their captain, waiting for his decision.

'Make your depth fifty feet.'

A few seconds passed while this order was acknowledged and carried out. Then, in a harsher and more urgent voice, 'Group up, speed seven knots. Come hard to port. Make your depth eighty feet.'

Triumph's deck tilted sharply downwards and the beat of her screws audibly increased. A few seconds later Woods' voice was drowned out by the propellors of one of the destroyer escorts passing close overhead. The thundering rattle of her twin screws was as loud and as insistent as the noise of a railway engine passing at full speed in a tunnel. Woods had time to bless his luck in taking *Triumph* down – the destroyer's propellors had probably passed no more than twenty feet above the boat's bridge. If he had kept at fifty feet, she would probably have rammed *Triumph*. Fortunately, the destroyer's passive sonar was deafened by the noise of water rushing past her transducer and by the racket of her own propellors.

Crash! Crash! Two violent explosions detonated astern of *Triumph*. All aboard could feel the acceleration as she was thrown ten feet towards the surface by the twin blasts. *Triumph*'s hull whipped like a diver's springboard. In her fore ends Petty Officer Frank Collison, in charge of the boat's torpedoes and sitting on the tiny perch by the tubes' firing levers in the small tube space, grinned at the dozen commandos picking themselves up from where the whipping deck had thrown them.

'Cheer up lads, that one was nowhere near. They'll have to do a lot better than that to get us.'

Woods allowed a minute to pass to put distance between him and the destroyer escort. He knew that the delay was robbing him of a shot at the battleship, but there was no way that *Triumph* could match the speed of the Italian squadron on her electric motors, much less catch up. He needed another look to see what was happening above him before he fired.

Triumph was in luck. Shortly after dropping the pair of depth charges, the squadron had altered course again, this time to port to head northeast and towards the entrance to Messina. The turn to port, and her relentless rushing on, had put the battleship well out of range but the stern of her two cruiser consorts was just within reach of *Triumph*'s torpedoes, and on a track close enough to offer a sporting chance of a hit. Woods turned to close, but again his speed disadvantage robbed him of a shot. The cruiser was heading northeast at eighteen knots, drawing quickly away from *Triumph* creeping along at seven knots in her wake. The range, already 3,000 yards, was opening at six yards per second. *Triumph*'s torpedoes ran at forty-four knots, twenty-four yards per second, so would gain on the cruiser at just eighteen yards per second, but by the time they had caught up with the cruiser their fuel would be exhausted. Speed and agility had trumped cunning.

But *Triumph*'s luck held good. The Italian squadron had to turn southeast to enter the actual strait of Messina. The second cruiser, too far away to identify, was now making that long turn to starboard. Woods decided to try and close the range by cutting the corner, turning east towards the strait and away from the squadron, hoping to arrive at a position from which he could fire at the last cruiser from the extreme range of about 7,000 yards (three-and-a-half nautical miles).

Here a new problem presented itself. The Mark VIII torpedoes used a compressed air tank to feed their diesel engines, and their maximum range was a function of how much air their tanks contained. For reasons not recorded, three days earlier Captain Raw's staff had ordered his flotilla's boats to reduce the air pressure in their torpedoes to 2,500 pounds per square inch.

The pressure reduction reduced these torpedoes' maximum range to just three miles – 6,000 yards. Woods' trigonometric brain had swiftly calculated that firing at a target 5,000 yards away which was sailing away from him at eighteen knots would give his torpedoes something like 7,000 yards to run in order to catch up. Six of his eight torpedoes were out of range. However, the two in tubes nine and ten, positioned outside the pressure hull near the bridge, were still at full pressure and had a theoretical range of 7,000 yards. There was no time for further deliberation.

'What's my firing track, Guns?' Woods asked Robert Douglas-Don.

'We're on it now, Sir. Bad solution but might be close enough.'

'Very good. Fire nine … Fire ten.'

Tubes nine and ten were just a few feet above the heads of the men in the control room. Two loud thuds of compressed air, fifteen seconds apart, announced the departure of their two torpedoes. A second later their diesel motors fired up and Woods could clearly hear the outboard motor noise of their propellors as they raced away to the east.

'Number One, take us down fast, eighty feet.'

Woods snapped the command because he wanted to get below his torpedoes' running depth, in case one of them circled back. By diving sharply after firing, *Triumph* would be below the torpedo's set depth and a circling torpedo would pass harmlessly overhead.

The excitement was over. Around the boat men mentally relaxed and allowed their adrenalin to soak away. Only those in the control room knew what was happening, but everyone could feel the beat of *Triumph*'s screws fall back to the regular slow swish of three knots. In the torpedo space the command 'secure tubes one to six, fall out from diving stations' marked the end of the engagement. No one was more relieved than the commandos, who had just heard their first depth charge and did not appreciate the experience.

In the control room, Douglas-Don was watching the hands of his stopwatch with intense interest. The firing range had been inexact, the run time not precisely known, and a hit was unlikely, but still, something might happen at around the seventh or eighth minute after firing. Leading Telegraphist Terry Crummey hunched over his asdic set, ears straining for even the slightest indication of a hit. Crummey, aged twenty-four, was a submarine veteran. He had volunteered for submarine service as soon as he could and was already a submariner at seventeen. Terry was also a war veteran. In his previous boat, *Spearfish*, he had experienced a thirteen-hour-long depth charge attack in which a German destroyer dropped seventy-nine carefully spaced and targeted charges on the submarine as she lay crippled with no power and no lights on the bed of the North Sea. After the attack ended, *Spearfish*'s artificers managed to get her to the surface where she was found by a destroyer and towed home.

Crummey reported a muffled detonation about three minutes after firing – much too early to have hit the cruiser. Probably a torpedo suffering a depth-keeping failure and diving to the seabed a couple of hundred yards below. As the clock ran past the maximum possible run time for the second torpedo, Woods ordered the boat to periscope depth and took a look. Backlit by the dawn sun he could just see two large ships about to disappear behind the headland outside Messina, with the battleship leading. Where was the third? Scanning the horizon astern of the squadron, the third ship, a cruiser, lay stopped in the water, a pillar of black smoke rising into the calm August air. *Triumph* had got a hit. Woods could see the destroyer escorts steaming at speed towards him, breaking into pairs and setting about 'plastering the area with depth charges. There was no organised hunt'.[7]

Triumph slipped quietly away to the north, untroubled by the counterattack. From start to finish the attack had taken just thirty-eight minutes. Having been awake all night, Woods, like his crew, was exhausted.[8]

'Pilot, you have the boat. We need to be off Furiano tomorrow morning. Number One, as soon as we're clear pass an enemy sighting report to SM10 using the mast aerial. I'll be in my cabin. Steward, please bring me a cup of tea.'

Torrente Furiano and Operation Walrus was waiting, and time and tide were pressing.

At midnight on 27 August, *Triumph* closed the beach at Furiano once more. Her casing was a Piccadilly Circus – eleven commandos, six Folboats, six explosive sausages, Petty Officer Telfer, the long ropes that the men would use to tow the two boats loaded with explosives, Thompson sub-machine guns, emergency rations, *Triumph*'s own casing party of half a dozen men, all tripping over each other in the pitch dark of a moonless night. The raiders were ready to launch on command when, half a mile from the beach, Able Seaman Geoff Brown, searching the night with powerful binoculars, whispered, 'Officer of the watch, Sir, port lookout. Small boat red four zero, range about 500 yards'.

Woods had to decide fast. The boat might just be fishermen, or it might be an Italian patrol boat. The operation was already late, and to abandon it now might mean giving it up completely if the weather turned against *Triumph* in the next two days. To fire on the unknown boat would give the operation away and might mean killing innocent fishermen.

'Stand by to ram.'

Running in complete silence on her electric motors, Woods first went astern to open the angle between him and what he was convinced was a patrol boat. The men and equipment on the casing were swiftly struck down below. *Triumph*'s 100-yard-long bulk swung smoothly onto a course to close the small, darker hump on the dark sea. And missed by a foot. As the boat began to slide down *Triumph*'s port side, Woods ordered 'Lewis Guns and small arms – engage'. A brief hail of .303 ammunition engulfed the boat. As it drew nearer, Woods saw with horror that it was just an innocent sailing smack.

'Check, check, check.'

The order to cease firing was instantly obeyed.

'Number one, take those men prisoner.'

It took some time for *Triumph* to bring the fishing boat, still under sail, to her bow planes from where her crew could be waved aboard under the muzzles of Thompson sub-machine guns. One man leapt into the sea to swim for what he was convinced was his life, but, after more delicate manoeuvring, he was grabbed by the neck and hauled up onto the casing. The six fishermen, two of them teenagers, were taken below. Two had been seriously wounded, and Lieutenant Michael Janvrin called Chief Petty Officer Reg Nott, the boat's coxswain and most senior NCO aboard, to help him treat the wounded, with the navy's medical encyclopaedia open on the wardroom table. Walrus was definitely off that night.

For two days *Triumph* cruised quietly and undisturbed off the north coast of Sicily to see whether her brief burst of fire had drawn any attention to the beach. Daylight was spent patrolling up and down the beach at periscope depth periodically examining it, while in the fore ends Michael Janvrin and Reg Nott did what they could for the two badly wounded fishermen. Able Seaman Luther Jones, who could speak Italian, became their sick berth attendant. As each day passed the air in *Triumph* became progressively more fetid, with yet another six more sets of lungs consuming oxygen and producing CO_2, now tainted with a sick smell of imminent gangrene. The beach remained quiet.

'We'll go again after moonset on Saturday morning.'

Woods was briefing Lieutenant Schofield in the wardroom. The commandos were delighted to hear the news. Not only would they at last do what they had come to do, but they would get a chance to stretch their cramped muscles and get away from the foul smell of their Sicilian companions' wounds in the fore ends.

At a quarter to one on Saturday morning the last Folboat was away. *Triumph* went slowly astern on her electric motors to clear the gaggle of boats and turned towards the horizon. She would sail five miles out to sea to charge her batteries and change her air, returning to a rendezvous one mile from the beach at half past three. The commandos had two and a half hours to paddle ashore, reach the bridge, demolish the pier and paddle back.

Ashore, the first part of Operation Walrus went smoothly enough but too slowly. Four men were left on the beach to guard the Folboats drawn up on the sand. The eight men of the demolition party found the bridge unprotected in the starlight. Petty Officer Telfer secured the sausages around the pier. The detonators and timers were set with a ten-minute delay, and the commandos retired a short distance to take cover and wait for the bang. When it came, the explosion was enormous, seemingly amplified by the darkness. After checking that the bridge was down, the demolition party rushed and stumbled the half mile back to the beach as fast as it could. It was already 3.25 am, and *Triumph* would be expecting them to appear a mile out at sea in just a few minutes. They were running late. The rush to the beach took fifteen minutes, but there, instead of their companions and the fleet of Folboats, Schofield found a stomach-lurching shock. The beach guards and two Folboats were gone.

It was now after the rendezvous time. Schofield knew that it would take half an hour to paddle his remaining Folboats the mile out to the submarine. Once out at sea, it would also take some time for them to find each other in the dark, since navigation on a dark shore was imprecise, and navigation of the Folboats themselves little more than guesswork. There was no time to search around for the missing men, and in any case their Folboats had disappeared as well. Schofield ordered his men into their boats and the party started paddling frantically out to sea.

The men on watch on *Triumph*'s bridge, three and a half miles offshore, could hardly miss the massive explosion. As soon as it was seen, Woods increased speed to twelve knots and raced for the rendezvous point, which he reached ten minutes later. The agreed recognition signal was one long flash on a blue torch from both submarine and commandos, changing to two long flashes when the boats had sighted *Triumph* (much easier to see from the Folboats than they were from *Triumph*). The landing party was under strict orders not to paddle more than a mile from the beach, to ensure that each group knew in which direction to search for each other. For twenty minutes Woods drifted in the pickup position, lookouts straining their eyes and ears into the dark for signs of the commandos. *Triumph*, on her electric motors, was completely silent. Of course, we know now that the main party of the commandos had barely got their canoes under way by that time, but Woods decided that perhaps they had inadvertently paddled too far out to sea, so he took *Triumph* another mile offshore, now flashing long blue dashes in all directions. As the commandos paddled seawards as hard as they could, at perhaps two knots, *Triumph* was matching their speed and direction. A low thick mist lay on the calm sea surface and wrapped itself like a grass meadow around *Triumph*'s waist.

After an hour of missing each other, by 4.30 am, marine twilight was breaking the night's shadow to the east, and in half an hour *Triumph* would be clearly visible to any Italian ship, aircraft or submarine in the vicinity. Woods and Janvrin were deeply uneasy – in the Mediterranean, *Triumph* had to be a creature of the night to survive, and both men had had personal experience of the cost of hanging around on the surface in daylight, with *Salpa*. It looked like the landing party had met with a mishap, and at the end of the day the survival of the submarine was much more important than that of eleven individuals, even if one of them was a member of his crew.

'Clear the bridge. Prepare to dive.'

Triumph's lookouts moved to the small open hatch in the bridge deck to descend to the warm fug below. Douglas-Don, the officer of the watch, closed the valve which sealed off the voice pipe to the control room and took a last look around the greying horizon. Two long flashes emerged from the surface of the mist, to seaward.

'Control Room, Bridge, belay the dive. I have a Folboat in sight ahead.'

In a rush, for the men on *Triumph*'s casing could now clearly see each other's faces in the growing light, a single Folboat was brought alongside the fore planes and two men were helped aboard. Twenty minutes later, still on the surface, *Triumph* sighted a second Folboat, with two more men from the landing party, fully five miles from the beach. These too were recovered and *Triumph* slipped thankfully back to her lair in the deep. Safely underwater, the men from the Folboat told their story. One of the Folboats with the explosive sausages had been upset in the surf. With three fewer sausages to carry, five men and two boats had been ordered not to land at all by Lieutenant Schofield, but to return immediately to the rendezvous point. After drifting around for hours, they were about to return ashore to give themselves up, when they saw *Triumph*.

Forty feet above their heads a very different story was playing out. Long after the war ended, one of the landing party left behind, who was captured next day by an Italian patrol, told of returning to the beach to find the guards gone. They paddled hard out to sea in the remaining Folboats, searching in the dawn mist for *Triumph* but were unable to find her. The mist lay thick but shallow – the commandos could see just the heads of their comrades sticking up, out of the mist, in plain sight, but not *Triumph*. The men nearly made it, for at the end of the night they could hear the compressed air rushing from *Triumph*'s ballast tanks as she dived at 5.30 am. Paddling back ashore to try and escape into the Sicilian countryside, the party of seven commandos and one very unhappy Petty Officer, was met on the beach by 'scores of trigger-happy Italian soldiers and Carabinieri. The game was up!'[9]

The exact details of how large the party was, who escaped and who was captured, remain confused. The patrol report, a memoir by a commando called Padgam and other derivative reports, conflict in many details. The commando, Padgam, reported that the beach party panicked when the explosion went off, imagining that the demolition party must have blown itself up in the blast. It is understandable that, after the war, no one was too keen to delve deeper into what might have been a mistake or might have been a failure of nerve. Whatever happened, it was a depressed and smelly boat that sailed back into Malta three days later, but the viaduct had been well blown. All the captured commandos survived the war. Taffy Telfer was invalided home in 1943 with meningitis, recovered and was back at sea in

HMS *Selene* by 1944. Given *Triumph*'s future, he was lucky to have spent two years in a prison camp.

Taffy Telfer was doubtless highly surprised, not to say outraged, at finding himself being processed into captivity.[10] Five hundred miles due east of Telfer, Atkinson and Craig had been busy processing themselves out of it, and it is to Athens in June 1941 that we will now return.

Chapter 9

Escape into Athens

The German occupiers of Crete were quick to move their thousands of prisoners north to the Fatherland. For sick and wounded men, they were very quick indeed. By the end of June's first week these were being flown by Junkers 52 to a prison hospital at Kokkinia, the Red Fields, that had been set up after the fall of Athens,[1] about midway between Athens and Piraeus.[2] There is no record of Atkinson or Craig being unwell, but they must both have contracted something, probably dysentery, for they turned up at Kokkinia, probably in the first batch of seventy-five sick men brought from Crete in the first week of June. Another of these men was Lieutenant Ted Cooper of the 5th New Zealand Artillery, who arrived in Kokkinia on 9 June. Cooper, at twenty-eight, the same age as both Craig and Atkinson, was born in Leicester, emigrated to New Zealand and was now back in Europe. With a large prominent brow, fringed by an already receding hairline and deep-set eyes, Cooper looked permanently worried. Well, he might have been, for he was suffering not only from dysentery, but also partial blindness. The three men might have considered themselves fortunate to be sent to Kokkinia. Unlike its sister camps, in which health, food and sanitation were all thoroughly neglected, Kokkinia was in an old stone military barracks which had been set up as a formal hospital with Greek and Allied medical staff. Its wards, made from the original barrack huts, were light, clean and airy, with proper beds and straw palliasse mattresses. Kokkinia was in effect two prisons, one being the hospital and the other an associated and nearby convalescent camp. The limited food provided by the German Army in both camps amounted to about 800 calories per day. Breakfast was mint tea. Lunch was a slice of bread and a piece of Feta cheese, and supper was another slice of bread and a helping of thin soup.[3] Rations were supplemented by donations from the Greek Red Cross, and prisoners were given a small allowance of German marks from their pay, with which they could buy additional food from a canteen, operated in the camp, where local traders sold fruit, wine and milk.[4] Men were allowed to write a short letter home every ten days, and replies (from the United Kingdom at least) arrived within six weeks, though Atkinson and Craig were not to be in residence long enough to enjoy them. Being only a few miles from Piraeus and Athens, the camps enjoyed fresh water and reasonable drains.

Another appeal, of the convalescent camp at least, was that inside the old, low stone wall that formed its perimeter, was just a single fence of barbed wire whose top strand could be reached with an outstretched hand. Local Greeks came and went with supplies and laundry. The entire camp, holding 1,000 prisoners, was guarded by just thirty Germans, of whom only four would patrol the wire at any one time. The houses and gardens of Nea Kokkinia (New Kokkinia) came almost up to the stone wall, which allowed messages, tobacco and food to be thrown across unseen. The prospects for escape looked promising. The first actual attempt was by two New Zealanders, who hid in bundles of dirty sheets that were heading for the laundry outside the camp. The bundles were left in the sun for two hours, nearly suffocating their occupants. When they were finally thrown onto the truck the escapers mistook the movement for evidence that they were outside the camp and emerged, to find themselves still inside the wire. They were arrested, beaten, and returned. They were lucky not to be killed – the Axis had quickly established that escapers would be shot on sight, and many Allied corpses littered the railway tracks from Kalamata and Athens to Germany. Commonwealth War Graves Commission records show that in the month following the fall of Crete, 223 Allied soldiers were killed in Greece and Crete, some of whom will have died of their wounds, but many of whom will have been shot while escaping. Contact with locals meant that an escaper could prepare the ground ahead of himself, to a degree at least, and the security regime was pleasingly lax. Atkinson, Craig and Cooper immediately began to plan their escapes. John Atkinson and Jim Craig walked the perimeter fence of the Kokkinia hospital prison together, trying not to make their close observation too obvious. In any given July, Athens is too hot to wander comfortably in the sun for any length of time, but July 1941 was notable for becoming one of the hottest summers anyone could remember. By mid-morning the men were already itching with sweat. At least the Germans had allowed the camp to use a local laundry service, and the heat was driving the wire sentry into the shade.

Kokkinia's fence did not look like much. A few strands of barbed wire, strung on posts, rose to about eight feet above ground. There was no cleared strip either side of the wire, and there were no guard towers or searchlights. Check parades had reduced from daily parades, in June, to twice-weekly parades, probably again because of the heat. Beyond the wire was a stone wall about the same height as the wire itself. The prison had been put together in a hurry, for men who were considered in no fit state to escape. Both Atkinson and Craig knew that their own recoveries from dysentery would soon become obvious to their guards, and that once they were visibly fit, they would be despatched to a camp in Germany, from which escape would be much more difficult. Time for action was slipping away.

The men in the camp already knew something of the lie of the land outside it. Most of them had passed through Athens or Piraeus on their way into Greece ten weeks earlier. Piraeus lay just four miles west of the camp, and Athens just six miles east – both little more than a short walk. A few miles south lay the Aegean Sea, whose coast was still littered with fishing boats and small cargo caiques which, with a little luck, could survive the sail across the benign summer Mediterranean to Egypt. Many men in the camp had friends or acquaintances in Athens and Piraeus from their short time enjoying their bars and brothels in March. New friends were also available among the local tradesmen who were running the camp market. The language barrier was porous, for many of the men in the camp had spent two months in Greece and Crete and had picked up some Greek, and it was commonplace to find Greeks who had emigrated for a while to America and even Britain, or had worked in British-owned merchant ships, and who spoke good or even fluent English. Kokkinia was receiving weekly visits from the wife of the head of the Red Cross in Greece, Mrs Zannas, always referred to in the record as Madame Zannas, who had brought not only substantial quantities of fresh food, but also mail, and even an old piano. Madame Zannas' husband, Alexis, had served as Minister for Air in an earlier Greek government and was a prosperous Salonikan. He was also, since 1940, one of SOE's Apostles – a covert group gathered to collect intelligence and carry out sabotage as opportunity offered. Zannas had spent much of April blowing up bridges around Salonika with the retired Canadian Salonikan Major Menzies, whose retirement job had been to look after the British war graves left by the Salonika campaign.[5] Here, Menzies cheerfully dug new graves to store the considerable quantity of explosives provided by Ian Pirie before the fall of Greece; those that would not fit were hidden in the crypt of Salonika cathedral by the Bishop of Kavalla. During the invasion, Zannas had demolished Salonika's docks, after which he had rushed south to Athens, ahead of the advancing Germans, to do the same to Athens' power station and fuel tanks. This latter job had been vetoed since the Greek government had sworn to protect them against the British with force, if necessary. Now, as the senior representative of the Red Cross, Mrs Zannas was in the Kokkinia camp on a more or less weekly basis.

Craig and Atkinson knew that they would not get far outside the camp without help. Between Mrs Zannas and the tradesmen in the camp's food market, they quietly made arrangements to meet locals outside the wire. Atkinson decided to team up with Lieutenant Ted Cooper. At the beginning of June, they had been treated together in the Polytechnikum Hospital in Athens. From there they were brought as convalescents to Kokkinia on 2 July, and over the next ten days had come to trust each other enough to lay a plan which might cost them their lives.

For the first two weeks of July the nights were brightly illuminated by a waxing moon. Atkinson would have liked to wait until the moonless nights of late July, but he, along with Cooper and Craig, were rapidly recovering from their dysentery and it was only a matter of time before they were swept off to a camp in Germany. The men chose the night of 16 July for their attempt. Moonrise was at one in the morning on 17 July. If they could get across the wire and the wall before that, they would have moonlight to make good their escape into the back streets of Kokkinia. At lights-out the men hid in the shower block near the wire, and as the 10.00 pm guard changeover took place they crept out towards it. Their escape almost failed immediately. With acute short sight, and almost no ambient light, Atkinson came within feet of walking straight into a guard. Stopping just in time, he waited for the guard to shamble off into the dark. Cooper snagged himself on the top strand of the wire from where he half fell and half jumped for the wall just beyond it. '[I] landed in a heap on the wall which proved to be only mud and rubble and collapsed under my weight with a noise which sounded like an earthquake! This woke up every dog in the neighbourhood and started what eventually became a very hectic evening'.[6]

Perhaps guided by the noise, and some swearing, Atkinson found his friend in the dark, and together they made quieter haste to get clear of the wreckage. The shower block was on the south side of the camp, and their plan was to reach the main railway line on its north side to jump a train heading north, perhaps towards the Turkish border. They were being optimistic to say the least. The route to Turkey was over 500 miles, and a train would have multiple stops and shuntings along the way, in which their presence aboard would almost certainly be revealed. In any case, selecting the right train, even if one passed by at night, would be a matter of blind chance, and there were plenty of other less helpful destinations that their train might be headed to, the most likely of which was Germany, since the Germans had already begun moving Greece's stocks of food, minerals and manufacturing equipment north to the Fatherland. Finally, if they did reach Turkey, they would have to cross a heavily guarded frontier and then still have 150 miles to travel to Istanbul. Both men were unfit and weak, having suffered dysentery (and in Cooper's case also temporary blindness), and been cooped up behind wire for six weeks half-starved with little exercise.

Nevertheless, they pressed on. Working their way around the camp, followed by an aggressive, barking pack of local dogs, they stumbled over a Greek family trying to escape the oppressive heat of the July night by sleeping outside their small house. Immediately realizing their predicament, the family hurried them inside. With daylight, Atkinson and Cooper could see from a crack in their window shutters, a German search party go from house to house on the other side of their road. That night, dressed in spare clothes lent by their hosts, they were taken the few miles to Piraeus to hide out again, and once more to watch the search party widen its net. Their luck held, their host's house escaped the search. But their hosts were agitated, Piraeus was the obvious place to look and was too small to allow them to melt into the background. The only practical answer was to get them to Athens, ten miles up the road. However, the roads to Athens all had roadblocks and vehicles were being searched, but it seemed that the suburban railway was not being watched. Atkinson looked almost like a Greek, but Cooper was a ginger-haired, light-skinned kiwi. Their host's daughters got to work with mascara and makeup to darken him into the local skin tone and dressed the men in scruffy cast-off clothing to give them the appearance of casual dock workers. On the morning of 19 July, Atkinson, Cooper and the two daughters of their host, bought tickets at Piraeus station and walked onto the platform.

Their blood froze. It was a Saturday. The platform for the Athens train was crowded with forty German soldiers heading for a day's leave in the bars of Athens. Off duty, happy and boisterous and with their thoughts on beer and female company, the troops paid no attention to any Greeks on the platform, and the four slipped quietly onto the train in the furthest carriage from the noisy party just before the automatic doors slammed shut with enough force to remove an unwary finger. The train's interior heated up quickly in the intense July sun. During the half-hour journey, Cooper was heating up too, and his makeup started to dribble down his face into his shirt; fortunately, the troops were far too happy to pay any attention and the party reached Athens without incident.

It must have felt extremely strange to Atkinson and Cooper. Here they were, in civilian clothes, probably for the first time in a year, surrounded by Germans, in a strange town whose language they could not speak, with street names they could not read, in acute danger of being identified. For the two soldiers, identification would probably mean recapture and a train to Germany, but for their two escorts, and probably their families, it might mean a swift trip to a firing squad. The tension must have been almost unbearable, made worse because they were unable to speak either to each other or their escorts for fear of being detected.

Reassurance was waiting for them at the platform barrier in Athens' main station. As the crowd of young soldiers powered into the morning sun, from off to one side a dignified, well-dressed middle-aged man, out for a morning stroll, looked pointedly in their direction. The man was Ghedeon Angellopoulos. Born in Soma, in western Turkey, at the turn of the century, as one of the million ethnic Greeks under Ottoman rule, Angellopoulos had been driven out in 1923 in the mass population exchange that followed the disastrous war in which Greece tried to expand into Turkey. During the war, Angellopoulos was more pirate and smuggler than patriot. He had led a band of guerillas whose mission was as much brigandage as defeating the Turks. When the Greeks lost, he sailed the few miles to the island of Mytilene, where he took up as a Greek Robin Hood, working on one hand as a highwayman and smuggler, and on the other as a one-man welfare service to the poor.[7] In 1940, Ian Pirie, MI6's man in Athens, recruited him into the Apostles, and with a nod to his classical education, and Homer's story of a man striving for years to return home to Greece from Troy, had given him the code name Odysseus. Odysseus brought his caique, which he sailed under another alias, Captain Stefanos. It was he who had provided the caique in which Pirie and his brand new wife had escaped from Greece in April, rescuing twenty-eight sailors from a sunk destroyer en route.

Odysseus made a discreet signal to follow, and a few minutes later the little group gathered out of sight in an alley near the station.

He spoke fluent, if accented, English.

'Are you alright?'

They nodded.

'We need to split you up. Many people have escaped from Kokkinia over the past week, and the Boche are running around like they stumbled on a bees' nest. It will be some time before we can get you back to Egypt. For now, you must hide.'

In fact, a total of thirty-seven men had escaped within a day or two of Atkinson, including Jim Craig, who we will soon find hiding in Athens. Cooper later reported that he knew of at least one spy, or colourfully termed stool pigeon, inserted into Kokkinia by the Germans to identify and report on escape attempts. This meant there was effectively no coordination between the dozens of men planning to escape. The stool pigeon, Charles Barthold, had rather given himself away by being allowed to leave the camp at night and drink in a local Kafeneion with the Germans. Two other spies were inserted but revealed themselves by their poorly accented English and were beaten up by some prisoners.[8]

Cooper was escorted to the house of a Dr Kotzias in an Athenian suburb. Here, he had an early encounter with the joys of infant childcare, for Dr Kotzias had dismissed his maid, suspecting that she was a security risk. Atkinson was luckier. Later that day he and Angellopoulos knocked on the door of a substantial town house at 9 Patission Street,[9] just around the corner from the Grande Bretagne Hotel, headquarters of the German occupation. It was opened by a slightly ageing, diminutive lady dressed in the grey skirt and jacket of a family nanny. To Atkinson's intense surprise he heard himself addressed in perfect cut-glass English.

'Oh, my dear, come along in now, quickly, quickly, the Germans are all over the place.'

The large front door closed out the hot midday sun, returning the hallway to its cooler state of elegant gloom.

'Please come with me, dear. Mr Ioannou is waiting in the drawing room and he's very keen to meet you. There's tea ready as well. I'm afraid we haven't got much lunch – it's very hard to find anything in the market at all these days. Captain Stefanos, there's something waiting for you in the kitchen.'

Atkinson mounted the grand main staircase in a daze of confusion. What was an Englishwoman doing living in this grand house in the middle of Athens in the middle of a war? He found out soon enough. His new host invited him to sit on the expansive leather sofa in the large front room on the first floor. Through the open floor-to-ceiling windows, the gentle noise of the Athens street drifted in, obstructed only by the half-closed shutters designed to keep the summer heat at bay. Athens was already much quieter than it had been in April. Petrol for private use was unobtainable, and many private cars and trucks had been requisitioned and loaded onto flatbed rail cars to he hauled north to help resupply Barbarossa. The business of the city was being conducted on foot or on bicycle, or on two-wheeled carts hauled by hand.

'Welcome to my house, Lieutenant Atkinson. I am honoured on behalf of Greece to host you here. My name is Mr Ioannou.'

Ioannou too spoke almost perfect English, though with a pronounced accent.

'I am a tobacco merchant. Was, a tobacco merchant I suppose, since I sold most of my product to English companies. We have a house in London, but unfortunately, we found ourselves here when the Germans came. I will shortly introduce you to Mrs Ioannou, and my daughter, Effi. You've already met Miss Morris. She is our nanny. She's been with us since Effi arrived, which makes it fifteen years, I suppose. How time flies by. The Germans tried to take her away, she's English, you know, but I sorted that with the commander of the garrison. She's much too old to go into internment, and of course she's completely harmless.' Ioannou smiled at Miss Morris as he said this.

'Apart from the four of us, and our cook and maid, there's no one else here, which means that you are completely safe, so long as the Boche don't take it into their heads to search the house. Do please sit down. Tea?'[10]

Atkinson collapsed onto the sofa, dazed by his surreal situation. Just a few days ago he'd been in a camp expecting to be loaded onto a cattle train bound for Germany, facing years in a prison camp. And now here he was, sipping tea with lemon, from a china cup, in a millionaire's drawing room, with an English nanny, just 200 yards from the German Kommandantur. War certainly delivered some surprises.

9 Patission Street became Atkinson's home and refuge for ten weeks. After a few days, the massive front door opened and closed again to reveal Ted Cooper, moved from the Kotzias house after being seen there by a police constable who had been persuaded to keep silent, but might change his mind at any moment. Food was in critically short supply, even to a man with the resources to pay for his shopping on the black market, so both Atkinson and Cooper's health relapsed. Atkinson suffered an attack of fever, and Cooper caught fever complicated by jaundice. Mr Ioannou paid for reliable doctors and nurses to care for them alongside the doughty Miss Morris. Effi Ioannou helped too. Cooper's ginger complexion was still a problem, so Mr Ioannou paid for regular visits to a beauty parlour with Effi where his skin was darkened and his hair dyed to a more Athenian black. Photographs were taken, and after a few weeks, and doubtless the giving of substantial bribes, both men had reliable identity cards that allowed them to walk Athens' streets and parks with more or less impunity. Effi took them to the cinema and to local cafes. In Ted Cooper's own words, 'we could quite pleasantly have spent the rest of the war on their hospitality'. Mary Cawias, another Athenian quoted in one memoir of the occupation, recalled 'one day, in the cinema, just further down the row from where I was sitting, an obviously British face was suddenly lit up. He had leant forward for a light and a German soldier who happened to be sitting next to him had obliged – and not noticed'.[11]

The risk of discovery, either in the street or following a house search, was pervasive, but there were too many houses in Athens for the occupiers to search everywhere. So long as they kept a low profile and shared their presence in Patission Street with the smallest possible number of people there was no particular reason why they would be discovered at home, and not much risk of discovery on their occasional forays out into the open.

Seventy years later, I visited Effi Ioannou, now Effi Kulukundis, in her home in Chelsea, west London, just 200 yards north of the Albert Bridge over the Thames. I found a tiny eighty-six-year-old with a sparkling eye and an engaging smile, completely in possession of all her wits. Over a cup of tea, we talked of Athens in 1941 and the house on Patission Street. Did she remember Atkinson? Effi's gaze defocussed slightly as she thought back over the span of a lifetime. She seemed temporarily lost for words. Saying nothing, she rose and disappeared into the back of her large and comfortable house. I heard her feet delicately climbing the stairs. I sipped my tea for a few minutes, wondering if she was alright. Perhaps a demand of nature had called her away. My thoughts drifted 200 yards west to the little Georgian townhouse in the same street, north of the Albert Bridge, in which I was born just fifty-five years before. I had spent the first twelve years of my life living two-dozen doors down from Atkinson's Athenian friend, without knowing it. The world can be a remarkably small place.

A few minutes later she came back into her sunny sitting room. Outside, the London traffic hummed to and fro to Battersea Park, where aged five I had taken my daily walk, with my own nanny, in the swinging sixties.

'Here he is.'

Effi was holding out a photograph, one of those very small black and white photographs from a 1940's Box Brownie camera. Just two inches by four, curling slightly, but clearly carefully looked after, perhaps in a shoe box, but not in an album or a frame.

'That's Atkinson in our garden in Athens.'

The photo showed a man standing with one hand in the pocket of the high-waisted baggy trousers that were the fashion in 1941. Mr Ioannou's trousers, I thought, tailored, quality wool cloth, perhaps bought on a trip to London. He was leaning slightly against a trellis, the other hand carelessly holding a cigarette, half smoked, its thumb hooked into his other pocket. He wore a dark shirt, open at the neck, and a white belt, and looked down at the camera which Effi must have been holding at her waist, looking down into the viewfinder on its top. The expression on Atkinson's face is serious, almost stern, as if he had been caught thinking about how to make the next move in his escape and had been distracted by Effi and her camera, while pacing to and fro in the little garden on a late summer morning. I handed the photo back to Effi. It had taken her just one minute to find it upstairs. Clearly, she remembered John Atkinson very well. One writer, in describing the experiences of an Australian serial escaper, reported that Atkinson became engaged to one of the Ioannou daughters (he doesn't report which one)[12] despite already being engaged in England to Josephine Wiscombe, who lived in Yeovilton Somerset.[13] I felt that I had stumbled on a private and precious memory.

Both Atkinson and Cooper had escaped in order to get back to Egypt and were also acutely aware of how much danger they were putting the Ioannous in by hiding in Patission Street. As the weeks passed the German regime grew increasingly harsh. On their arrival in April, the occupiers had decreed that it was their intention to treat Greeks as friends, and that the Greeks should treat them as protectors from exploitation by the imperial-minded and exploitative British. Greek soldiers, who it will be recalled, were sent home on leave while Lustre Force retreated pell-mell to the beaches, were permitted to travel home in peace. German soldiers were under orders to salute Greek army officers and to rise from their desk chairs when receiving Greeks in their offices. German propaganda initially stated that Germany respected the Greeks, who had fought hard in the line of duty. These German attempts at civility and respect were not reciprocated, not least since Greeks could see their commercial and agricultural assets being looted day by day. Greeks for the most part treated the Axis occupiers as if they were invisible. The occupiers reacted quickly, and not warmly. A curfew was imposed from 10.00 pm to dawn with a threat to shoot to kill transgressors. All weapons were ordered to be handed in, on pain of death. All radios were restricted to listening to the Athens station, and a decree was circulated forbidding aid to escaping British troops – of whom some 2,000 were scattered around the centre and south of Greece.[14]

Most Athenians delighted in breaching all these decrees. Each day's bright Mediterranean dawn brought its crop of walls painted with large *Ohis* (No, as a reminder of Metaxas' firm 'No' to the Italian ultimatum of October 1940), or with large 'V's' for victory, reflecting the dit-dit-dit-dah 'V' in morse that preceded each night's radio broadcast from Cairo. The Greek flag still flew, for now, over the tomb of the unknown soldier outside parliament at Syntagma Square, albeit alongside a Swastika. Each sunset, the two flags were lowered together in front of a crowd of Greeks, at least until a party of patriots stole the swastika flag from the Acropolis, after which the Greek flag disappeared from public view. Faced with passive, insolent resistance, German troops quickly grew hostile, aggressive, and then violent.

'A German Officer hit a friend of mine who happened to take off his hat, and the German was deceived and saluted him in return. "I will not stand to be mocked" the German roared. [I] explained that we had not even noticed him. He was surprised to hear German and went off cursing.'[15]

The corrosive, permanent threat of discovery at Patission Street was one problem for Atkinson and Cooper. Another was that food supplies in Athens were running out. By the end of September, poorer people were beginning to show signs of incipient starvation. Meat, olive oil, flour, bread and butter disappeared from the markets. Atkinson and Cooper knew that they had to get back to Egypt, or risk seeing their hosts starve in order to feed them. Fortunately, Odysseus had been busy working towards to the same goal. Smugglers, at least in Greece, appear to be a gregarious species. In his twenty years of sailing his caique around the quieter islands of the Aegean, Odysseus had befriended another rogue, Harry Grammatikakis. Odysseus was an Anatolian and more than half a Turk, and so something of an outsider in mainstream Greek society. Grammatikakis was another, for he was a Cretan who had only become a Greek at the age of twelve, when Greece wrested Crete from Ottoman possession in the 1912-13 Balkan Wars. Now, thirty years later, Cretans still thought of themselves as Cretan first, and Greek a distant second. History does not relate where the two men met, but it was probably on some dark night on the placid Aegean Sea unloading crates of untaxed cognac from one caique to another. Greek Director of Naval Intelligence, Vice-Admiral Panos Konstas, later said of Grammatikakis, 'Harry is of Cretan descent, a real pirate guy, sea dog, enthusiastic and adventurous, and most suitable for a risky assignment'.[16]

Grammatikakis, like all good smugglers, had a caique. He also had the look of a movie star. A long, oval face with soulful eyes that suggested an ability to be a rogue or a lover, as he wished, a full lip beneath an aristocratically straight nose was rounded off by a sharp but handsome chin. Harry would have looked completely at home in the team photograph of the cricket first XI in one of the major English public schools. With a girl in every port, Harry of course had one in Piraeus, a young lawyer called Alexandra Bourbouras.[17] Alexandra knew Odysseus too, and probably all the Athenians active in helping Allied troops escape. She let Harry know that a caique was needed to carry an escape party to Egypt and placed a party of six escapers in his care. One of the six was Jim Craig, of the New Zealand 22nd Battalion, who had been hiding in another house in Athens almost as long as Atkinson. On Friday 26 September, a taxi arrived at Patission Street. Miss Bourbouras, tense with apprehension, was trying to look as calm and natural as she could when she rang the doorbell. Atkinson and Cooper were already waiting in the hall, with Miss Morris and all the Ioannous fussing around them with sandwiches wrapped in brown paper and a flask of tea. Effi was probably in tears, perhaps imagining that she might never see Atkinson again, though that fear would sadly prove unfounded. The two escapers climbed into the old taxi to find Craig and three other men already ensconced, along with Miss Bourbouras' brother, Adamantios. There was no time for friendly greetings – the party needed to put space between itself and the heart of the occupation as quickly as it could without drawing attention. The taxi itself was a red flag, in a city with almost no available petrol. The group of six young men together, even in civilian clothes, was another. In the words of Ted Cooper, 'We were all dressed in various forms of camouflage and I am afraid looking like a real band of cut-throats'.[18]

One of the six , Flight Lieutenant Henry Daston RAF, had grown up in Istanbul and spoke fluent Greek. He sat in the front passenger seat of the taxi. There were two Italian checkpoints on the way to their rendezvous with Harry's caique. At each of these Daston, Bourbouras, her brother, and the taxi driver began a vociferous 'family argument' in fluent Greek to distract the guards from the band of suspicious-looking men in the back seats. When the guards tried to interrupt the row, demanding identity cards, Bourbouras shouted the demand back to the rear seat passengers without breaking the stride of her domestic yelling. These were passed forward in a bundle, with the aim of minimizing the scrutiny that the guard would give them and their subjects. The ploy worked, twice, despite the men in the back sweating profusely and losing their hair dye and makeup in rivulets down their shirts.

Once the second checkpoint was passed, the taxi had only twenty miles to drive to a drop-off point eight miles from the small bay where Harry's caique was due to pick them up. These eight miles the party walked, though they walked many more because Bourbouras had brought only a small-scale tourist road map which led them first to the wrong bay, and then to a narrow escape from a German coastal gun position. This was the first serious walking that any of them had done since their capture, and their leg muscles must have felt the pain. It was dark by the time they found themselves slipping and sliding down a steep hill to a small beach a few miles north of Lavrion. A stab of panic must have struck when they realized that they were not alone. The bushes behind the beach were alive with men hiding, waiting for the same caique. Harry, with an eye to the main chance, had maximized his revenue by selling every square foot of his caique to men heading south.

By September 1941, the movements of caiques between the many islands of the Aegean were strictly controlled by the Axis. Caiques were essential to the economy, being the only means of bringing supplies to the islands and exporting their production of wine, fruit, eggs, lamb and olives to the markets of the mainland. Each sailing needed explicit permission. Harry Grammatikakis had obtained a permit to carry forty-five Cretan ex-soldiers from the mainland back to their homes in Crete in the caique *Koimisis tis Theotokou* (the Dormition of St Theotokous) 'borrowed' from the Fourourakis brothers. His plan was to leave Piraeus with these legitimate passengers late on that Friday and pull into the bay four hours later at nightfall, since movement after dark was prohibited. Here he would load his additional passengers, unseen, and sail at dawn south and east towards Crete. Atkinson and his fellow escapers were stowed in the small, smelly forepeak of the caique, reeking of old fish and squalid nets. Crete was too far away to make in a single daytime sail, and in any case, the Italians had set up a control point on the island of Paros, about midway between Crete and Athens, where Harry's permit required him to check in en route. Obviously, he could not pass the control point with his escapers aboard, so a few miles before he slipped into a bay to land his illegitimate passengers before checking-in his legitimate ones at Paros. During the war, Greece's islands were so thinly populated that the chances of being observed off any given beach were effectively nil.

Harry, it proved, was very happy to mix business with pleasure. The drop-off beach was also home to a young lady with whom he was having a passionate affair, and he lingered on Paros for four days while the escape party of Allies and Greeks hid in a nearby house. The next part of the journey went smoothly. After crossing the hundred miles of sea between Paros and Crete in an easy day's sail, Harry arrived off Heraklion on Crete's north coast. Here, he offloaded his legitimate passengers from one side of his caique, while his escape party slipped into a dinghy on the other side to hide out in a shed ashore while the caique was inspected and passed by the German guard party. In the small hours of the next morning, Harry reloaded his escapers, slipped his mooring and puttered out to sea in darkness, this time heading for Alexandria.

The voyage to Egypt was a very different proposition to island-hopping in the Aegean. After coasting the 150 miles off the north side of Crete, at a safe distance from observation but not from a patrolling bomber, Harry had to turn southeast for 300 miles, at least forty hours if nothing went wrong. The first 100 miles of this, ten hours under power, was in daylight across waters under constant air patrol. Something very quickly went wrong. Unnoticed by Harry or his passengers, the caique's single engine's water circulating pump failed at around midday on 2 October. The single-cylinder diesel engine gradually overheated until, in a shower of sparks and smoke, its cylinder head cracked and it stopped. In a rising equinoctial sea, adrift in bright sun and in plain sight of passing aircraft, the situation must have felt desperate. Harry may have been a rogue, but he lacked nothing in resource. As the boat rolled heavily in the beam sea, he dismantled the engine and used a heavy hammer to beat a rough seal into the cracked cylinder. With the engine reassembled, he found it would run successfully at low power, allowing the *Theotokus* to sail at a walking pace towards Alexandria. Someone in the party had saved his infantry compass from being confiscated by his captors. Knowing that Alexandria lay roughly southeast, the *Theotokus* plodded on, running short of fuel, food and water. So long as they kept heading in the generally right direction, they could not fail to hit Africa, though it was anyone's guess whether they would hit land occupied by British or Axis forces since no one aboard had recent information on the state of the North African campaign. The compass had no luminous dial, so at night Craig navigated by keeping the Pole Star between the backstay and the engine exhaust pipe to give *Theotokus* a course of roughly southeast.

The slow and rough voyage dragged on for almost a week, with rationed water and no food. After a day or two, the risk of being seen by an Axis aircraft diminished, but the possibility of being attacked by the RAF rose. At any moment the repaired engine might fail beyond resurrection. *Theotokus* had a stumpy mast but no actual sails or rigging, and the possibility that they might lose power, and drift hopelessly to die of thirst just a day or so away from safety, must have played on the minds of all aboard. Craig and Atkinson were some weeks away from meeting their new friends in *Triumph*, but it would not have cheered them to know that for this frightening and uncomfortable week she was alongside *Medway*, her people feasting on the delights of an ample galley and Alexandria's cheaper cafes. Craig knew that if they kept heading southeast, they would eventually have to hit Africa, but it was not until 8 October that the African coast came in sight – a low featureless sandy shore, empty of people or structures that could reveal who was in occupation. The crew of a passing dhow suggested that east would be better than west and provided some welcome fresh water. Dusk was falling as Alexandria crept over the horizon. The escapers were fortunate. Alexandria was blacked out at night because of regular air raids, and the *Theotokus* might easily have sailed right past it in the dark, leaving them adrift offshore with no water and perhaps only a few days to live. However, here they were, with safety in sight. But how to enter the heavily guarded harbour? The answer appeared quickly. Two warships[19] were approaching the harbour's floating boom. Another man of the escape party, the New Zealander Corporal Bert Haycock, used two vests as naval semaphore flags to signal their situation and ask permission to fall in astern and follow them in.

'Welcome,' was the short but reassuring reply.

Once in Alexandria harbour the crew of the *Theotokus* found themselves somewhat abandoned. No one seemed to care much about this leaking caique, puffing black smoke and settling lower in the water as night fell. Craig looked around the harbour and decided to head for the largest warship he could see, which happened to be the battleship *Valiant*. He asked Harry to pull alongside her embarkation ladder at whose head stood a midshipman on deck watch, bursting with unjustified importance, regarding the scruffy *Theotokus* with some disdain as she and her crew of dirty men in civilian clothes and twelve-day beards approached its immaculate teak and brass boarding platform. Cooper climbed its steps to find the quartermaster, a young Able Seaman, at its head. 'With all the authority I could muster under the circumstances (with water and fuel oil pouring out of my civilian clothes and wearing black hair and 12 days growth of ginger beard), I asked him to find the Officer of the Watch.'[20]

Within short order the Greeks in the escape party were taken to *Valiant*'s Marines' Sergeants' mess for drinks, food, showers and fresh clothes, probably in that order. Atkinson and his fellow escapers were interrogated first, before their hosts realized that they too were in urgent need of the same succour. *Theotokus* survived her near-sinking, probably due to the swift attentions of *Valiant*'s duty watch. Atkinson and Craig had been away for 131 days, and were heartily glad to have purged their double defeats by returning to the war.

Chapter 10

Coney Island

During the first three months of 1941, the secret departments in Cairo had been heavily distracted by the need to support a rag-tag invasion of Italian-occupied Abyssinia, under the leadership of the hypnotically dedicated Orde Wingate. Wingate christened his little army 'Gideon Force' and co-opted the deposed emperor Haile Selassie to accompany his invasion.[1] The secret activities of Gideon Force were led by Major Tony Simonds, G(R)'s man in Cairo. Through a combination of aggression, guile and luck, Wingate took Abyssinia from the Italians on 6 April – the day Marita's divisions crossed the Greek border. Exhausted by his crusade, Wingate returned to Britain to recuperate, leaving Simonds to join MI9 in Cairo.

Simonds faced a problem of almost insuperable size. MI9 had only come into being a scant year ago. Its first job, large enough by itself, was to indoctrinate every man in the Allied forces in Africa (some half a million) in 'escape-mindedness'. The aim of escape-mindedness was not so much to recover captured men, as to force the enemy to devote large forces to guarding prisoners of war, taking them out of the fighting line. Alongside mental attitudes, MI9 was also tasked with training men in escape techniques and tactics, and with designing, procuring and then issuing escape equipment such as maps printed on silk, and tiny compasses that could be hidden about a captured man's clothing for use in an escape.

As if this was not all enough to keep him busy, Simonds' next task was to interrogate every man who managed to escape. The aim of these interrogations was to gather operational intelligence (the locations of enemy units and equipment, their state of morale, their efficiency and so on), collect information on escapes to help subsequent escapers, and to detect men who were not really escapers at all but had been inserted into escape lines so that they could arrive in Cairo and then fade into the background to spy on the

Allies. It was thanks to this task that Harry Grammatikakis' escape party found itself heading for Simonds' office.

MI9 took great care to prevent returning escapers from inadvertently revealing critical facts of how they had escaped and who had looked after them. Once MI9 had taken charge 'we had military police all round us. They would let no one close to talk to us. We had already been told that we were to keep our form of rescue and all connected with it a secret, because other attempts were to be made to pick up others ... Police were with us in each truck and at the station we had a special carriage at the end of the train with police back and front'.[2]

The interrogation took days, for each man had to be questioned at length, and their accounts cross-referenced. Units had to be contacted to verify identities and the circumstances of their original capture. New kit had to be issued, back pay handed out, and medical conditions treated. So, it was not until ten days after they had wearily climbed the wooden steps to *Valiant*'s quarterdeck, that the escape party posed for a photograph with their saviour, Harry Grammatikakis. In this photograph, Atkinson stands on our left. A tubby-faced young man with the beginnings of a moustache. His experiences since June left him looking thinner and more thoughtful – perhaps he was thinking of the girl he had left behind in Patission Street. In the middle of the group, arms folded in the same linen suit he had been wearing in a prewar photograph, and which he must have picked up in Paros and brought with him in *Theotokus*, hair neatly coiffed and oiled, stands Harry himself, looking seriously, almost fiercely, not at the camera but down at the photographer's feet. Harry is the only man in the group not smiling, as if he knew that too much serious business lay ahead for humour. Perhaps he was also realizing that after leaving Greek waters without a permit, he might not be able to return openly to Greece for the rest of the war, and that he was alone and penniless 400 miles from home and from the girl he loved.

The rest of the group are smiling broadly. Unlike Harry, they were home, or at least among friends. Jim Craig is sitting in front of the group, nearly laughing with happiness. To his right, the second seated man is described as Ted Cooper, but that is almost certainly incorrect. Cooper was in his twenties and a second lieutenant, with a single rank pip on each shoulder. The second man in the photograph is in his late thirties or early forties. His uniform clearly shows three rank badges on his shoulders, probably the crown and two pips of a colonel. It seems much more likely that the second man is Colonel Tony Simonds, commanding officer of MI9's office in Cairo. It was in MI9's hands that Atkinson, Craig and Grammatikakis would spend much of the rest of 1941, carried to and from Greece by the men of *Triumph*, and to their ultimate fates.

With recent and very precious knowledge of conditions and people in Athens, Craig, Atkinson and Grammatikakis had joined the secret world in Secret Building as soon as they arrived in Cairo. Though they were formally in the hands of MI9, and had been interrogated by Colonel Simonds on their escapes, SOE (competitive as ever) quickly identified them as possible agents for reinsertion. Colonel Pearson of SOE invited Atkinson and Grammatikakis separately to his Cairo flat to talk over opportunities and possibilities. Of Atkinson, Pearson later wrote 'I had many conversations with him. I did not like him. He was undoubtedly clever and pleased with himself. He was critical, and not always with justification'.[3] Pearson was more impressed with Grammatikakis. 'I suggested that we pay him a retainer. Before we were able to arrange this he was interviewed by MI9 and taken into their service'. SOE had let these two plum agents slip between its fingers into the hated hands of MI9. Pearson clearly loathed Colonel Simonds, describing him in a memorandum as '[joining] MI9 after a brilliant career in Abyssinia, the report of which, written by the Colonel himself, may doubtless be found in the archives of the Middle East'.[4] A later attempt to rectify the loss of two possible agents, and pay Simonds back for his sticky-fingered behaviour, would result in disaster for all involved.

The antipathy between SOE and MI9 was real and visceral. In Cairo, MI9 was just one of four secret organizations (the others were SOE, 'A' Force tasked with deception operations in the desert, and MI6) who competed for the limited resources available for secret work. The Gaberdene Swine (SOE's senior officers in Cairo) were especially competitive, not just with the other secret organizations, but among themselves. SOE was also actively at war with the Foreign Office in London, whose official policy supported the reinstatement of the King of Greece into a constitutional democracy. SOE had quickly realized that the king had no support at home and that the best opportunities for setting their corner of Europe afire were offered by a mix of communists, socialists and republicans who hated their exiled king. Simonds was ambivalent as to who helped his escapers, but could not afford to be completely agnostic towards SOE since it was larger, richer and noisier than MI9 could afford to be, and was competing for submarines, gold sovereigns and agents constantly. Money was a vital resource. Escaper interrogations revealed that food supplies were disappearing in Greece, and that its urban population was facing starvation – in the mountainous countryside Axis rule barely held and food was less hard to come by. Greek families, hiding escapers, desperately needed money to buy food on the black market. Paper money was inflating at near hyper-levels, so what the escape network needed was gold, in the form of British sovereigns.

There were other demands on the secret funds allocated to MI9 and SOE. Just a week before *Theotokus* limped, spluttering and leaking, alongside *Valiant*, Sammy Woods had brought his submarine back to Alexandria after another successful mission to deliver an SOE landing party to Axis territory, this time to Yugoslavia. Greece was not the only Balkan country to have fallen swiftly to the Axis in April 1941. We saw that Operation Marita had begun with a wide right hook from Bulgaria, through Yugoslavia, and into northern Greece. On 6 April, Yugoslavia had been a neutral state. Eleven days later, it was a subject state of Germany whose young king, Peter, and his government had fled to London. The situation that ensued made even the complexities of Greek domestic politics look simple by comparison. The occupied country contained populations of ethnic Serbs, Croats, Slovenes and Albanians who in principle all hated each other because of the oppressions they'd each inflicted on each other since the ejection of the Turks. To add to the toxic brew, there were competing populations of Christians and Muslims and, since 1921, an active and growing communist underground. In Croatia, a pro-fascist organization (the Ustase) was conducting a murderous campaign against anyone who opposed it.

Tasked with 'setting Europe ablaze', SOE in Cairo had responsibility for Yugoslavia, but no idea where or with whom to begin. SOE did not just hate MI9, but also on occasion the Foreign Office. In Yugoslavia, the Foreign Office agenda was to ensure the return of King Peter after the war, while SOE's agenda was to ally with, and support, whoever could create the most trouble for the German occupiers. King Peter had no support base in his kingdom, so that meant allying with one or another group of republicans. The distraction of generating sabotage and subversion in Greece had fully occupied SOE over the summer of 1941, so it was not until early autumn that attention was given to subversion in occupied Yugoslavia. As in Greece, the collapse of the state had been so swift that no residual SOE network existed. SOE in Cairo knew no one in Yugoslavia, and nothing about who might be in a condition to create trouble for the Axis. What was needed was agents on the ground with gold and a radio. The only way to get them safely into Yugoslavia was by submarine – a round trip from Malta of 1,200 miles. With its necessary day-night routine, evasive routing, the distractions of attacks along the way, and the need to spend at least a day preparing and carrying out the landing operation, a submarine could plan on advancing just 120 miles per day, making a simple landing of half a dozen men a two-week operation. The little U-class boats were too cramped to operate for that long with passengers and Folboats so far from Malta. Happily, for SOE and Captain Raw, in the middle of September, while Atkinson and Cooper were cautiously slipping out from the house on Patission Street to Athenian cafes and cinema shows, *Triumph* had just returned to Malta and was ready for her next operation.

Before April 1941 Yugoslavia had figured low in the agendas of both SOE and MI6, the Secret Intelligence Service. MI6, however, had the good fortune to recruit a young British mining engineer based in Montenegro into Section D, its small sabotage section, in 1939. This man was Duane Tyrell Hudson. Aged thirty, and using the much simpler first name Bill, Hudson had lived in Yugoslavia since 1935 with his young Russian ballerina wife. He was employed to manage an antimony mine. Here, he had become fluent in Serbo-Croat, had engaged in a little anti-Axis shipping sabotage with limpet mines, and had managed to escape Yugoslavia for Cairo just ahead of the invading German Army. SOE Cairo flew Hudson to Malta on 13 September to join *Triumph* with three Yugoslavian army officers, one of whom was a trained radio operator.

Often special operations arranged in a tearing hurry misfired, but on this occasion the operation, codenamed Bullseye, proceeded without a hitch. *Triumph* sailed after dark on 16 September, and four days later Hudson and his three companions landed at the southern end of the Adriatic at Petrovac, opposite Bari and just 140 miles north of Corfu. They were laden with two suitcase radios and a hoard of British gold. The archives do not tell just how much gold, in the form of sovereigns, Hudson was given to take into Yugoslavia. After the war, he admitted he had buried stashes of sovereigns around Yugoslavia with the intention of returning in peace to recover them for his personal use. One article, in a major newspaper, claimed that he took £80,000 in sovereigns (equating to some £4 million today). At gold prices in 1941 (about £2 for a sovereign weighing eight grammes), that would have implied some 40,000 sovereigns weighing over 700 pounds, plus the weight of their containers – an unlikely burden for four men who were also lugging two radios, weapons, ammunition and food. It would also have been two months' entire budget for SOE Cairo. The story may have grown over time. Another story of Hudson's war cited him as a partial inspiration for James Bond.

If he took a stash of gold sovereigns with him in 1941, Hudson did not appear to use it to buy a comfortable life. Discovering that Yugoslavia's two resistance leaders, Tito and Mihailovich, were as much at war with each other as with the Germans, he retreated into hiding in the mountains, spending the winter of 1941/1942 starving and freezing on a diet of nettle soup. Hudson's misery was prolonged – he was not exfiltrated from Yugoslavia until early 1944.

Triumph returned, from dropping Hudson and his golden hoard, to Alexandria. It's possible that her officer of the day had seen *Theotokus* puffing her way alongside *Valiant* at sunset, and wondered what she was and from whence she came. Her passengers would soon find their way into her little wardroom, for Colonel Simonds' busy mind was thinking about how to solve a massive problem.

By the end of May 1941, something like 2,000 Allied troops were in hiding in Greece and Crete. No one knew the exact number, for no one knew for sure if a missing man was hiding, captive, or dead. The Red Cross, responsible for tracking prisoners of war, was gradually getting on top of the problem, but communications had to pass through neutral states by slow post. By the end of September, 1,100 escapers had already trickled back to Cairo in stolen caiques, or through Turkey, or in one of His Majesty's submarines, and what was certainly clear from the interrogations so far was that there were many hundreds more, scattered around Greece, who needed help to get home.

Simonds did not just have to worry about time and money – he also had to think about the legal status of escapers. The law of armed conflict, as it stood in 1941, held that an escaped soldier could move about occupied territory in civilian clothing without being automatically treated as a spy or a saboteur, and therefore without being shot out of hand on recapture. This protection – which was generally honoured by both German and Italian troops until the middle of 1943[5] – disappeared if the escaper armed himself or used lethal violence to defend himself from recapture. In November 1941, the GOC of the Italian occupation forces in Greece, General Giovanni Magli, wrote a detailed memorandum to Italian army headquarters on this subject: 'for the simple fact of not wearing uniform, the enemy soldier does not as a general rule loose [sic] his status of legitimate belligerent ... and therefore assumes the status of prisoner of war'.[6]

An SOE agent, on the other hand, inserted into occupied territory, bristling with weapons and fully prepared to use them, was usually uniformed on arrival and thus a legally permitted combatant entitled to protection as a prisoner of war if caught. However, the practicalities of survival in occupied territory swiftly led SOE agents to swap battledress for local dress, at which point they became saboteurs and were liable to death on capture. Simonds' problem was that it was difficult for occupation troops to work out whether a man, captured in civilian clothes, was a legal prisoner of war or a non-legal saboteur, spy or terrorist. Hence the work of SOE had the potential to make the work of MI9 extremely difficult, not to say dangerous. SOE was not the only source of difficulty. MI6 and the Foreign Office desperately wanted to know what was happening in the political sphere of occupied Greece – who was up, who was down, and who should they focus their attention on when the Axis left and a political vacuum emerged? These questions lay firmly in the field of spying, and it was accepted by all that a captured spy had no rights to protection.[7]

By autumn 1941, the flow of escapers from Greece had slowed. The Axis had taken effective control of Greece's inter-island caique traffic, which made the theft of a caique almost impossible. Harry's borrowed caique was the last arrival on record.[8] Escapers knew that if they managed to cross the Aegean to Turkey, they would generally be handed over into the care of the British Embassy and permitted to travel by train, south across Syria and Palestine to Cairo. The route had only recently been opened. Until May 1941, Syria and Lebanon were Vichy French territory and were openly hostile to Britain. A British force invaded on 8 June and took control of Syria on 14 July, after an extremely violent campaign that saw some 200

Allied troops killed in action. However, with caiques strictly controlled, the only options open to escapers were to find a caique captain willing to risk his life by hiding men aboard and hope that the Axis searches did not find them, or to steal a small boat and either row or sail across 150 miles of open water to Turkey. Both happened, but in small numbers. What Simonds was thinking about was how to increase the flow of help into Greece, and men out of it.

Since the first rescues at the end of May, submarines had been the obvious answer. The torpedo compartment of a large submarine like *Triumph*, could squeeze fifty or more men in for the ten hours needed to voyage to the relatively safe waters between Crete and Egypt, while providing them with food, water and lavatories. In extreme circumstances, a boat could carry double that, but no one would plan for that many since the submarine would be completely unable to fight or flee with that many people cluttering up her tiny hull. The challenge was coordination. Simonds' discussions with Captain Raw, who effectively decided where Alexandria's submarines went and what they did when they got there, had resulted in a clear conclusion that he would not hazard one of his precious boats close inshore for less than twenty escapers. Raw also refused to commit his boats to exact places and times for picking up men; if the rendezvous was compromised, the boat would certainly be ambushed on the surface in waters too shallow to allow her to dive, and would be lost, or even captured. In any case, it was almost impossible to communicate a fixed rendezvous to a group of escapers hiding out in multiple homes and caves around Greece, and the probability that word of the rendezvous would leak, perhaps via one of the false escapers being fed into the network by the Axis, was a near certainty. After discussing the challenge, Simonds and Raw agreed that what might work was to collect parties of escapers in a single place, out of sight of the Axis, and keep them there until a submarine chose to arrive, unannounced and unexpected, to lift them home as if on a magic carpet. But where?

That bright October morning of the group photograph, the answer to 'where?' had just left Simonds' office in search of lunch, in the unlikely form of Harry Grammatikakis. Harry had spent some ten years threading the islands and inlets of the Aegean, carrying cigarettes and whisky out of sight of the authorities. He had grown particularly fond of the island of Paros, partly because it sat conveniently at the centre of the routes between Athens,

Turkey, Crete and the tip of the Peloponnesian fingers, each of which lay just 100 miles, and a night's sail away, but more particularly because he had formed a close personal relationship with a girl in the main port of Paros. Since the arrival of the Axis, Paros had acquired a new appeal. Axis controls allowed caiques to sail relatively unhindered and uninspected for up to twenty-four hours from their home port. With sailing prohibited at night, that meant six hours out and six back, all in daylight, which was not enough time to make a full trip to and from Paros. But if a caique broke the no-night-sailing rule (which was relatively safe since Axis navy patrols did not have radar and were too few in number to cover much of the Aegean anyway), a caique could sail from Piraeus, or one of the small harbours south and east of Athens, in daylight, pick up escapers at a quiet beach, reach Paros, drop the men off, sail back, and be back in its home harbour within twenty-four hours and the Axis none the wiser.

Paros, about the same size and shape as the Isle of Wight, was too well populated to serve as a hideout for a large group of escapers, and, as a large busy island, had also been given a garrison of a whole battalion of Italian troops. With these men, and the local population, concentrated on Paros' north coast, a hideout on Paros would have to be on its south side, as far away as possible from the port and the garrison, adding an impossible three or four hours to the round trip from Athens. However, just west of the main island of Paros sat the much smaller and largely unpopulated island of Antiparos ('Anti' in Greek meaning 'opposite'). The north head of Antiparos is separated from Paros by a narrow strait, a little less than a mile wide. The island then stretches five miles southwest, widening to two miles at its end, from where a narrow deserted peninsula points southeast two miles into the Aegean. At the southwest end of Antiparos lies a large, sheltered bay with a half-mile-wide entrance to the open sea. The bay is sheltered from the west by the even-smaller island of Despotiko then, as now, deserted. Harry had made a habit of using Antiparos, and the bay at Despotiko, for smuggling. He now suggested to Colonel Simonds that it would be ideal as a hideout and collection point for escapers. A caique (breaking the no-night-sailing law) could sail from Athens to Antiparos, and back, inside the required twenty-four hours. The bay was generously large, big enough to allow a 100-yard-long submarine safely to enter, manoeuvre and leave in complete darkness. At the head of the bay a 600-yard-long beach, perfectly sheltered from all directions, would allow Folboats to land and pick up men and equipment regardless of the weather outside the bay. The island itself was almost unpopulated, had no garrison, and was twelve miles by sea from Paros harbour, which meant two hours of slow sailing. Therefore, if an Italian patrol left for Antiparos by boat, a fast runner could carry the news of the approaching problem to men hiding on the island and arrive ahead of the patrol.

Antiparos was unguarded but not completely deserted. A Paros lawyer, Tzavellas, owned a comfortable medium-sized house 300 yards across flat open ground from the beach. A handful of other houses were scattered on the hillside. The Tzavellas house still stands today, a sprawling one-storey building with small rooms and twisting passages. If supplied with food, clothing, a radio and spare fuel for caiques, a very large party of escapers could be assembled on Antiparos and hidden for weeks while waiting for a submarine to turn up out of the night. Simonds reasoned that Antiparos could become a vital part of the escape network, a veritable base indeed. If the Antiparos cake needed any icing Harry provided it, by telling Simonds that he also had a pair of caiques at moorings in Despotiko bay, waiting to be used for the Athens shuttle.

On 5 November Colonel Simonds met Captain Raw in *Medway*. At Raw's side was his newly appointed operations officer, Sammy Woods, promoted to Commander in the June promotions round.[9] Sammy was by now an experienced beach operator and had just handed over his beloved boat to one of *Medway*'s spare submarine commanders, Lieutenant Johnny Huddart, who had not yet commanded an operational submarine. Huddart sat quietly to one side.

'It's perfect,' Woods opined.

'We can get in and out easily, there are no obstructions for a boat to worry about, it's completely sheltered, so whatever the weather is doing won't be a problem. And once we've picked up a party of escapers, the journey home presents no navigational problems.'

Raw looked at Simonds.

'How do we know that the island has no garrison or guards?'

Simonds tensed. In truth his only source of information was Harry Grammatikakis, whose reliability was far from proven and who had last seen Antiparos two months before in September. Harry was not at the meeting, but Simonds knew that Raw would want more than the word of a single Greek smuggler of uncertain reputation.

'We are sure, Sir, we received confirmation by radio three days ago that Antiparos is unguarded.'

This was a flat-out lie. Simonds knew that Raw did not know that there was not a single operating radio station in the whole of Greece and its islands. He also knew that while Antiparos was unguarded, Paros, just across the water, had a large Italian garrison. The statement that Antiparos was unguarded was as much hope as certainty. But Simonds' plan depended entirely on being given access to Raw's submarines.

'Very good, if you're certain, then we can go ahead.'

Simonds relaxed. With the Navy's blessing, the plan looked like working. One problem remained.

'We can't predict how long it will take to get a large enough party of men together on Antiparos, so we'll have to be ready to provision them with food and clothing while they wait. We'll also have to land enough diesel to refuel the caiques, because they will only get enough from the Germans for day-sailing. Can you help with those, Sir?'

Raw looked thoughtfully at Woods. Both men were doing the maths in their heads. If Antiparos was hiding say forty men, and they had to wait for several weeks before a submarine could schedule a diversion on her way home from the Aegean, the escapers would need close to 100 pounds of food per day, perhaps for forty days, plus fuel for cooking. A single caique trip to Athens would need an additional thirty gallons of diesel, and there might be a dozen round trips between supply drops. Simonds had also discovered that a large party of escapers was hiding out around the southern tip of the eastern-most finger of the Peloponnese, around the port of Neapoli, so men would be coming in from the west, as well as the north.

To set up a base for escapers, a submarine would have to drop at least three tonnes of stores using her Folboats, which could carry no more than 200 pounds per round trip. Given a long night, an early start, and a late finish, it should just about be possible. The delivery submarine would have to unload some of her spare torpedoes and take three fit men from Courtney's Special Boat Section to do the rowing. But it should be possible.

Raw made a decision.

'We'll do it. Sammy, who do we have ready for sea at the moment?'

'Well, Sir, I'd normally say *Triumph*, of course, but she's just left for the Aegean to drop off two parties of agents for SOE. She won't be back until around 4 November, and it will be two weeks after that before she's ready for sea again.'

Woods looked at Simonds.

'Tony, I imagine you're in a bit more of a hurry than that?'

Raw saw Simonds' reply before he spoke it.

'Yes, we'll need to get on with it sooner than that, Sammy. Who've we got on hand?'

'*Thorn* has just come in, Sir. She's new to the Med, only done one real patrol so far, but this one shouldn't present her with major problems, and it will be a good opportunity for her to learn about beach operations in a relatively safe place. I think she can be ready to go in a few days.'

Simonds found himself holding his breath. If this came off, a large part of the problem of getting men out of Greece would be solved.

Raw sat back in his swivel chair and took a last long look at the chart. Would Antiparos be as safe as Simonds said? Sammy was an old hand at beach landings, perhaps the most experienced officer in the Mediterranean. He was also a cautious bird – he'd kept his submarine alive for ten months in the most dangerous waters in the war. Sammy would be on hand to give a thorough briefing to Robert Norfolk, *Thorn*'s commanding officer, who had already practised with Folboats. There were hundreds of men hiding in Greece in homes and farms whose hosts were running the risk of death if discovered by the Axis. He shivered a little. Give me a submarine, any day, he thought.

'We'll do it. Sammy, make it so. Tony, send over the stores as soon as you can so we can get them organized in *Medway*. And please get your chaps here too, for a planning session. We'll need them aboard as soon as possible.'

Aboard *Medway*'s picket boat, carrying him back to the Alexandria corniche and his staff car, Simonds was elated. Setting up a base under the noses of the Axis to bring his men home! What a coup. Security was vital, of course, and he was already listing a set of code names in his head. Simonds was an enthusiast for Hollywood and gangster movies. Greece would be called Hollywood. The base would be Coney Island, after the New York beachside funfair. The island itself would be Harlem. Athens would be named Eton. Rhodes was Bray.[10] The caiques would be referred to as Films. If Atkinson could be persuaded to return to Greece to help round up escapers, he would be codenamed Durbin, after the actress Deanna Durbin, a slightly sarcastic nod to his rather soft and round looks.[11] The escapers and evaders (evaders were men who had never been captured) would be collectively referred to as Elks. And the plan overall would be Film Plan Number 2 – Film Plan Number 1 was a simpler plan to use Turkey-based caiques to collect small groups of escapers on the west coast of the Aegean.

Simonds was acutely aware that Coney Island's success depended on his ability to assemble parties of escapers safely in Antiparos. In October 1941, there were no functioning radios operating in Greece. That night, though Simonds did not know, *Triumph* was landing two agents and a radio at the very top of the Aegean, near the monastic peninsula of Mount Athos, but they were hundreds of miles north of Athens and the Peloponnese where escapers were actually congregating. The only way to organize escapers to reach Antiparos was to send men into occupied Greece and gather them up. Harry Grammatikakis had already volunteered. It was obviously essential that the men sent have some pre-existing relationships, contacts and knowledge of Greece, and ideally some Greek language skills too. Another benefit of sending men who had already escaped from a prison camp was that, if they were caught by the Axis, they were already on record with the Axis and the Red Cross as men on the run, and so were protected by the Geneva Convention from being treated as spies or saboteurs. The small detail that they had made it to Cairo, and returned, would have to be concealed to protect their lives.

The obvious answer was to send back some of the men who had arrived with Grammatikakis. The natural hierarchy of the army dictated that the men should preferably be officers, or at the very least senior sergeants. They would also need to be released by their parent units. As Simonds was driven back to Cairo, through the autumnal cool of the Nile Delta, his thoughts on who to send turned naturally to Atkinson and Craig. Both men enthusiastically agreed to take part in the Coney Island plan. It was agreed that, while Atkinson headed to Athens to collect escapers, Craig would take charge of the men, stores and the radio on Antiparos. Two sergeants, John Redpath of 19th Army Troop of the New Zealand Expeditionary Force and Sergeant Alan Empson of 18th New Zealand Battalion, would join the party. Redpath had arrived in Cairo after escaping from the holding camp at Galatas on

Crete. He had sailed from Crete to Cape Malea at the southern tip of the Peloponnese, had hidden around Cape Malea for a month, and had then stolen a small caique to sail to Alexandria.[12] His job at Coney Island was to sail one of Harry's two caiques west to Cape Malea, the nearest finger of the Peloponnese, to rescue the men he knew were in hiding around the cape and its port town of Neapoli, and bring them back to Coney Island.

Three tonnes of food and fuel duly arrived alongside *Medway* for loading into *Thorn*. When all was stowed in her torpedo compartment, which was filled almost to overflowing with boxes of canned food and tins of diesel and paraffin for cooking, Atkinson and his companions dumped their diminutive personal kit in *Thorn*'s wardroom and Petty Officers' mess as she slipped her berth at midday on 10 November and headed north for Antiparos. Everyone knew that the timetable was uncomfortably tight, more so because *Thorn* had been delayed on her way to Antiparos, first by an order to provide some submarine-hunting practice to a destroyer off Alexandria, and then by accidentally misfiring a torpedo whose detonation nearly sank her. It was, therefore, not until midnight of 14 November that *Thorn* glided into Despotiko Bay, landed her men and stores and sailed on for her patrol. The original plan was that *Thorn* would spend eight days patrolling the Aegean, hunting for targets, at the end of which she would return to Despotiko Bay to pick up whoever the Coney Island party had managed to collect. In truth, the navy saw Coney Island as a nice-to-have bonus to a patrol, rather than its main object. A tense discussion in *Thorn*'s wardroom, as she sailed to the Aegean, bought Atkinson an extra day of time in Athens. Atkinson knew he had just nine days to sail secretly from Antiparos to Athens, make contact with Odysseus, the Bourbouras siblings, and the Ioannou and Zannas families, and get them to warn and collect as many men as they could, preferably at least twenty, then assemble those men in secret, proceed through the checkpoints around Athens, load them onto Harry's caique and sail them, again in secret, to Antiparos.

Thorn's wardroom hosted another tense discussion the next day. As the group made detailed plans for who was going to move where and when, Harry confessed that he had been a little optimistic in telling them that he had two caiques standing by at Antiparos. In fact, what he had, he said, was friendly captains who might, or might not, have a boat to lend. This created a two-headed problem. Not only was it highly uncertain that Harry could get his hands on a boat at all, but to have any chance, he would have to cross from Antiparos to the main harbour at Paros to get any, adding several hours of travel and inevitable negotiations and bargaining to the task. Then, assuming he was successful, he would have to bring the caique back to Antiparos to pick up Atkinson. Jim Craig, in command of the expedition and in acute pain from two broken ribs, must have been close to exploding with frustration. This increased a few days later as he examined the landing beach through *Thorn*'s periscope. 'The beach where he informed us we could land and hide all our stores in the bush was found to be a very small beach entirely exposed to the sea, with no bush whatsoever, with just a few odd bits of scrub around the beach, which would not have permitted us to hide any of our stores there'.[13] In truth, Jim Craig's view on the beach's shelter was unfair, and reflected his lack of experience of the sea; the landing beach was as sheltered as any beach accessible by submarine could be, but his frustration with Harry Grammatikakis was probably breaking through as he typed the report a couple of months later.

At midnight on 14 November Harry paddled ashore in one of the Folboats, with instructions to wake up his friends and bring them back with fishing boats to help unload the stores. Harry, however, had something else on his mind. As soon as his feet touched the beach, he was off across the island to row over to Paros where, he hoped, his girlfriend was waiting for him. He did manage to get the fishing boats moving. In less than an hour, they were bumping alongside *Thorn* in the dark, being loaded with cases of food and the Coney Island radio set. Multiple shuttle trips were needed. As daylight approached, many tins of fuel remained to be landed, but there was no time to make the several more trips needed. Remembering that diesel is lighter than water, *Thorn*'s casing party roped the dozens of tins together, lowered them gently into the sea and the fishing boats towed them, clanking like a string of goslings, to the beach.

Here, the frantic work continued. A tonne and a half of food boxes had to be lugged by hand in darkness to Spiros Tzavellas' house. Spiros and two friends were on the beach to help Craig's party, as well as two of the men from the Special Boat Section, but even so, it took hours of stumbling around to get everything stowed. Dawn's greyish tinge could already be seen above the large hill in the centre of the island, and there was no time to carry the fuel tins to the house as well. The beach party stashed the 150 tins in whatever scrub they could find while Lieutenant Norfolk paced *Thorn*'s tiny bridge trying to hide his worry, silently urging them to get a move on. It was already daylight when *Thorn* recovered her Folboats and SBS paddlers, and thankfully weighed her anchor to slide silently back out to the safety of deep water on her electric motors.

The landing party had been working flat out all night and was exhausted. Craig called a short rest and then took stock. The first task was to get the fuel tins into better concealment. Since they would have to be carried back out to sea to refill a caique, the obvious answer was to bury them on the beach. With this done, and the food hidden in the Tzavellas house, there was nothing to do but wait for Harry to return with at least one, hopefully two, caiques. 15 November passed. Then 16, and 17, with no Harry. Each day lost made the Athens pickup voyage less likely to succeed. All four men on Coney Island must have been climbing the walls with frustration. On 18 November they cracked. Spiros Tzavellas agreed to travel to Paros to find out what had happened to Harry and give him a spirited reminder of his promises to Craig and Atkinson. History does not record what passed between them when Spiros found Harry, but Spiros was back at his house that night with the reassurance that Harry would arrive in the morning, with a caique and permission to sail to Athens. It would take a little time to load the extra fuel required, but after that was done, Atkinson could get moving.

But did he now have enough time? *Thorn* would return twice, first on the night on 22 November, and again the following night. If he left Antiparos at around midday on 19 November, and if Harry brought a fast caique, capable of sailing at ten knots, Atkinson might reach Athens, ninety miles away, before midnight the same day, but more likely sometime during the day of 20 November. To be back in Antiparos by midnight on 23/24 November, he and his party of Elks would have to be under way well before sunset on 23 November, giving him just seventy-two hours to round up and move twenty men from multiple hiding places in secrecy. The plan was extremely risky. Haste would displace caution, and the smallest slip might result in the deaths of many Greek civilians hiding men in attics and cellars. Bad weather (and this was November, when weather in Greece can be as bad as anywhere) might also disrupt the plan, as could an inconvenient Axis patrol boat, or a breakdown.

On the positive side of this fragile balance sheet, if Atkinson missed *Thorn*, which seemed more than likely, there was an ample supply of food, cooking fuel and even alcohol in the Tzavellas house to keep the escapers warm and fed until another submarine could arrive. The Coney Island plan had been designed to be flexible, though Colonel Simonds had probably not factored Harry Grammatikakis' love life into his risk assessment. Neither Craig nor Atkinson lacked guts or determination. They decided to go ahead with the plan as originally conceived, working with all haste and trusting in luck to bring it off.

The morning of 19 November brought autumn sunshine, Harry Grammatikakis, and one caique, the *Despoina*. Craig and Atkinson conferred. The Coney Island plan had two legs, one to Athens and the other to Cape Malea, and needed two caiques. But here was Harry with just one. Which destination worked better? There were probably more escapers in Athens than around Cape Malea, and their hosts were in considerably more danger of discovery, since they were working under the noses of the enemy and, were surrounded by starving people who might betray them, for the reward of food, given half a chance. They decided that Atkinson would take Harry and the single caique to Athens. Atkinson had left and Craig was relaxing in the Tzavellas house early in the evening of 19 November, imagining that his troubles could be set aside for a few days at least, when a new bombshell knocked at Jim Craig's front door.

In the gathering winter evening, Craig found two locals, Agapitas and Antonias [14] from Paros, in a highly agitated state. Once he had got them to speak slowly enough for him to understand what they were saying, a frightening picture emerged. Harry, who had spent three days in Paros in the arms of his lover, had been hanging around the harbourside cafes where, as the evenings wore on and the ouzo took hold, he had boasted too loudly that he had landed from Egypt, in a British submarine, with a party of soldiers. The story got worse. Harry had not just one girlfriend in Paros but two. He was engaged to one, but the other was now pregnant and had heard the talk of submarines and soldiers. So had her mother, and she sent Harry a message that, unless he left his fiancée and agreed to marry her pregnant daughter, she would inform on him and his British friends on Antiparos to the Italian garrison.

Jim Craig's blood must have frozen. By now it was dark, but his visitors were sure that an Italian patrol would arrive on Antiparos in the morning. The Tzavellas house was stacked with more than a tonne of boxes of food, weapons, ammunition and a radio. What on earth should be done? Tzavellas came to the rescue.

'We have an old well nearby. It's dry now, that's why Antiparos is so empty – not enough water – but we can throw everything into the well and cover it with earth.'

There was no time to spare. Tzavellas, Craig, Sergeant Empson and Sergeant Redpath threw themselves into the task. The well was 300 yards away, but by midnight it was full, the house was empty, and the landing party was ready to leave. The diesel was already buried, and too bulky to move in the time available, so it was left where it was. A short way across the bay from the Tzavellas house lay the small empty island of Despotiko, about 500 acres of rough scrubby brush. Its chief appeal was that it was not Antiparos. Craig and his landing party were rowed across the bay by Tzavellas and disappeared into the scrub. Tzavellas returned home to await the Italians. While they hid, the group discussed what to do next. The consensus was to entice Harry's inamorata to Antiparos, perhaps with the promise that he was about to return, and there to take her prisoner and then to Egypt.

The pale winter sun of 20 November brought no Italians, but it did bring Agapitas and Antonias, who were asked to put the abduction plan into action. An anxious day and night of waiting and hiding followed, but by nightfall still no Italians had appeared. What was happening in Antiparos, and would Atkinson suddenly appear with a caique of escapers needing food and shelter just as the Italians decided to turn up too? Despite the gathering cold, Craig and his men remained on Despotiko, trying to keep as warm as they could and doubtless missing the fireside of the Tzavellas house, whose smoking chimney they could clearly see across the bay.

Another dawn brought another story. Agapitas and Antonias landed on Despotiko beach and hurried to tell it. They had spun the pregnant girlfriend a tale. Harry had been called away on urgent business (that part at least was true) but had left a message with them that he would marry her on his return in two or three days' time. She was content, and the Italian garrison therefore blissfully ignorant of what was happening on Antiparos.

But where was Atkinson? It was already 21 November. *Thorn* would return on the following night. Would there be any escapers to evacuate?

All day on 22 November, Craig, Redpath and Empson watched the bay. At hand was a signal flag, borrowed from *Thorn*'s wireless office, with which they could show her that they could see her periscope. At midday they sighted a periscope moving slowly through the water. It could only be *Thorn*. Hoisting their flag to show that they had seen her, Craig flashed a message in morse, with a signal lantern, that Atkinson had not returned. *Thorn* had no way of transmitting a morse light from her raised periscope, so could not signal back a reply. Craig knew that she would follow her orders to surface that night and take the landing party back to Alexandria, with or without Atkinson. That left him the rest of the afternoon to debate his next course of action with his sergeants. Although under strict orders to return with *Thorn* whatever happened, Craig was not a man to follow orders blindly if the circumstances had changed materially. With tonnes of stores on hand and men to be rescued, he and Sergeant Redpath debated the various mechanics of setting up a new base, 100 miles west, on Cape Malea. Redpath and Empson knew the ground well, having hidden there for a month or more that summer, and a Malea base would be safer from the dangerous entanglements of Harry Grammatikakis. The commanding officer of *Thorn* had told them he would be as happy picking men up from there as from Antiparos. The men agreed to put the alternative plan to *Thorn* when she surfaced at midnight and see what transpired.

It only remained to wait and see if Atkinson arrived with a party of escapers. At midnight, Craig, Redpath and Empson were enjoying their first properly cooked meal for a week, in the burrow-like comfort of *Thorn*'s wardroom, after the special treat of a hot shower. Discussion of the combination of possibilities continued. Lieutenant Norfolk told them that his orders did not allow him the time or discretion to divert to Cape Malea, and that they must either stay on Antiparos or leave with him that night as ordered. He was keen to get going, for his boat was at her most vulnerable floating in the shallow waters off Despotiko beach. Atkinson had not shown up, so why wait? A compromise was reached. *Thorn* would leave Antiparos for a few hours and sail out to sea, to charge her batteries in deep water where she could dive if an Axis patrol appeared. At 3.00 am she would return to the bay until an hour before dawn, which was due at 7.09 am. At 6.09 am she would head for home.

As Craig and Empson dragged their rowing boat down the beach to the gentle surf at five minutes to six, they heard the chug chug chug of a single cylinder diesel engine enter the bay from the north. Atkinson had returned. Everything seemed to happen at once. *Thorn* drifted into sight, a black hump in the fading starlight gliding in from the south, and took Atkinson's caique alongside, with Craig's rowing boat. Twenty men clambered thankfully across from the caique onto *Thorn*'s casing, delighted to be away from the fish-reek of her hold and into the submarine reek of diesel, oil, boiled vegetables and unwashed men. Atkinson, elated at his first successful mission for MI9, wolfed a meal in the wardroom while Craig told him the sorry tale of Grammatikakis' love life. With a complex love life of his own in Athens, perhaps Atkinson sympathized. The idea of moving the base to Cape Malea was swiftly discarded when Atkinson reported that his collection effort in Athens had borne a rich harvest. In addition to the twenty men he had just brought, another forty were expecting to sail to Antiparos in just a week. It was too late to change all the arrangements. Harry must get back to Athens as quickly as he could, and the risk of being found by the garrison of Paros would just have to be borne. The original plan, for Sergeant Redpath to take some stores to Cape Malea and establish a second base, would still be used if a second caique could be found; in the meantime he and Empson would stay on Antiparos and await the arrival of the forty escapers. Harry too would stay. Craig and Atkinson took Harry aside and ordered him, in the clearest way they could, that under no circumstances was he to visit Paros.

With these orders and plans laid, *Thorn* thankfully closed her hatches and dived. Behind her the pre-dawn twilight outlined the features of the three men left behind on the Antiparos beach. Redpath and Empson returned to their beds in Spiros Tzavellos' house. While they slept, Harry stole Redpath's revolver and set off to Paros on a personal mission.

Chapter 11

Just One More Patrol

Sydney Raw's submarines were increasingly busy on special operations. While *Thorn* was waiting off Despotiko beach for Craig and his escapers, *Triumph* was creeping into another bay just 100 miles south of Antiparos to spend the first night of her new patrol on a task that was now routine, dropping another SOE agent, Royal Artillery officer Chris Woodhouse, west of Heraklion on Crete. Though her crew were now experienced veterans in the subtle art of beach landings and pickups, her captain was not, for Sammy Woods had handed his boat over to one of the 'spare COs' aboard *Medway*. Under this odd but practical arrangement, the Flotilla staff, living in the depot ship, kept almost an entire reserve crew of men aboard in case of illness, promotion or exhaustion. Men were swapped into and out of actual submarines as circumstances dictated. Included in the spare crew were two or three command-qualified officers, since it was an accepted practice that a submarine commanding officer might ask for a temporary relief if he felt that he was unfit, through extreme stress or poor health, to carry out a patrol safely, or might actually be ordered ashore for a while if Shrimp or Raw thought he needed a rest. So much of the stress of a patrol, and especially an attack, fell on the commanding officer personally, that it was commonplace for a man to step back for a couple of weeks while the spare commanding officer took over.

Johnny Huddart was a veteran of the submarine service, having joined it at the age of twenty-three in 1934. Huddart had a reputation as a party animal, with a very easy-going attitude to life. While he passed his command qualifying course (the 'Perisher', which still runs today) in early 1940, there appear to have been questions about his fitness to undertake long patrols in contested waters, and he found himself always on reserve crews or in command of training boats for short periods, even as short as a fortnight. Until October 1941, Huddart had been based in the Clyde, as reserve commanding officer, in the submarine depot ship where new boats were worked up for war.

In October he was appointed to *Medway*, where he arrived just as Sydney Raw was wondering who to appoint to *Triumph* to replace Woods. He had hardly unpacked his gear when he was given command.

In his first operational briefing, Johnny Huddart heard that he was not expected to do much actual fighting in his new command. The standard operational assignment for a submarine at the time was a year. *Triumph* had left Scotland in November 1941 and now, after twelve months of active patrols, she was beginning to fall apart as equipment started to wear out and break. Her crew too was close to wearing out. Over the past year they had spent some 150 days at sea, under permanent threat of a quick and unpleasant death from mining, a torpedo or a bomb. They knew the risks they were running intimately, having inflicted death by the same means on two dozen ships and one Italian submarine. Death was no stranger to them; by November 1941, 1,330 submariners had been killed, about half of the total men in the service in September 1939. In a service of just 2,600 men, the dead were not just remote names on a list, but old friends and shipmates. The psychological burden of their loss must have weighed heavily. At the start of 1941, when they sailed into the Mediterranean, *Triumph*'s men were privately expecting not to survive the year. Now, in November, to their collective surprise, they were all very much alive – though they had lost one of their shipmates in Malta and another to capture ashore in Sicily. Huddart brought with him a thrilling piece of news. After one more short patrol in the Aegean, starting on 20 November, they would be sent home, starting with a quiet passage to Gibraltar, under strict orders to attack nothing and engage no one in action, followed by a crossing of the Bay of Biscay, an 'up homers' passage along the channel and then, under escort, to arrive at Fort Blockhouse at Gosport, opposite Portsmouth.

The prospect was thrilling. Survival was, probably, as surprising as it was welcome. Once home, *Triumph* would disappear into a dockyard for a refit. Her men would have three- or four-weeks' home leave. They would then scatter onto various promotion courses. Michael Janvrin, her second in command, would do the Perisher and be given his own command. Robert Douglas-Don would return to sea as a second-in-command of a new boat. Everyone aboard would take a step up and a few months later find themselves in one of the T-class boats now coming out of the builders' yards at a rate of one a month. The two most senior NCOs, the coxswain, Reg Nott, and the chief artificer, Tommy Phillips (Chief Tiffy to his men), would probably go ashore permanently to train a new generation of submariners. Lieutenant Denys Wright, her engineer officer, would certainly join a flotilla staff as the engineer lieutenant commander for a group of boats. The atmosphere in *Triumph* was like a boarding school at the end of term.

Secrecy demanded that no one in the boat tell their families or wives what was afoot, but hints were dropped. Douglas-Don wrote home on 15 November 'we have been told to expect a sudden move any time between tomorrow and the next few months ... a fortnight's leave, six weeks perhaps in dockyards and then out here again'.[1] Leading stoker, John 'Topsy' Turner,[2] wrote home to his wife Eileen in Blackburn, 'It's all downhill now, kid, so keep smiling and we shall soon be counting the weeks instead of years. Our Jack will soon be two now. It will seem strange seeing him running around but he will soon get to know his dad when I get home'.[3] Anything more obvious would have been censored by Turner's department head, Denys Wright.

Aboard *Medway*, Topsy Turner bumped into an old shipmate, Sydney Hart, who had just been drafted to *Medway* as reserve crew. Hart wrote after the war, 'I walked down to my mess in Medway, colliding with Stoker Topsy Turner en route. Topsy gave me the interesting news that ... he was going home. 'Off ashore to buy a few presents for the folks, and such', he said'.[4]

With home in sight, *Triumph*'s crew took the opportunity to stock up on gifts, food and drink for families in rationed Britain. Men were allowed to bring home whatever they could afford to buy and stow on board. A memoir, from another submariner who survived the war, relates how the wireless office staff, with more spare space than any other man on the boat, stuffed the nooks and crannies of their office with green bananas in hopes that they would survive the month-long voyage home. Officers stocked up on sherry and gin. Everyone bought souvenirs, filling their lockers aboard *Medway* with pyramids, camels and mummies. No one could be sure how much leave they would get between the end of their last patrol and setting off for home, so the buying frenzy started early.

Huddart granted everyone five days' leave to give his men a chance to see the sights of Egypt before they left. Until then, most men had been too busy to make the day-long excursion to the pyramids. Artificer Fred Wilkinson had been a ten-year battleship man who volunteered for submarine service in 1940. The staff in *Medway* requisitioned an RAF lorry to carry a party from *Triumph* to the pyramids. They took a photographer with them, with a high-quality glass-plate camera, who snapped the group at the end of their visit. Wilkinson was in the party and ordered a print of the photograph. A quarter of the ship's company signed up for the trip, and the photograph, left in Wilkinson's locker when *Triumph* sailed on her last patrol, survived to come home with his effects. The group look fit and happy, even the men, perched unsurely on two camels, in the back row. Ted wrote home hinting to his wife Muriel that she might see him soon.

Triumph's last patrol, or at least the patrol that was supposed to be her last, passed without incident. On the night that Atkinson was rushing back to Antiparos with his twenty escapers, *Triumph* was landing Woodhouse on a Cretan beach west of Heraklion. By now, the exercise was routine, though new to Johnny Huddart. Two weeks of quiet patrolling followed, with no targets, no counterattacks and no dramas. It was almost as if the war had decided to give her a break as she prepared to go home. Returning to Alexandria, at midday on 11 December, must have felt very much like the end of a long and terrifying journey.

Until a few days later. Two weeks before, *Thorn* had returned from Antiparos with the news that a large party, of up to forty men, was expected at Antiparos any day and would need picking up. Coney Island had been provisioned for up to fifty men for a couple of months, but would need resupply since these escapers, if they were there, would have eaten half of the entire stock by the end of the year. MI9 was requesting another two-way trip by submarine, with a stores' drop on the outward trip and a pickup of escapers on the return journey a fortnight later. *Thorn* was already booked to make another patrol in a week, too soon for MI9 to collect and pack five tonnes of stores and get them to *Medway*. The situation was made more complex because Simonds was working on Film Plan number one, using caiques on Smyrna to do pickup runs around the Aegean; he was probably trying to add another two or three tonnes of fuel to the Coney Island stockpile to refuel his growing flotilla.

Triumph's men, living in *Medway*'s comfortable mess decks, with a few hundred of their shipmates from other First Flotilla submarines, were probably well-supplied with gossip, always called in the navy the 'buzz'. They were preparing for their voyage home, stowing souvenirs and personal stocks of food and drink wherever *Triumph* offered an unoccupied nook or cranny. A few days before their return to Alexandria, a momentous event had taken place: the Imperial Japanese Navy had carried out a surprise attack on Pearl Harbour. As they tied up alongside *Medway* on 11 December, they heard a disturbing combination of happy news and a disaster. That morning, Germany had declared war on the United States, which meant that the full weight of the US Navy would now be on their side, but just yesterday, the Japanese Air Force had sunk two battleships, *Prince of Wales* and *Repulse*, killing nearly 1,000 of their shipmates and friends.

The start of a war between Britain and Japan would have momentous consequences for every man aboard *Triumph*. In 1940, the Admiralty had pulled the whole of its Far East submarine flotilla back to the Mediterranean. Now, it urgently wanted some of those submarines back in the Far East to protect the naval base at Singapore and disrupt Japanese plans to enter the Indian Ocean in strength. Captain Raw knew of this order in advance – signals had flashed between Admiral Max Horton, at Northways in London, and Alexandria for the past ten days, over what and who to send, trying to balance the need to cover the Mediterranean with the new need to cover the Far East. With this problem looming, and the need to resupply Antiparos and pick up the men who must by now be there, could he afford to lose one of his best submarines to a voyage home? Especially one which had more or less invented the beach operation and had proved herself expert at its execution? The answer was clearly no. Days passed as Johnny Huddart and his men waited for the final order to leave. On 22 December the fateful news arrived. Two boats, *Trusty* and *Truant*, would detach for Singapore immediately. With every other boat either at sea, or about to sail to support the blockade of the Afrika Korps, there was only one choice for the second operation at Coney Island. The buzz probably reached *Triumph*'s ship's company before Johnny Huddart announced the order to them, in *Medway*'s onboard cinema. Just one more patrol, then home. The operation had a new name. It was to be called Operation Isinglass.

The outline of Isinglass was a repeat of Film Plan Number 2. *Triumph* would load five tonnes of food and fuel for Coney Island, embark Atkinson and Craig, drop them at Antiparos on the way to her patrol area in the Aegean, and then, ten days later, return to Antiparos to pick up whatever escapers had found their way there. While *Triumph* was away hunting Axis merchant ships, Atkinson and Grammatikakis would sail to Athens to round up a new group of escapers while Craig took charge of whoever was already on Antiparos. If a second caique could be found, Sergeant Redpath would sail west to Cape Malea to collect escapers from there. As far as it went, Isinglass was uncomplicated, at least for *Triumph*. It quickly became much more complicated when Colonel Pearson of SOE became aware of it, and more complicated still when Harry Grammatikakis in Antiparos returned to his old ways.

Pearson's job was at heart simple: raise hell in Greece. However, it was made more complex by the fact that, even by December 1941, SOE had very little idea of what was happening among Greek underground networks. SOE knew that these were forming in confusingly large numbers, but had no clear idea who was in which network; what a network's ideas were for the political future of Greece; how effective each network might be; whether they had been infiltrated by Axis intelligence; whether they extended beyond the narrow confines of Athens and Piraeus; or whether they knew what Cairo wanted them to do. Behind SOE, the Foreign Office had very clear ideas of who it wanted to support: the King of Greece and his government-in-exile, then hanging around Cairo where they were trying to confine SOE support to people they knew would support the Royal cause.

What Pearson needed was a man with existing relationships with leading members of the Greek underground in Athens, who could meet with them without the need for verification, who could appear in Athens with a credible claim to represent British policy, and cut through the confusion to bring back to SOE a usable chart of who was who and what was what. And of course, he needed to get that man to Athens, and back, quickly. Only one such man was available – John George Paterson Atkinson, currently in the employ of MI9 and a regular visitor to Secret Building in Cairo. Stifling his distaste for Atkinson's character, Pearson set out to recruit him into SOE.

He found a willing audience. Atkinson was nothing if not keen to fight the Axis and help his Greek friends. Over whiskies in his Cairo flat, Pearson laid out his needs and his plan, and Atkinson volunteered without hesitation. To Atkinson, the large distinction between 'escape and evasion' and 'sabotage and subversion' were probably invisible, and if visible, probably unimportant – the enemy was the enemy and must be fought in every way available. Pearson laid on Atkinson a fearsome prohibition against revealing his SOE tasks to Colonel Simonds, on the overt grounds of operational security, but in reality, because he knew that Simonds would forbid Atkinson from mixing rescue with sabotage and might even forbid him from going altogether. The vicious enmity between the secret organizations was alive and well. Pearson's instructions to Atkinson were essentially simple: while he was in Athens, he should visit and talk with every one of his underground contacts and discover their agendas and loyalties in the domestic political sphere. To Atkinson's own contacts, Pearson added the small list of people in Athens that SOE knew, or believed, were active in the underground. Atkinson, lacking the classic Greek education that those around him all seemed to have had, struggled with the Greek names on Pearson's list. Unable to memorize them there and then, he wrote them down in a black pocketbook for later study.

Pearson had another agenda. The only way in which SOE could communicate with Athens was by radio. At present there was a single British radio in Athens, but it lacked a functioning code and a time-date-frequency communications plan. Any group that controlled a radio had a good chance of controlling the agenda and the actions that would follow – who would receive gold sovereigns, explosives, limpet mines and arms. Pearson was desperate to get another radio set, and a loyal SOE radio operator, into Athens to work with whatever underground group SOE decided to support. Just a week before, his first attempt to insert a radio and operator in Greece had misfired, when his man, John Lekkas (codenamed Kip), had been taken prisoner.

Operation Isinglass offered a gold-plated opportunity to deliver another radio and operator and would be a substantial operational coup for SOE. Pearson had a man ready too, a Greek Cypriot called Kosta Kypriades, trained and ready to move under the code name Diamond. Pearson wanted no chance of objections from MI9, so he kept his plan for Kypriades secret until the last moment. Kypriades was to appear in *Medway* on the day she sailed with secret orders to join her for passage to Antiparos. Simonds was not to know, and nor was he to have the chance of obstructing Pearson's plan.

Triumph's men now knew that they would not be going home until after this next 'last' patrol. While the buzz was rushing around *Medway*'s mess decks, a new reason for staying in Alexandria arrived. On the night of 19 December, the Italian submarine *Scire* launched three human torpedoes at Alexandria. These were modified torpedoes, with seats from which they could be steered by their suicidally brave pilots. When they arrived at their target, the pilot would dive to the seabed, detach the 660-pound warhead from the nose of the torpedo, set a timer, and retire. The warhead was large enough to cripple a battleship or sink a cruiser. The harbour at Alexandria was protected by a floating boom, from which hung a massive steel mesh net. That night, a squadron of cruisers and destroyers entered the harbour. The human torpedoes followed them in while the boom was being towed back into position. Two warheads were laid successfully underneath the two largest ships in harbour, the battleships *Valiant* and *Queen Elizabeth*, where they detonated at six the next morning. *Queen Elizabeth* was hit in her boiler rooms and was without power. *Triumph* and *Trusty* were immediately ordered to sail across the harbour, come alongside her and connect their powerful electric generators to her switchboard. *Triumph*'s men must have given a collective silent groan. Would they ever be allowed to go home?

Trusty left Alexandria three days later for the Far East, while *Triumph* moved back alongside *Medway*, where her crew became fully occupied in offloading some of their reload torpedoes to *Medway*, to make space for the tonnes of stores to be stowed away in the fore ends. With the stores came Craig and Atkinson, the latter hefting a large leather suitcase whose contents he jealously guarded from inspection. Christmas Eve brought more arrivals. In *Valiant*, now completely disabled and resting on the seabed just a few feet below her keel, a young midshipman was due to spend three months serving in a small ship to broaden his experience. This was a standard part of a midshipman's training and was usually spent on a destroyer. A recent Admiralty Fleet Order had allowed midshipmen to choose submarines instead of destroyers. This particular midshipman, George Waterall, had already told his training officer of his plan to enter the submarine service and requested that he spend his small ship time in one. *Valiant*'s Captain, Charles Morgan, most likely called on Captain Raw to ask his opinion of the idea – submarines were known to be extremely dangerous, and it would hardly help a young midshipman's training and career if he died during it. Happily, Raw had an ideal opportunity for the young Waterall. *Triumph* was a crack boat, highly competent and a proven survivor. She had one relatively quiet and short patrol coming up with some exciting special operations off a beach in Greece, after which she would sail quietly home. Back in the United Kingdom, Waterall could be drafted to another boat, perhaps a training boat, to finish his three months and then he'd find his way back to *Valiant*.

After all, the latter was sitting on the bottom of Alexandria harbour and was going nowhere further than a floating dock for several months to come. The matter was settled. George Waterall, probably bursting with excitement, brought his kit over to *Medway* on Christmas Eve, to spend Christmas Day with his new shipmates.

Another new arrival in *Medway* needed submarine experience too. Lieutenant Arthur Collins had joined the naval volunteer reserve in 1937, from his job working in a bank in Essex. In January 1940, he was mobilized to take command of the motor fishing vessel *Deo Volante*, working as a water taxi for the fleet in Scapa Flow, and then the drifter *Coldsnap*. Most of the navy's submarines in 1941 had navigating officers who were RNVR officers. There were many similarities between the navigation of yachts (where RNVR officers had generally learnt their navigational trade) and the navigation of submarines. Both moved painfully slowly, usually at a walking pace, close to the hazards of shore, heavily affected by the whims of currents and tides, and with very limited physical facilities in the way of equipment and space. RNVR navigators proved particularly adept at navigating submarines (*Triumph*'s navigator was the RNVR Lieutenant Alf Peterkin). Arthur Collins was appointed to *Medway* as a spare navigator, arriving by RAF bomber from Gibraltar on 19 December. It was an indication of his importance to *Medway*, that he was given a precious place on an air crossing of the Mediterranean, and that his presence was needed sufficiently urgently to run the risk of two night flights past the entire Mediterranean Axis air forces. On 21 December, Arthur wrote home to his mother 'the messing [aboard *Medway*] is very good indeed – eggs and fruit are abundant … bananas and oranges too, and a squeezed orange is brought to me every morning by my servant in lieu of morning tea. It was seventy degrees in the shade today and I did the quarterdeck watch in monkey jacket and no pullover or overcoat. *What* a change from Scapa!'[5] Raw and Woods considered how to break their new arrival into the reality of submarine operations safely and gently.

'We don't want to have him sitting around doing nothing, Sir. May I suggest that we send him out with *Triumph* on her patrol after Christmas? I can't think of a better tutor than Alf Peterkin, and he will learn a great deal very quickly.'

'Splendid idea Sammy, make it so.'

Yet another pair of passengers joined *Triumph* to help load her stores, but these were familiar faces. The movement of five tonnes of fuel and food from submarine to beach was a significant task requiring up to fifty round trips by Folboat (fewer if Spiros Tzavellas still had his rowing boat, but which could not be counted on). *Triumph* could not come much closer than 200 yards to the beach, for fear of running aground, so the Folboats might have to paddle a total of some ten miles together. Sailors were generally not very fit. The navy provided physical training instructors (nicknamed then and now 'Clubs' after the Indian clubs that they loved to toss). However, the average sailor treated Clubs and his physical training (PT) with humorous disdain, and instructors, or PTIs, found themselves concentrating on training up ships' sports teams. Submarines fielded few sports teams – given half a chance, a submariner would prefer to spend his leisure time lifting pints not weights. It was therefore vital to provide two fit men to paddle the Folboats to and fro, and it had become standard practice to draw these from Roger Courtney's Special Boat Section. Christmas eve, therefore, saw Bombardier Alf Child and Corporal Clive Severn, of the Northamptons, climbing *Medway*'s accommodation ladder with their small kit bags. Ahead lay the pleasant prospect of Christmas dinner in *Medway*'s generous mess decks – called Christmas Big Eats by sailors and served by the wardroom officers. Both men were experienced beach operators and were probably more excited than apprehensive about what would happen on the forthcoming patrol.

The Big Eats of Christmas Day were just a happy memory for *Triumph*'s crew as they filed down the ladder to *Medway*'s mooring trots to board their boat for her last patrol before sailing home. The boat's wardroom was filled to overflowing with Craig, Atkinson, Atkinson's mysterious suitcase, George Waterall, Arthur Collins, and at the last minute, without warning, Kypriades and his suitcase radio. Severn and Child were settled in their two messes forward. The fore ends were a heap of boxes and tins smelling of leaking diesel (the fuel tins were famously flimsy, and this was long before the 8th Army had copied and adopted the more robust German fuel containers that we still use today known as Jerry cans). On the bridge, Johnny Huddart gave the orders to get his boat under way.

'Let go headrope. Let go all aft. Slow ahead port. Stop port.'

Triumph's 300 feet swung slowly off her berth, on the long wire leading from her bow to the stern of the boat next door, which acted as a spring. When her stern was pointing clearly out into Alexandria harbour, the order came

'Let go forespring. Slow astern together. Attention on the upper deck and face to starboard. HMS *Medway*.'

The men on the casing dropped their wires on the deck and lined up to attention, facing their comfortable depot ship. Leading Seaman Don Hutchison raised a silver bosun's call to his lips, gripped the notched ring between his teeth, and blew a single piercing call – the 'still'. The men on the casing came to attention. The officers on *Triumph*'s crowded bridge, Lieutenant Robert Douglas-Don on the fore casing, and Midshipman George Waterall on the aft casing, all saluted. *Medway*'s quartermaster echoed the 'still' on his call, and the dozens of men on her decks came to attention in response. On *Medway*'s bridge wing, Sydney Raw and Sammy Woods returned the salute. Seeing this out of the corner of his eye, *Medway*'s quartermaster blew the two notes, high-low, that marked the 'carry on'. This was echoed by *Triumph*, and as the whistle's shrill falling note echoed into silence on the crisp winter's air, her casing became a hive of activity as ropes and mooring wires were coiled down into the spaces between her casing and her pressure hull, and men disappeared down her hatches to the warm diesel-scented fug below.

'Slow ahead together. Pilot, give me a course for the boom please. Number One, you have the ship. I'll be in my cabin if you need me.'

Triumph was once more going to war. It would be her last departure.

Chapter 12

Operation Isinglass

We need now to leave *Triumph* sliding out to sea and go back a few weeks and a few hundred miles to Antiparos, on the morning of 24 November. *Thorn*, with Atkinson, Craig and twenty-three escapers aboard, was already thirty miles away to the southeast, dived at eighty feet and sailing peacefully towards home. The boat was quiet throughout. Having spent the entire night awake and in a state of high apprehension, her crew and two dozen passengers now slept where they could, most of them on her hard deck plating.

Sergeant Redpath, on Antiparos, could enjoy little relief, but he did manage to get to sleep after his night's hard labour. This was to have a rude ending. 'When I woke at 11 am I found that while I was asleep Grammatikakis had gone to Paros'.[1] The moment that Redpath had dropped off to sleep, Harry had heeded the siren call of his two girlfriends and disobeyed Craig's direct order to stay in Antiparos, and had filched Redpath's revolver. Worse, when he arrived in Paros, Harry sought out his pregnant girlfriend's mother and threatened to kill her if she carried out her threat to tell the Italians about Coney Island. The threat backfired. As soon as Harry left her house, the mother-in-law wrote a note about Coney Island and delivered it to the garrison's officers. Paros is a small town today and was even smaller in 1941. Harry heard about her betrayal almost as soon as she made it and left town in a hurry to hide in a church in the hills behind Paros. Meanwhile, a patrol was detailed to sail to Antiparos to check out the claim.

At last Coney Island had a little luck. The garrison always used the same caique to move about their islands, and its owner knew about Coney Island. As soon as he received the order to pick up the patrol, a runner was despatched the three miles overland to the narrow strait between the two islands from where word could be passed to Spiros Tzavellas that a patrol was coming. With clumsy delaying tactics on the patrol's caique, and with deliberately slow progress once under way, news of the patrol reached

Redpath and Empson a full hour before the patrol itself, giving them time to clear out and hide on Despotiko. The patrol landed, searched around for a while, found nothing of significance and left. The Grammatikakis bullet had been dodged.

A few days of peace and quiet followed, until 28 November when a caique put in to Despotiko Bay from Crete, en route to Athens. Even though she was carrying three Italian soldiers, her captain decided that it would be safe to add Harry to his crew – one more Greek passenger did not seem to matter, so Harry emerged from his hiding place and slipped aboard. Redpath and Empson had a radio set and had been briefed that a submarine, at that time probably *Truant*, though no names would have been shared, would call at Antiparos some time after Christmas. That gave Harry a clear month in which to gather escapers in Athens and bring them to Antiparos. The Coney Island plan looked like it might actually begin to work properly, if Harry could keep his mouth under control in the cafes and bars of Athens.

When he reached Athens, Harry knew where to begin the work of collecting escapers because his Athens girlfriend, Alexandra Bourbouras, was one of the key people in the escape network. Alexandra shared a house with her brother, Adamantios Bourbouras, at 12 Favierou Street, a ten-minute walk west of the Ioannous at 9 Patission Street. Alexandra told Harry that a party of some two dozen escapers had been warned to move at short notice. It took a week to organize the dangerous task of moving these past the guard posts around Athens, to a quiet beach, and of course Harry had to find a caique as well. So, it was not until the morning of 9 December that they were ready to move. Alexandra had four of the escapers hiding with her and her brother, and had just arrived at the house of her friend and co-conspirator Catina Doussi in Sotiros Street, at the foot of the Acropolis, probably to carry out the next step of the escape plan, when she was betrayed.[2] Within a couple of minutes of closing Catina's front door, seven Italians barged in. Too stunned, and probably terrified, to take any action, Alexandra and Catina were taken in handcuffs to the headquarters of Italian Counter Espionage at Panepidistimou Street, by a Warrant Officer called Cavini. At the same time, another group of Italians was breaking into the Bourbouras' house at Favierou, where Adamantios was drinking tea with the four escapers. The Italians were determined to find out where the rest of the escape party was hiding. For most of that day they tortured the Bourbouras siblings by hoisting their bare feet off the floor in handcuffs and beating the soles of their feet. 'They thrashed my bare soles with a double belt. I remember only that the belt had metal pieces inserted. The pain was excruciating, and punishment went on for a long time, before the whip was exchanged for one which caused [even] more pain'.[3] When the siblings passed out, they were revived with a bucket of cold water to their faces. Adamantios must have been released afterwards for we find him being re-arrested in March 1942 for producing an underground newspaper, for which he was tried and sentenced to twelve years in prison.

Harry had been warned of the betrayal by Athens' chief of police, a man called Evert.[4] He arrived at the Bourbouras' house a short while after Adamantios and the four escapers had been dragged away. He knew that eighteen more escapers, who had already travelled to Anavissos, twenty-five miles south along the coast towards Cape Sounio, might very well have been betrayed too. With a feeling of dread, he rushed to Piraeus in the hope that he could sail the caique he had acquired down to Anavissos and reach the escapers before the Italians did. Finding that his caique had not yet been given permission to sail, Harry spent most of his remaining cash[5] chartering, though in reality buying outright, the fastest motor launch his network of smuggling contacts could provide. For once, Harry focussed on the primary objective. Losing not a moment, he headed southeast to Anavissos, where he found, to his relief, that his escapers were still free. The record does not reveal whether they had, in fact, been betrayed or not. Either way, sailing overnight at his best speed, Harry and his party arrived at Antiparos at dawn on 10 December. The Bourbouras siblings would spend the rest of the war in prison, but survived to tell their story to war crimes investigators in 1945.

At this point the narratives, recorded later by Harry and by Sergeant Redpath, diverge violently. Harry's story, recorded in 1942 by SOE in Cairo, when there was no one around to gainsay it, had him nobly sailing back to Piraeus for food and fuel, returning later to find that the escapers had been living large on the supplies of rum landed by *Thorn* and *Triumph*, and were carousing around Antiparos like a crew of sailors on shore leave. Harry accused Redpath of becoming so drunk that he had to be carried to bed on several occasions. In Harry's narrative, Coney Island was 'blown' by these drunken antics. His story does not stack up. Coney Island had no need of either fuel or bread from Athens because ample supplies of food and fuel lay buried either in Tzavellos' well or on the beach. And in any case, food in Athens was almost unobtainable; the population of the city was actually starving. The escapers, having spent six months surviving in hiding under the noses of the Axis, would hardly have relaxed to the point of partying in plain sight, especially with the imminent arrival of a submarine, and with an Italian garrison twelve miles away in Paros.

Redpath's narrative, recorded after his second escape (from Italy) in 1943, is very different and not complimentary to Harry. The eighteen escapers, brought by Harry, were sent up to a deserted house belonging to an islander called Baba Manoli. Perhaps the Tzavellas house was too small, and too likely to be visited and searched by another Italian patrol. Perhaps it was occupied by Harry's pregnant girlfriend, who had been told by his friends that she would become his wife and had relocated to Antiparos to be with him when he returned on 10 December. Redpath was expecting, or perhaps hoping, that a submarine would return any day between 10 and 14 December. For three days a party of escapers climbed 500 feet to the top of the highest point of Despotiko to send the agreed signal to tell a lurking submarine that men were ready to leave.[6] We know now, though Redpath did not, that plans in Alexandria had been hijacked by Pearl Harbour and that no submarine would arrive for another fortnight at least.

When no submarine appeared, Redpath was not a man to sit around. He immediately sent word around Paros that he was looking for a caique in which to sail to Turkey, 100 miles to the northeast. A reasonably fast boat would be able to cover the distance in a single night (it was the middle of winter, guaranteeing ten or eleven hours of darkness). However, the close community of Paros caique owners and skippers were wary of getting involved in any venture that involved the unreliable, unpredictable and indiscreet Harry Grammatikakis, especially one that put their boats and thus livelihoods at risk, not to mention their lives. Harry offered to travel to the neighbouring island of Naxos to see if he could obtain a boat there instead, with a large sum of money drawn from Redpath's stock of cash. Redpath reluctantly handed over 30,000 Drachmae (about £60 in 1941, or £3,000 today) in notes. Harry, glad of an excuse to be away, left post haste, but not for Naxos – by the end of the day he was back in Paros with his fiancée.

Ten more days passed, bringing neither submarine nor caique. Harry arrived back to find that Redpath was negotiating with the captain of another passing caique to take his escapers to Turkey. Having now run out of cash (Redpath reported he spent what was left on buying goats and vegetables for the men hiding on Antiparos, though it is not clear why the rations in the well were insufficient),[7] Redpath promised the caique skipper that he would be well paid on arrival in Turkey. For some reason Harry clearly wanted to avoid Turkey at all costs[8] so argued vigorously that it would be better if the caique took them all to Alexandria. Redpath saw immediately that a 400-mile voyage across the full width of the winter Mediterranean in a small caique might be suicidal, and an agreement was struck to sail next morning for Turkey. That night, Harry took the skipper aside and persuaded him that he could obtain a large payment for the caique from sources in Athens (probably taking the name of the British in vain) with much less risk. When dawn broke on 29 December, Redpath looked out into the bay for his caique. It had sailed in the night, taking Harry with it, who was no doubt relieved to be away from his tangled love life. We can imagine Redpath's state of mind that morning. Harry had proved erratic and unreliable, and at times dangerous. Coney Island was out of cash. A suspicious garrison of Italians was on a nearby island, where Harry's girlfriend's mother might at any moment denounce the escapers again. The promised submarine had not arrived. He was responsible for the safety of twenty men, including himself and Empson, in the middle of winter with food running out. His situation must have felt disastrous. Redpath's report makes no mention of access to a radio, for reasons which are not clear. It is, therefore, likely that Redpath had no idea that at that moment *Triumph* was halfway across the Mediterranean and sailing as fast as she could for the very beach on which he was standing.

By now the routine was familiar. At 10 pm that day, Johnny Huddart conned his boat on her electric motors towards the beach opposite the Tzavellas house on Antiparos. The night was cold, very cold, and the men on the bridge were wearing thick submariners' jumpers, whose original pristine white was dulled by grease and diesel smoke to a musty grey. Huddart bent to the voice pipe located under the break of *Triumph*'s bridge.

'Depth?'

A metallic distant voice came back from the red-lit warmth below.

'Five fathoms, shoaling slowly.'

'Very good. Let go. Two shackles. Away Folboat.'

This last to Lieutenant Douglas-Don, invisible on the casing below. With a quiet 'let go, veer cable to two shackles' to Able Seaman Geoff Brown, standing at the windlass control rod, *Triumph*'s anchor dropped from its snug housing in her raised bow into the sea grass at the bottom of Despotiko Bay. Fifty yards of heavy cable clanked behind it. There was no one on the beach to greet them, for no warning had been passed of her coming. Corporal Clive Severn and Douglas-Don lowered themselves into the Folboat which had been swiftly launched off the fore planes by the casing party and paddled into the starlit night. Behind them, *Triumph*'s off-watch men were stacking cases of food and tins of diesel on her casing, passing them hand to hand from the cavernous mouth of her torpedo loading hatch. There was a hurry, five tonnes of stores needed to be loaded into boats and paddled or rowed ashore in the next five hours.

Once ashore, Douglas-Don stumbled quickly through the night to the Tzavellas house, whose red paint loomed grey in front of him. It too was dark, for there was no reason for its occupants to linger awake into the cold small hours.[9]

'Halt. Who goes there?'

Robert froze in place. Of course, a party of escapers would post a sentry in case of a surprise visit by an Italian patrol, and the briefing back in *Medway* had made very clear that Coney Island had been equipped with a supply of Thompson sub-machine guns and ammunition. Douglas-Don could feel his hair standing on end, imagining the small black muzzle of a machine gun pointed at his stomach and a frightened squaddie's finger on the trigger. This was not how naval officers were meant to go to war.

'It's all right soldier, hold your fire, the Navy's here.'

It took just a few minutes for the sentry to wake Redpath and then run up to Baba Manoli's house to rouse the other escapers. The words 'the Navy's here' was all it took to drag them from sleep and get them moving to the beach as fast as they could in the dark. The beach was already a hive of activity. The two Folboats were shuttling food as fast as Severn and Child could paddle. Spiro Tzavellas had roused the few local fishermen on the island who were adding their fishing boats to the job. Boxes of food were stacking up just above the gently lapping surf. Redpath took charge of his men.

'Come on lads, let's get these boxes to the house over there, quickly now. And for heaven's sake keep the noise down.'

A shuttle of boxes, followed by cans of fuel, quickly fell into order. Off to one side stood a huddled group of dark shadows, clearly in conference. Craig, Atkinson and Kypriades had found their way ashore in one of the fishing boats, with the heavy leather suitcase radio and Atkinson's suspiciously bulky personal suitcase. Redpath stepped away from the supply line to join the group. He quickly narrated the dramas of Grammatikakis and his love life.

'I'm very glad to see you both, Sirs. Things have pretty much gone to pot here. It will be a huge relief to get everyone off the island and on the way home.'

It was not exactly clear who, between Craig and Atkinson, was in charge. Both men were lieutenants, but in different units and different armies. Their ordered tasks were clear, Craig would stay on in Antiparos and Atkinson would head straight to Athens to find more escapers, but the question of seniority had not been properly anticipated. An additional complication had appeared during *Triumph*'s quiet three-day passage from Alexandria. Probably because of the wardroom chat, in which Craig had become aware that Atkinson had taken on a secret job for SOE, while on the MI9 payroll. He had brought this question into the open, and an acrimonious discussion had ensued. Atkinson revealed that he was not just going to Athens to find escapers but also had a list of political people to meet, and a list of questions to ask and requests to make. Craig was furious, seeing, quite correctly as it would later transpire, that mixing sabotage with escape would endanger the people in the escape network. Craig, of course, did not know that two of them were already being tortured in an Athens prison. The list of people that Atkinson planned to talk with in Athens included people who had helped Craig escape, for as far as SOE was concerned, it was not too fussy whether it got help from the escape network or the political network, and in any case, Athens was so small and so closely networked, that everyone there probably saw no great distinction either. Apart from the added risk, Craig was furious that Atkinson was in effect stealing his precious contacts for sabotage work.

'Have you got the list with you?' Craig demanded, angrily.

'Of course not,' snapped back Atkinson.

He was lying. The list of names, not encoded in any way, was in a small black notebook in his battledress pocket. It is likely that Atkinson had made strenuous efforts to commit the list to memory but had been defeated by the strange and unfamiliar Greek spellings and transliterations. Most of the people on his list, he had either not met, or had met too briefly to allow them to lodge firmly in his memory. The list was not Atkinson's only secret. In his suitcase was also a large sum of cash in gold, notes of what he was to ask the people he would meet, and a bottle of lethal curare, for use in some future assassination.

Now, on the beach, tempers were rising. Redpath was for abandoning Coney Island. Craig tended to agree, especially in light of the dangers created by Harry's love life and the fact that Harry had disappeared with the only available caique. While fleetingly there, Harry had reported the betrayal and arrests of Alexandra and Adiamenos Bourbouras. This must have hit Craig hard, for Alexandra had become his friend and co-conspirator, and having spent two months in Athens he could easily imagine what was now happening to them. Who knew what secrets the Italians had managed to beat out of them by now? Atkinson was for staying on. He had two missions to complete in Athens, plus a radio operator to deliver, and some way would be found of getting him there. As they argued the options in heated but whispered tones, a sixth shadow joined the party – Lieutenant Johnny Huddart.

'What's up, gentlemen?' he asked, in his characteristically relaxed, almost humorous way.

Atkinson and Craig spoke over each other to explain their views of the situation.

'I'm sorry chaps, but no one's going home tonight anyway. We've got a ten-day patrol to complete, and I can't do that with the fore ends full of your chaps. We don't have enough air in the boat to stay dived all day with them aboard, or enough food to feed 'em.'

Huddart's next words were recorded a few months later by the serial escaper Francis S. Jones.[10]

'You chaps had better stay here. I'll be back in ten days, and you'll be in a Cairo nightclub three days after that. It's a promise.'

Redpath's heart sank. He had been promising his escapers for two weeks that a boat would come in, pick them up, and they'd be home in Egypt in no time. The submarine was here all right but was going to sail without them. He did not relish breaking the news. Most of the escapers had been on the run for six months, and many came from units famous for their willingness to disobey orders from officers, especially British officers, and to use their fists to get what they thought they were entitled to. Craig was almost equally alarmed. If the escapers were going to stay on Antiparos for ten days, then it was his duty to stay with them and take charge, whatever the risks caused by Harry's indiscretions. There was a chance that another party would arrive from Athens in the meantime, and he would need to be here to take charge of them too. Finally, there was still the need to establish another escaper base on the Malea peninsula on the Peloponnese.

Redpath lowered his voice further.

'I understand, Sir, obviously it's up to you, but I think there might well be trouble when I go and tell the lads what's going to happen. May I suggest that we wait until you can get all your crew clear of the beach? I can't speak for what might happen otherwise.'

In his mind the picture arose of a riot, or even a panicked capture of some of *Triumph*'s crew as hostages in a demand to be taken on board. Frightened, tired men can be unpredictable.

Huddart paused for a moment's thought. This was completely out of his experience of highly disciplined sailors who would suffer any privation required of them without complaint and follow orders without argument.

'Yes, I agree.'

'Guns, when we've finished unloading, get the Folboats and Severn and Child back to the ship, make sure that you are aboard before them. Sergeant Redpath, I think it's down to you to explain what will be happening. Your men won't like it. Tell them that we have another special operation to carry out first and can't take them aboard now. We *will* be back in ten days. Tell them that the navy is always on time. And wish them a happy new year from *Triumph*'.[11]

The work of lifting the tonnes of food and fuel ashore took the rest of the night. Although the noise level on the beach rose hour by hour, the two dozen men worked unmolested by Italians, who were probably starting their welcome for the new year early in the bars of Paros. The men on the beach were indeed not happy – a near-riot ensued, but the issue was settled by the shrinking black hump of Johnny Huddart's submarine, fading into the grey dawn. One good thing had happened. *Triumph* had landed a new supply of rum. Redpath's escapers toasted the new year, with their two new officers, and then sought their bedding rolls to catch up on the night's sleep.

No one on Antiparos knew that they would never see *Triumph* again.

Chapter 13

Disaster on Antiparos

As far as they knew, most of the men hiding on Antiparos believed that they had ten peaceful days ahead in which they simply had to stay warm and hidden. Atkinson and Kypriades, the radio operator, were desperate to get to Athens to round up more escapers and make contact with the resistance; however, when they woke around midday of 30 December, they were without either Harry or a caique. They were stuck, for now at least. Craig, hearing the report of Harry's complications in Paros, quickly decided that they needed to vacate Antiparos before the garrison at Paros finally decided to come and search the island, but there was no way of moving further than Despotiko. The two officers, and Sergeant Redpath, fretted over their plans for a week, until Harry's love life once more dictated events. On the morning of 5 January 1942, a breathless sentry arrived at the Tzavellas House with electrifying news. A caique, the *Despoina*, with a large squad of soldiers was heading for the narrows between Antiparos and Despotiko. With no time to lose or wonder why friends in Paros had not sent word, Craig and Atkinson locked up the Tzavellas house and took to the hills, from where they could watch events. The Italian patrol, led by Lieutenant Gali, had broken with the normal protocol, and had commandeered *Despoina* just an hour before. *Despoina* belonged to Baba Manoli, who was now skippering his passengers towards an island he knew only too well was populated with escapers, for they were hiding in his own house. Desperate to buy them time, Manoli contrived to tinker with *Despoina*'s engine to stall it and then delay restarting it for as long as was safe with an Italian rifle pointed at him. He bought just enough time for the escape party to scatter before *Despoina* puttered into the bay.

On Antiparos the patrol searched around the house for a while. Lieutenant Gali found Spiro Tzavellas outside his Red House and suggested that they go inside for a drink. Knowing that the house was full of British stores, Spiros pretended that he had mislaid his key, and that the house was locked. Both were patently thin excuses, but Gali must have decided that this was not the moment to force an encounter with whoever was at home, sitting by the fire whose smoke was billowing out of the Red House chimney. Craig reported afterwards 'an hour later they left the island, and in my opinion seemed to be very suspicious'.[1] He was right. The patrol had noticed empty discarded packets of British cigarettes around the beach and house, probably thrown down carelessly during the unloading a week before. Clearly something was up.

Craig, Atkinson and Redpath had a heated argument about what to do next. Craig was for moving men and some supplies across the bay to Despotiko. Atkinson was more martial, voting for armed resistance, with the two dozen men and ample supplies of arms and ammunition landed by *Thorn* and *Triumph*. Craig prevailed, not surprisingly since it was obvious that the patrol was just the tip of a much larger Italian spear located only a dozen miles away. However, the time taken for the argument proved fatal. Harry's girlfriend's mother had continued to make trouble. She believed that Harry was now hiding on Antiparos (in fact he was in Athens), and once more told the Italian commander that British escapers were hiding on Antiparos. Gali's patrol had been a reconnaissance. Another patrol of eighteen men was detailed off for a night-time raid.[2]

At 2.00 am Craig, Atkinson and Sergeant Redpath, asleep in the Tzavellas house, heard a vigorous banging on the front door. Dragging themselves from sleep, they dressed quickly in darkness. Spiro Tzavellas bought them a little time while he clarified what the Italians wanted through his locked door. With an electrifying cold shudder Atkinson remembered what he had stashed in his suitcase – his notebook. He must have realized at this point that if captured he would appear very clearly as a spy and saboteur and would face a firing squad. Capture was not an option. Atkinson belted his service revolver around his waist and prepared himself for the coming confrontation. At last, he had the opportunity to fight the Axis face to face.

The two officers could easily follow what was happening downstairs. Tzavellas unlocked his door and a few of the Italians came into his parlour. Here they found Kypriades, groggy from sleep, on a sofa. Spiro Tzavellas introduced him as a relative – perfectly plausible on the face of it, so long as no one found the radio. The two Greeks were taken outside and the house was surrounded, while four Italians, led by Lieutenant Carlo Ribolzi, began to search the house. Ribolzi was a popular officer with his men. Knowing that they would be in their room within a minute, Craig hid behind the swing of the door with a Thompson, planning to take the searchers hostage and bargain their way out of the house. Atkinson, probably in a high state of excited agitation, compounded with deep alarm, drew his pistol and waited in front of the closed door. Redpath also armed himself with a Thompson.

The men did not have long to wait. A minute later, Ribolzi opened the door of their room and shone his torch into the darkness. Atkinson took aim and fired a single round. The .45-inch copper-jacketed bullet hit Ribolzi full in the chest, throwing him back into the small lobby outside the door. Electrified by the sudden and unexpected shot, the three Italian soldiers hurriedly left the house, encouraged by a burst from Redpath's Thompson over their heads. It was time for the three men to leave too. Stepping over Ribolzi, Atkinson saw him fumbling in the badly lit gloom with what looked like a grenade. He coolly aimed his Webley service revolver at Ribolzi's chest and fired again. Then chaos ensued. The crash of glass revealed a volley of grenades flying into the house from outside. Throwing the bedroom door shut again, the men dashed to the window of their room. As they struggled with its latch, two grenades crashed through the glass, fell into the room and burst with sharp cracks. The men fell out of the window and ran for the beach as more grenades fell about them.

In the darkness and the panic, Atkinson lost contact with Craig and Redpath. Reaching the beach, Craig realized that they were not being pursued, perhaps because of the presence of the Thompson. Redpath had received a shrapnel wound in his leg, but was still able to walk, so he and Craig decided to climb up to Baba Manoli's house, gather up the escape party and some food, and retreat into the scrubby hill in the centre of the island to watch and wait. Forty-five minutes later saw the party of two dozen escapers hiding in dry scrub shivering in the dark as their adrenalin cleared. No one knew where Atkinson had got to. At about 4 am Kypriades stumbled across their position. He had managed to give his guards the slip in the chaos of the hunt and with great presence of mind had returned to the Tzavellas house to remove the two suitcases (the radio set and Atkinson's suitcase), which he gave to Baba Manoli to hide.

The morning of 6 January brought half of the Paros garrison to Antiparos, who split into patrols and began to search the island. Antiparos is a small island, until one tries to search every nook and cranny of it, when its 10,000 acres of herby scrub[3] provide an almost infinite number of hiding places for twenty men – though as far as the Italians were concerned, they were only looking for two, at least one of whom had a machine gun and was prepared to use it. Search patrols returned for the next three days, but without success. Perhaps Craig and his escapers would get away after all? Craig badly wanted Atkinson's suitcase for the stash of gold sovereigns in it which might ease the passage home on a caique. He was out of luck. The Italians had already arrested Baba Manoli and beaten out of him the location of his hiding place. Atkinson's suitcase and the radio were now being inspected by very angry officers, for Lieutenant Ribolzi had died of his wounds the night before.

The food that the escapers had been able to grab as they fled Baba Manoli's house ran out on 8 January. On the night of 9 January, the first night on which *Triumph* was to return, Craig and Redpath, stomachs rumbling with hunger, lay on a high hill overlooking the entrance to the bay and flashed their recognition signal seawards with a torch. There was no response. The same happened on 10 January. By dawn on 11 January Craig knew that, for whatever reason, they were on their own, apart from the permanent presence of Italian patrols on the island. In the middle of that day, Craig and Redpath watched as a new caique sailed into the bay. One man aboard it must have had a near heart attack when he rounded the point. Expecting to see an empty bay he found several caiques and an E-boat at anchor, and hundreds of Italian troops milling around and searching the island. That man was, of course, Harry Grammatikakis, returning at last from his Athens trip. A burst of machine gun fire over the heads of the men in his caique, who were Cretans being carried home with permission, persuaded the caique's captain not to turn and run. While the captain was being questioned by an Italian officer, Harry quietly slipped over the side into the freezing cold Aegean and swam for Despotiko, his back cringing at the expectation of a burst of machine-gun bullets from the E-boat. None came. Shivering with cold, Harry crawled ashore and disappeared into the wild scrub of Despotiko.[4]

Three more days passed in which the search continued without success, and the escapers slowly starved. Having had nothing to eat for over a week some of them cracked. Two men, who had been on sentry duty, noticed a pair of sheep in a pen on the flats inland of the beach and, at the end of their watch, they sneaked down to take them prisoner. The men were not sneaky enough. They were seen by Italian sentries, fired on, and then captured. For the first time the Italians must have realized that they were not just hunting a couple of saboteurs. Redpath recorded that the location of the hideout was beaten out of the two unfortunate captives. That seems likely for ninety minutes later it was surrounded by a ring of soldiers. Luckily, the light was failing so the Italians waited overnight for the dawn – the saboteurs were still armed and dangerous, after all. Craig ordered his party to disarm and scatter, if they could, through gaps in the siege, but within a few days the entire party had been rounded up and transported to a nearby island, Kythnos, for interrogation. Francis Jones, who had been in prison there for three months, told of their arrival: 'Four new men came into our cell, and a bigger party of twenty went into the strongroom next door. All bar two of the newcomers had been captured on an island called Antiparos'.[5]

According to Harry's own SOE interview later in Cairo, which has to be taken with several pounds of salt, he hid on Despotiko for at least four days, waiting for Antiparos to clear of Italians. Once they had found Craig and his men they left, and Harry swam first to Antiparos, and then to Paros to hide. Here, he hid for four months, in spite of having a reward on his head of £50,000 (in today's money), plus food for the duration of the war. His future mother-in-law, Maria Tsadani, who had now been revealed in Paros as the source of the betrayal of Coney Island, once more found out where Harry was hiding and told the garrison. Harry was ever a slippery character. As a patrol broke down the front door of his hiding place, he was slipping out, naked as the day he was born, onto the roof to escape.[6] Harry got away. Stealing a rowing boat, he managed to reach Turkey in May 1942 and from there Cairo, where he was interviewed by SOE in June 1942. He'd had enough. Wanted in Athens, Paros, Crete and probably Turkey, and with an impossibly tangled love life, in December 1942 he requested permission from GHQ Middle East to travel to the Belgian Congo to live with 'his father in law'.[7] This appears to have been granted, though there is evidence that after the war he returned to Paros where he died at a ripe old age.

Craig and his men came tragically close to being rescued before they were captured, by a man they knew nothing about. Captain Michael Parish of the Sherwood Rangers was sitting on the neighbouring island of Poliagos with a large caique, fuel and food enough to carry the whole escape party home but was running down the clock to the day on which he had been ordered to go to Antiparos.

Parish had joined a territorial cavalry regiment in 1938, because he thought 'I had much better be carried by a horse than march on my own two feet'.[8] At the age of twenty-five Parish had started his career mining in Rhodesia, returning as soon as war broke out. Posted to Egypt, GHQ Cairo soon worked out that traditional cavalry was probably not going to be of much use against an armoured enemy equipped with machine guns, and that there were insufficient tanks with which to equip a territorial yeomanry regiment, so Parish's company was detailed to become coastal defence gunners. In February 1941, Parish found himself manning a six-inch coastal defence gun overlooking the coast of Crete, near Maleme. Parish had watched the entire airborne invasion of Maleme, from fifteen miles away, through the crystal-clear lenses of his Barr and Stroud binocular rangefinder. He knew that the range of his six-inch guns was two miles less than that. Seeing German aircraft landing without hindrance, he requested permission from General Freyberg's headquarters to increase the cordite charges in his guns so that he might hit the runway with his massive shells, at the risk of damaging the guns. Permission was refused. A few days later, Parish blew up his guns anyway and evaded capture, eventually reaching Turkey on 4 September and Cairo on 17 October, where he was quickly recruited by Colonel Simonds to run a caique-based escape route. The Antiparos plan was 'Film Plan Number Two'. This new plan was Film Plan Number Three, to be based on the Cypriot port of Paphos.[9]

It took four months and multiple flights between Cyprus and Egypt for Parish to requisition and assemble the large quantity of stores, arms and ammunition to equip his force of two caiques in Paphos. 'It was all very different to one's regimental discipline; I was on my own, I was my own master, I could walk into the Foreign Office or the Ordnance Department and order more or less whatever I wanted, and it would come in double quick time.'[10]

By the end of the year all was ready. Parish left Paphos in the 200-tonne caique *Agios Demetrios*, in company with the smaller *Evangellistria* on 1 January 1942. In his memoir of the war[11] Parish reports that he had explicit orders to rendezvous with Atkinson, and a party of escapers, on 27 January.[12] Today this appears odd. On 1 January, Atkinson was expecting to travel to, and return from, Athens, in time to meet *Triumph* on the night of 9 January. That plan only misfired when Lieutenant Ribolzi arrived on Antiparos in the small hours of 6 January. How would a rendezvous for 27 January have been set a week before? Atkinson's detailed orders for Isinglass have been lost to the record, but with Parish set to visit Antiparos sixteen days after *Triumph*'s pickup on 9 January, the most likely answer is that Atkinson radioed Cairo for instructions when *Triumph* failed to arrive, and was ordered to remain in Antiparos to make another run to find and rescue escapers in the two weeks between that and Parish's visit. There would have been no pressing reason for Atkinson to return to Cairo instead – he was fully equipped, supplied and trained to keep making visits to Athens, and, in addition, in Athens he would have access to Kypriades' radio through which any changes to his orders could be transmitted.

Transferring their kit to the *Evangellistria*, to help their concealment, Parish sailed slowly towards Antiparos. They were in no great hurry, sailing at night and stopping at deserted islands along the way to stash stores, money and fuel as they went.[13] On 11 January, when Harry was sailing into a crowd of Italians on Antiparos, and Craig and Redpath were hiding and starving in its wilds, Parish, knowing nothing of these events, was just seven miles away, heading for another deserted rocky islet, Poliagos, two hours' sail from Despotiko Bay. Here, he stayed for ten days, running down the clock until his planned rendezvous on 27 January. A few days before the rendezvous, Parish decided to make the short crossing by night to Despotiko. Arriving at dawn he found four Italian armed schooners already in the bay. He hastily withdrew behind a headland and into a small bay. One of Parish's crew, a Greek tug-boat captain and smuggler called Vernikos, volunteered to row over to find out what was happening. Half an hour later, Parish watched through binoculars as Vernikos was captured. After about an hour, Parish saw Vernikos being rowed away under Italian escort. He decided to rescue him, but as *Evangellistria* closed on the rowing boat, Vernikos made vigorous 'go away' signals. The Italians had clearly been deceived by Vernikos into believing that he was a German, and Vernikos was keen to avoid a confrontation (perhaps expecting that he would be the first person shot in a firefight). Vernikos did manage to update Parish with what he had found out. 'Keep away. Durbin (Atkinson) has been captured. The island is empty.' Four days later, Parish was back in Turkey, reporting to the consul at Izmir that the Antiparos base's cover had been blown and that Atkinson was in enemy hands. The news reached Cairo next day, but Simonds had no idea that Atkinson had been captured with both his notebook and operational orders intact.

What had happened to Atkinson? We know only from third-hand reports, shared in whispers by the men in that Kythnos cellar. Atkinson had been hit by a grenade blast, probably the one tossed into his bedroom in the Tzavellas house, breaking his leg in two places. Unable to move he had been swiftly captured, with his precious and disastrous notebook. We shall return to what happened to Atkinson after that shortly, but for now, his capture presented Craig and Redpath with a potentially lethal threat. Atkinson would clearly appear to the Italians as a spy and a saboteur. In his pocket was a list of names of the Greek resistance. In his suitcase was a large sum in gold, a list of operational instructions on whom to see in Athens and what to tell them from SOE, a bottle of lethal poison and a quantity of dynamite. The operational instructions are no longer to be found in SOE's files at Kew, but they were quoted in part at the 1942 trial of two SOE agents in Athens: 'An Association has been created in Athens; the chiefs are Major Tselos and Captain Condouriatis. The Aims are (A) to create an information service throughout Greece in order to collect the information in behalf of the Allies; (B) to prepare sabotages; (C) to organise a revolution against the occupying forces in due time'.[14] As if that were not enough, Atkinson had also brought with him a personal diary which recorded his escape from Kokkinia and mentioned other Allied agents in Greece by name.[15] In his other suitcase was a radio. If Atkinson was a saboteur, then surely his companions were too? Craig and Redpath desperately coordinated a story to save their lives. Craig had been captured in uniform and simply denied all knowledge of his companion's mission. He was, he stated, operating a British base on Antiparos, an outpost well within the laws of war, and was therefore a legal combatant. Redpath had been captured in civilian clothing, but the two argued that men in an outpost are entitled to wear plain clothes when off duty. They also argued that housing escaped prisoners was a legitimate act of war. Craig had a nasty moment when it was discovered that he had been in the camp at Kokkinia, but he argued that there was nothing intrinsically illegal about a man escaping and then returning to active duty.

The question of their status hung over Craig and Redpath's necks like a headsman's axe for several weeks, during which their lives truly hung by a thread. Eventually they heard that they were going to be treated as prisoners of war. It later became clear that it was not just their arguments and their story that had saved their lives. Atkinson, perhaps realizing that his own status was beyond saving, and that the Italians wanted just one life to pay for Lieutenant Ribolzi's, had made clear that he was the secret agent and that the others were what they claimed to be, soldiers fighting under the protection of the Geneva Conventions. Perhaps Atkinson was also beginning to realize the scale of the disaster he had brought down on his friends in Athens, and had some element of self-recrimination in mind. The Italians immediately realized the significance of the papers they had captured. Here, in plain language, was a detailed analysis of everyone in Athens prepared to work underground to resist the Axis, or at least everyone on the liberal, democratic or royalist side of the underground fence, along with a detailed set of instructions for Operation Isinglass.[16] Better still, no one in Athens knew that the list and the instructions had been captured, which allowed Italian intelligence to delay rounding them up while they were put under surveillance.

However, Athens was a small and gossipy town, so it only took a few days for news of Atkinson's disastrous mistake to leak out. On 5 February, Station 333, the radio set left in Athens in May 1941, transmitted a signal to Istanbul with news of the capture of an unnamed British officer in Antiparos. 'In fight with Italians he was wounded and arrested. In his hands found note writing following quote must meet in Athens Captain Coundouriotis and Tselos and come to understanding with them for organization espionage service sabotage groups and revolt against conquerors … officer brought bottle strong venom [the curare poison]'.[17] Three days later SOE Cairo signalled back to Istanbul that the (unnamed) man did not belong to SOE (the first of many SOE evasions in the weeks to follow) but admitting that he had with him a memorandum that corresponded with the report from 333 and that, worse, he had a list of all of the known possible leaders of the Greek political underground in plain language. 'He had with him … a list of pseudonyms and en clair names of the following Zannas, Lekkas, Spyromiliou, Dracos, Politis, Chrysanthos, Manettas, Pangalos, Agrios, Kannelopoulos, Tselos, Condouriotis, Zarinos, Nikotsara'.[18] These fourteen names comprised the whole of the liberal/democratic/royalist community of resistance leaders. When we read them today and picture trying to commit them to memory in a hurry and under great stress, it is possible to sympathize with Atkinson for taking them ashore, if not for allowing them to fall into Italian hands.

Perhaps equally disastrous, and the source of even more bitter accusations against the men of Secret Building, was the disappearance of *Triumph*. The last anyone had seen of her was the white spray of her main ballast tanks venting as she dived in the grey light of the morning of 30 December. Huddart had sent a brief signal home that the beach operation had been completed successfully. Since then, nothing had been heard. *Triumph* was scheduled to return to Alexandria on 14 January 1942. As day followed day without her return, the tension and feeling of doom in *Medway* must have risen to breaking point. Each evening might find her flashing her recognition signal to the ship guarding the entrance to Alexandria's submarine sanctuary. Boats occasionally arrived home late if they were damaged or had some machinery fault, but each day that passed lessened the probability of a return.

One man in *Medway* must have suffered particularly acute agony – Commander Sammy Woods. For Woods had led the sixty-four men in *Triumph* personally for a year, through acute danger and in happy parties ashore. He knew every man personally, and, as far as the separation of rank permitted, was a friend to each one. These were his men, his team, his family. Their work in the Mediterranean was done. He had brought them through almost intact, a unique achievement in December 1941. They deserved to go home but now would not. Whatever happened to them, he should have been with them, and taken whatever fate came along with them, or perhaps used his superior skills and experience to lead them to safety.

Sydney Raw waited a week. On 21 January, he finally accepted that *Triumph* had been lost. That must have been a black day aboard *Medway*. *Triumph* had dodged every shell, every bomb, every mine and every depth charge that the Axis had thrown at her. She had been just about to go home. Her shipmates in *Medway* had the awful job of clearing the lockers of her crew, packing up anything that would not rot for despatch, by the long sea route home, to their next of kin. A submariner recalls doing this for another boat in Malta: 'About four of us … were given the job and on cutting the locks off started to put their belongings into their kit bags. On opening the lockers, we were confronted with photographs and letters from their wives, girlfriends and mothers, as well as their personal clothing and mementoes that these friends of ours had in their lockers; one could not help reading some of the letters and wondered how this poor bastard had died. Would we very soon face the same fate?'[19] The process was doubly painful for *Triumph*'s shipmates, for their lockers overflowed with gifts and souvenirs intended for friends and family. Woods sat down to the appalling task of writing sixty-four letters of regret to the families of his men. Many of the letters from Woods have survived, and even now, eighty years later, they radiate sadness. So close, and yet so far.

What had happened to *Triumph* was an unanswered question, which remained so for eight decades. Before answering it, we need to travel back to Atkinson and what happened next in Athens.

Chapter 14

Disaster in Athens

Almost exactly a year after his capture, John Atkinson was carried into the dock of a military court in Athens to stand trial. With one leg amputated, and the other still unable to bear his full weight, he was permitted to sit across the courtroom from the three senior Italian officers who would form his judge and jury.

It had not been an easy year. Badly wounded in both legs and unable to walk, Atkinson had been taken first to an Italian hospital in Rhodes for treatment to his legs, then in May 1942 a post-war report has him in the punishment cells of Averof prison in Athens. 'He was immediately isolated in the underground dungeons of the Averof prison without adequate medical assistance … his crutches were removed and the sentry put on guard in front of his door was ordered to refuse him any help whatever, so that he was obliged in his condition to crawl back and forwards a distance of about twenty yards in order to get a drink of water.'[1]

The regime in Averof prison was brutally cruel. The prison (built in 1892) had three blocks, each of three floors of cells, and a basement. Atkinson was in the Italian block. The other blocks were the German section for men and a second German section for women prisoners. Averof was essentially a civilian prison, rather than a prisoner of war camp, located just a mile from the Ioannou house in Patission Street. All that remains of it today is a single marble pillar in the courtyard of the Athens Supreme Court complex which was built on its site in 1972. Relatives of prisoners were permitted to bring food parcels into the prison and have one ten-minute visit each week. Naturally, Allied prisoners had no relatives in Athens.

Italian Contra Spionaggio (CS, the Italian counterintelligence unit, led by Colonel Arturo Scatini and Captain Alfredo Pizitola) treated all recaptured Allied soldiers as spies and saboteurs until they proved themselves innocent, along with any Greek civilian they found helping them. Inmates were crowded ten to a cell of seventy square feet, designed for a single occupant, no beds or bedding were supplied. Men were not allowed to look through their cell windows. The Italian guards were promised a fortnight's leave if they managed to shoot a prisoner breaking that rule.[2] The daily ration provided somewhere in the region of 300 calories. Contra Spionaggio held suspects at Averof, but tortured them at its headquarters in a nearby hotel in Hermes Street, around the corner from the prison itself. Only once it had satisfied itself that it had insufficient evidence that a man was working as an agent, was he released into the PoW system. For men who infringed its rules, Averof had a punishment cell, a basement cellar flooded with water to prevent men from sleeping for days on end. One man, the Australian Kevin Walsh, spent thirty-seven days here after a failed attempt to escape.[3] Beatings were commonplace, Red Cross parcels were stolen by the guards and looted, while outbound mail was stolen and shredded.

Despite being badly injured, Atkinson was tortured for a month or so, by the Carabinieri Mareschiallo (Warrant Officer) Michaelo Defacio, who 'was known amongst the prisoners of Averof prison as the most brutal and cruel of interrogating officers'.[4] The torture, being kicked in the legs, kidneys and stomach by a pair of guards, was essentially gratuitous – Atkinson's notes and notebook told Contra Spionaggio everything it needed to know. Averof's guards had more than beatings to offer. A steel belt with sharp prongs fitted on its inside circumference was gradually tightened around the victim's waist. Men were hung from the ceiling by their feet for long periods. The most inventive form of torture in Averof was to have splinters of pine wood inserted beneath a man's fingernails, where they became infected from the sticky pine sap.[5] Defacio was vociferous in demanding that Atkinson pay for Lieutenant Ribolzi's life with his own, and it seems likely that his treatment of Atkinson was more revenge than an attempt to learn anything new or useful about MI9 or SOE. Perhaps Defacio suspected that Atkinson's mind contained secrets beyond his revealing notes and list. *We* know that was true. Atkinson's list of names lacked one important entry, the Ioannous. Despite days of torture, Atkinson kept the name of the Ioannou family locked inside his head, or perhaps his heart.

Atkinson's torture caused his wounded leg to become re-infected. At least one prisoner had already been kicked to death by Corporal Bianchi, the prison medical orderly, as punishment for asking for medical treatment in the middle of the night. It seems likely that Atkinson was moved, to keep him alive for a later trial, and after about a month in Averof he was taken across the square to the Elpis civil hospital in Athens[6] where one of his legs was amputated. He was still at Elpis as late as August 1942, since the International Red Cross reported seeing him there on that date, and was probably still there in October because he was seen there by a MI9 agent, who reported in Cairo at the end of 1942: '[Atkinson] is well and cheerful despite the condition and privations ... he needs money badly [to buy black market food] and this we are continually trying to get to him, but contacts are difficult'.[7] In a memorandum written on 15 October, Colonel Simonds refers once more to Atkinson being in Averof prison, so it seems likely that he was moved back around this date to the rather less salubrious hospital ward in the prison.

Athens was a small town, and Atkinson found that one of his nurses was Alexandra Bourbouras, who he had met during his stay in Athens, but who had been captured just two months before. It is likely that he was able to pass news of his arrival and his unfortunate position to the Ioannou sisters through her. At this stage, his fate was not completely sealed. Three other SOE officers had been captured elsewhere and were being held in Averof. One, Captain Savage, had been landed by *Triumph* in October 1941, but had been discovered and caught within weeks. Two others, Frank Macaskie and Richard McNabb, had been caught elsewhere. Macaskie's story, of being a simple escaper, was somewhat compromised when the Italian officer in his prison on the island of Kea, presented him with a photograph of him shaking hands at Cairo station with Tony Simonds (Cairo was well supplied with people who wanted to end British rule and were prepared to support the Axis with a little local espionage).[8] All three were now being held and investigated as potential saboteurs. The Italian authorities were surprisingly legalistic and balanced in deciding who was a saboteur, seeking and weighing all the evidence that they could find. While the regime inside Averof was excessively cruel, there was no fixed assumption that the three officers were agents, though their chances of survival did not look promising. In Egypt SOE and MI9 were making strenuous efforts to tip the scales in favour of a decision that the three were legitimate prisoners of war. The files at the National Archive contain multiple telegrams to and from the Vatican, whose Papal Legate was acting as go-between, seeking to swing the decision away from saboteur and towards legitimate combatant. Cairo did not just resort to persuasion but included open threats. Three Italian saboteurs had been captured in 1941, parachuting behind Allied lines, and were now being held in much the same legal limbo as Savage, McNabb, Macaskie and Atkinson. Cairo openly discussed threatening these three prisoners with death if any one of their men were harmed. There is no doubt that the four agents knew something of what was happening behind the scenes, given how leaky Athens was. SOE in Cairo was prepared to use any means at hand to save its men, signalling on 3 March 'We should also attempt to bribe judges or police'.[9] In the summer of 1942, Atkinson was visited in Averof by Monsieur de Bavier, the Swiss Chargé d'Affaires,[10] who took the trouble to visit the Italian diplomatic plenipotentiary in Athens, Ghigi, and suggest to him that killing Atkinson would bring inevitable repercussions from the Allies. Ghigi replied that 'in any country a civilian who kills an officer is sentenced to death'.[11]

One report from the time suggests that Atkinson was confident that his life would be saved by these manoeuvres[12] and that he approached his trial with some degree of confidence. In the case of Macaskie there were also elaborate plans to affect his rescue by force. So, it was probably a reasonably optimistic young man who sat in the dock that morning. He was also encouraged, for the court was open to the public, and across it he could see Effi Ioannou trying to look insignificant.

Within days of the discovery of his fatal papers, Contra Spionaggio had begun to round up the people named in his memorandum. The net was inefficiently thrown. Major Tselos (SOE codename Sugar) had managed to evade arrest. Tselos was a prominent royalist army officer, and therefore a favourite of the Greek government in exile and the British Foreign Office. He was also the principal contact that Atkinson had been tasked to meet, and Kypriades and his radio were intended for his use. Tselos worked under another leading royalist, Professor Panayiottis Kanellopoulos of the Athens University (codename Cuthbert). Kanellopoulos was regarded in Cairo as the leader of the royalist movement and had been invited to come to Cairo to take up a cabinet post in the king's exiled government. Together these two men offered the best, if not the only, chance for London to build up a royalist, or liberal democratic, resistance network in Greece. Kanellopoulos too managed to avoid the Italian net, arriving in Turkey in April 1942, but the hopes of a royalist resistance left Greece with them.

There were a few successful arrests. Captain Coundouriotes (codename Prometheus II) of the Royal Hellenic Navy, was seen in London as a major operator in sabotage, and was also in control of Station 333, operated by a man whose codename was Niko but whose real name has not survived the war. Dr Bourekas and his wife were established members of the escape network, at first in Salonika and later in Athens. Dora Nikotsara had been working as a messenger for Colonel Bakirzis (codename Prometheus I), who was a prominent leader of the democratic Venezelist faction. Alexander Zannas, former Minister for Air and head of the Red Cross with the SOE codename D/HG50, was arrested on 22 April 1942. He and his wife were senior representatives of the Red Cross but also diligently working to smuggle escapers to MI9's rescue lines. It was to Zannas that Atkinson was bringing his bag of gold, to help buy food for men in hiding. With these arrests, the democratic Venizelist resistance also expired.

By January 1942, Athens, along with the rest of urban Greece, was in a state of forced starvation. German troops had commandeered supplies of food on an industrial scale for despatch to the fatherland. 'The Germans have taken 60 per cent of the wheat crop. Where [troops] are stationed they take all available eggs and supplies of meat. The whole of the petrol and leather in the country has been taken to Germany. In Athens all the gold rings, except wedding rings, have been taken from the women. A number of church bells have also been sent to Germany.'[13] Allied forces were blockading Greece by sea. Food shops were empty, and the population of Athens was living on a few hundred calories per day. 'In Athens people collapsed in the street, swelled and went black all over their bodies. German trucks went round several times a day collecting the dead.'[14] No one was counting exactly, but post-war estimates suggest that the Axis occupation killed 400,000 Greeks – one tenth of the population – the great majority by starvation.

Maria Cawias, who later married a man who finished his diplomatic career as British Ambassador to Washington, wrote afterwards 'at that time I remember corn bread, coffee made out of toasted chick peas and dandelion leaf salad were our staple diet. Sometimes a friendly Rumanian Embassy official who lived in our building would add something to this sparse menu, or rich relatives who had found some delicacy on the black market would invite us to a meal … passers-by, their clothes hanging limply away from their skeletal bodies, would sway and drop down dead. Their lifeless limbs, sprawled out on the pavement like those of a severed puppet, seemed unreal.'[15]

Another name on the list, Lekkas (SOE codename Philon), was the wireless operator landed by *Triumph* in October 1941 with Captain Savage. Atkinson did not know that Lekkas was already dead, having been shot when discovered moving his wireless set from Athens to Piraeus. Giannis Politis, a Greek diplomat whose fate is unknown, was the head of an Athens resistance network called Ali Baba, as well as the Kyrou network, with two other men named on the list, Archbishop Chrysanthos and General Drakos.

SOE's memorandum on the fates of the men on Atkinson's list denies knowledge of the rest of the people on it, perhaps because they were names provided to Atkinson by Tony Simonds of MI9, but equally probably because SOE's administration in Cairo was chaotic, with codenames being allocated but not recorded for many agents. There are several signals in the archive dedicated entirely to untangling this mess, and it is likely that the writers of the memorandum simply did not know, for example, that Giannis Politis was an agent or what his codename was. We know from Craig's operational report that, when he saw Atkinson's list in *Triumph*'s wardroom, sailing from Alexandria to Antiparos, he was furious that Atkinson had used names of people in the escape network without permission from either himself or Simonds.

The disaster in Athens in 1942 was a time-bomb that only really exploded in 1944 when the German occupiers left Greece, the Italians having surrendered to the Allies in September 1943. For the two years since Atkinson's capture, resistance in Greece had been effectively monopolized by the communist party, who latterly had spent as much time killing or disarming non-communist resistance networks as they had fighting the Axis. Because the leaders of the moderate resistance were either dead or in prison, courtesy of John Atkinson, or exiled, there was no one in a position to oppose the communists, and no one outside the communists to whom Cairo might supply arms or money. As the last German troops left, the communists stepped up to take power, and it would take a five-year civil war and a backstairs agreement with Josef Stalin, before Greece attained peace and a non-communist government in 1949.

Sadly, for Atkinson, what he did not appreciate as his trial approached, was that he would be tried not just for sabotage, but also for murder. The Italians wanted blood for blood, in particular for the blood of Lieutenant Ribolzi. The case appeared clear. Atkinson had been in plain clothes in Italian-occupied territory, an escaped prisoner of war, and therefore not entitled under the law of armed conflict to use lethal force, or indeed any force, to remain at liberty. In this position he had cold-bloodedly killed a man, and under the Italian interpretation of the law, that made him a murderer.

Atkinson's tragedy was that SOE and MI9 quietly agreed. Strenuous, and ultimately successful, efforts were made to establish that Savage, Macaskie and McNabb were legitimate combatants and therefore prisoners of war with rights and protections, but a May 1943 memorandum, in SOE files, reveals that it had already come to the conclusion that 'it strikes us that the Italians were determined to take revenge for the death of the Italian officer, and made the worst of the circumstances of their case against Atkinson'. It goes on to say: 'It does not seem likely that any protests would have deterred them from carrying out the sentence. The additional charge of espionage could we suppose have been supported by the discovery of the list of names Atkinson carried with him.'[16] Atkinson would receive no help from home in his coming ordeal, but there was no one to tell him that sad news.

The record does not show why it took nearly a year to bring Atkinson and his network to trial. A decision must have been taken early to try the resistance network in a single trial, and in public. Perhaps a quarter of the period was spent with Atkinson in hospital, and perhaps the Italian command decided that they would prefer to try a man who was visibly fit and healthy. What we can see from Italian records, captured and translated after the war, is that the prosecutions were prepared with great care and in great detail. While other people who were tried in Athens reported court procedures that were run with indecent haste and little care (defence counsel were junior officers, appointed on the morning of trials), it seems that the Italian command in Greece wanted to run a show trial, and to demonstrate that it was capable of due legal process. Another delaying factor was the capture, over time, of additional members of the escape network and the resistance, with each new arrival delaying the trial date to allow a new case to be built. For example, the trial report in SOE's archive narrates that Angellopoulos had been left at liberty for three months, while he was covertly followed to reveal other members of the resistance. Perhaps, too, the high command was noticing signs that Italy might fall out of the war and was keen to use a strictly legal process in order to head off the retribution that might follow when the Allies won. Italy did indeed make peace with the Allies just seven months after the trial. Or perhaps the men who made the decision simply believed that revenge was a dish best served cold.

The long gap left time to plan escapes, and plans were indeed laid, but at least one plan, to spring Dora Nikotsara from Averof, was detected and stopped when she confided it to an Italian stool pigeon.[17]

What we do know for certain is that on 9 February 1943 the court assembled at 91 Patission Street, a few hundred yards from the Ioannou house at number 9. The circularity of his journey must have struck Atkinson hard, even harder when he looked across the court room that morning to see Effi Ioannou in the public gallery. Opposite the dock sat the judges – General Geraldo Magaldi was in the chair. Magaldi was a hanging judge, described in a post-war criminal affidavit as 'a wild beast'[18] who worked to prevent people on trial receiving any form of natural justice. In one trial of four men, when the prosecutor demanded a death sentence for one of the accused, Magaldi simply condemned all four. Even the Italians in CS and the Carabinieri called Magaldi 'The Executioner'. Magaldi hated both Greeks and British, perhaps because he had already lost four sons to the war.[19] There was no jury. These three men would determine life or death for the thirty-one defendants crowded into the dock (eight more were being tried in absentia, including Kanellopoulos and Tselos). The central figure in the trial was Atkinson, dressed in a borrowed officer's uniform, with Kypriades in support, also in uniform. In addition, the dock contained Alexandros Zannas of the Red Cross, Ghedeon Angellopoulos, Condouriotis, Dora Nikotsara and Spiro Tzavellas. On trial as well were the Pateli brothers and Tzantanis, the crew of the caique which brought Lieutenant Ribolzi's patrol to Antiparos. For most of the defendants the charges were of espionage or aiding escapers. Atkinson's charges included the murder of Lieutenant Ribolzi.[20] Atkinson is reported by witnesses to have been optimistic that he would not be condemned to death, though he will have known through the prison grapevine that just two days earlier two men, the New Zealand Private John Stuart and a civilian Tony Handkinson, who was in some unknown way working with Stuart, had been shot at Kokkinia for killing an Italian soldier during their capture in 1942.[21] Atkinson had shared a cell with Stuart and the news of his death must have been intensely alarming, for Atkinson was charged with the same crime.

One of the accused, Constantinides (alias George Stevens), made a set of revealing and accusatory statements to the Italians, which he later retracted. However, the damage was done, but not to him as he was sentenced to just eight years imprisonment.[22] Over the two weeks of the trial, Atkinson's notebook, captured on Antiparos, was filed in evidence against him and against the members of the underground he mentioned in it. One note reminded Atkinson to expressly thank Zannas for the information he had provided to Cairo about Athens rail and shipping movements, and for unnamed acts of sabotage he had either carried out or ordered. The evidence was damning. So damning, and so unlikely in the hands of a British officer, that a rumour briefly circulated in Athens that Atkinson was a double agent for the Axis. Perhaps equally painful, for Atkinson and Spiro Tzavellas at least, was that the man responsible for bringing the Italian patrol to Antiparos in the first place was not in the dock alongside them. In January 1943, Harry, slippery as ever, was in Cairo, trying to get permission to put as much distance between himself, the war and his complicated love life as he could.

Faced with irrefutable written evidence, Atkinson must have decided that to deny his actions and plans was pointless, and probably even irritating to the three men who held his life in their hands. So, when asked by the prosecutor Major Porgio if he had met Zannas on previous visits to Athens he admitted he had. This openness did not play well with his Athenian audience: 'public opinion about his dealings did not change in the least … people also believed and said that Atkinson only behaved the way he did hoping to get a lighter sentence'.[23] Italian military tribunals may have lacked a jury, but this one did not lack thoroughness. Detailed accounts of major trials were preserved, stored in Italy and captured by the Allies after the war. These show that each piece of evidence was examined in detail and cross-referenced with others. The records that have reached the National Archives at Kew show that there was no presumption of guilt, and that evidence was tested for corroboration from other sources. In one case, in the trial of Private William Ditchburn of 25th New Zealand Battalion, a note about radio schedules found concealed in his belt, convicted him of espionage while in civilian clothing, but as he had not succeeded in his aim of getting the note to Cairo, he was sentenced to imprisonment rather than death.[24] Ditchburn's three co-accused were acquitted as the court decided that there was no evidence that they knew anything about the note. In an odd bureaucratic addition, Ditchburn was ordered to pay the expenses of his trial, though from what resources is not shown. The trial of Captains Savage and McNabb, alongside fourteen Greeks, contains sixteen narrative foolscap pages of facts and law. Some of Magaldi's trials might have been kangaroo courts, but the major ones were not.

But General Magaldi, the Beast, was determined to see Atkinson die anyway. The trial lasted four days. Magaldi dismissed two of Atkinson's defending officers for taking up too much of his time with their arguments. It may be significant that the detailed report of Atkinson's trial, is not to be found in the Advocate General's records at Kew. On 18 February, Magaldi condemned eleven of the accused to death. Atkinson headed the list, seconded by Kypriades. Also condemned were Alexis Zannas, Spiro Tzavellas, three Pateli brothers and Francis Tzantanis, (all part of the crew of Ribolzi's caique), Kostas Arvinatopoulos, George Kapoutsos and Dora Nikotsara. Nikotsara was invited to plead for clemency, but with magnificent courage she flatly refused to do so. Fortunately for her some friends did so on her behalf, and the tribunal, perhaps revealing some innate Italian sexism masquerading as chivalry, commuted her sentence to imprisonment. Zannas did plead for clemency and his sentence was also commuted, possibly because of a rumoured large bribe. Kondouriotis was sentenced to thirty years in prison in Italy.

Once the verdicts were passed, General Magaldi lost little time. His standing orders were to refer death sentences to the General Military Prosecuting Office in Rome for review. It was highly likely that this office would defer the actual killing of Atkinson, as it had done with another death sentence, Captain MacAskie's, who survived the war. But Magaldi was having none of that – Atkinson would die, and soon. An appeal for clemency was filed for the Pateli brothers[25] and Dora Nikotsara, but Magaldi was intent on not letting Atkinson escape his net. Atkinson had just the weekend in which to bring himself to terms with his fate. The verdict must have come as a terrible shock – reports from Athens at the time tell that he was expecting to be imprisoned, not shot, for few Allied prisoners were actually killed by the Italians, then or later. Atkinson would not have been human if he hadn't spent much of the week contemplating a whole set of what-ifs. What if he had followed Craig's advice and allowed himself to be captured without resistance that night? Like Craig and Redpath, he would have been judged a prisoner of war and would now be in a camp in Italy. What if Craig had followed his advice, and used the full force of his and Redpath's powerful Thompsons to fight the Italian patrol? With another twenty men a short distance away, they might well have prevailed, perhaps taken the survivors prisoner, stolen the *Despoina*, loaded her up with food and fuel and sailed as fast as they could for Alexandria, to return to a hero's welcome. What if he had simply not volunteered to come back to Greece at all? He might have fought out the war in his RASC company, with a reasonably high chance of survival, returned to Greece afterwards to find Effi, and lived a long and happy life. At least, he must have thought, he had made sure that Jim Craig and Redpath had escaped his dreadful fate. He might have felt bitter rage at Harry Grammatikakis, whose antics had brought the Italians down on their heads in the first place. And what if he had taken swifter action to move from Antiparos to Despotiko? Ribolzi's patrol would have found an empty house and perhaps left. Ah, Ribolzi. Did Atkinson think about that unfortunate man's fate? It is highly likely that in his short RASC career, with only a few days under fire on Crete, Atkinson had never in fact taken a man's life. To kill another human being is a terrible thing. Atkinson had not just killed a man but had killed him from three feet away while he lay on the floor at his feet, deliberately aiming at his beating heart, pulling the trigger, watching the man's body flinch as the heavy bullet sank into it, and seeing the man's blood flooding onto the floor at his feet. It must have been clear to Atkinson that it was that act, much more than his work for SOE, which was the reason for his own rapidly approaching death. Did Atkinson regret Ribolzi? It was his duty to fight and kill the enemy, and Ribolzi certainly fell into that category. But had it truly been necessary? Would it have been better to run, or to surrender? Was the whole affair worth a life, indeed now many lives, since half a dozen of his companions were heading to their own deaths because of him? Did Atkinson feel guilty about Ribolzi's death? Did he feel that it was some form of justice to forfeit his own life in return? We have no letters from Atkinson to tell us what was in his mind on that last weekend of his life. While the record tells us that his next of kin was his fiancée Josephine Wiscombe, in her English red brick terraced house in Yeovilton, we don't know if he was thinking of her, or of Effi Ioannou. Those last three sleepless nights can only have been a tortured time of regrets and thoughts of other possible lives that he might have lived.

The cold bright Greek dawn on Monday 22 February brought a scene which was becoming familiar in Athens. Tzavellas, Kypriades and one of the Pateli brothers were marched out and tied to posts in the grounds of the Kokkinia prison by a squad of Italian soldiers. Atkinson, unable to walk or even stand, was carried out and tied to a prison chair. The soldiers, who had doubtless been well-briefed on the killing of Lieutenant Ribolzi, lined up ten metres from their victims. A priest was ready by the condemned men, though we don't know what they asked for or were given. The men must have had bone dry mouths, hammering hearts and faltering knees. A later eye-witness report of the killing told, though, that they showed no outward signs of the dread or panic that must have been pouring through their adrenal systems. It is probable that Atkinson was the first to be shot – as the leader, the most culpable, and the only officer in the group. His body was thrown into a shallow grave in the 3rd Cemetery of Athens,[26] and moved after the war to the Phaleron War Cemetery in Athens.

Atkinson's story was over. We don't know if he knew what had happened to *Triumph*. In January 1942, there might have been four reasons why she would have failed to return to the rendezvous in Despotiko Bay on 9 January – weather, breakdown, sudden new orders or knowledge that Coney Island had been 'blown'. A fifth possible reason was enemy action. In any case, Atkinson was already a prisoner by the time the rendezvous came and went.

But what had happened to *Triumph*? For eighty years the answer to that question was a matter of speculation, until one summer's day in 2023.

Chapter 15

Missing, Believed Sunk

Triumph was due back at Alexandria on 14 January 1942. When she did not appear as expected, each day that passed carried a growing burden of dread. *Triumph*'s crew were not just colleagues, but close friends of every man aboard *Medway*, especially Sammy Woods, who had lived with, and led them, for a year. After a few days it was clear that she was unlikely to return, for if she was still heading home, she would have signalled to explain her tardiness. For a few more days the possibility existed that her crew might have been captured after an unsuccessful battle (*Cachalot*'s crew had been taken prisoner just five months earlier). If that had happened, news of it would have filtered through to *Medway* by one route or another within a few days. And then for a few days more there was the possibility, more remote, that she had sunk but that some men had escaped. That too happened, though usually with no more than a handful of survivors.

On 21 January, with *Triumph* a week overdue and no claims of an action emanating from the Axis, Raw and Sammy Woods wearily accepted the most likely outcome – that *Triumph* had been lost with no survivors. Formal letters were drafted and sent out to the relatives of her crew – mostly parents, and a few wives. Pay was stopped and war widows' pensions begun. Sammy began the awful task of handwriting sixty-four letters of sympathy, made more awful by the very personal nature of his own sense of loss of people he knew very well indeed. Raw took on the even worse task of writing to Midshipman George Waterall's parents. He had allowed Waterall to join *Triumph* for a few months because she was a crack boat, heading home, and at the least risk of being lost. It was bad enough to lose her crew, but to lose a man who was barely more than a child, and at the start of what was looking like a first class career, demanded a personal note, he wrote: 'I cannot mention the name of the submarine in this letter, but she was one of the best, if not the best, in the flotilla, and her officers without exception were amongst the finest that I had'.[1] Personal effects were packaged up and sent home by surface mail around the Cape of Good Hope (and we know that these arrived for many relatives today still have them). And then life went on.

Loss of a submarine had already become commonplace in the Royal Navy by the start of 1942, and losses would continue until the very end of the war. Britain lost eighteen more submarines in 1942, fourteen in 1943, five in 1944, and its last, one boat, in 1945. Including *Triumph*'s, submariner losses after January 1942 totalled 1,481 men.[2] Death in action was not a surprise in itself, but what was uniquely painful about deaths in submarines was the black hole left by two questions: where and how? Despite the very large numbers of men and women killed in the war, the location and reason for each death is remarkably well-known, for units and comrades who survived usually reported with precision what happened to a man and where it happened. Men killed on land were usually buried with some visible marker. Men killed in surface ships had no grave, but the exact positions of their ships were usually known to within a tenth of a mile.[3] After the war the Commonwealth War Graves Commission picked up where it had paused in 1939 and began to search for and re-inter every man and woman lost, no matter where they were. But a submarine on patrol made a particular point of *not* reporting her position, sometimes for weeks at a time. If a boat transmitted a signal home its bearings could be triangulated by the enemy to reveal her precise location, so the rule was to transmit only in exceptional circumstances. A submarine was usually given an operating area exclusive to her for a week or even a fortnight. Her commanding officer was left to choose where in that area to hunt, without reference to home or reporting of his decision. So, when a boat failed to return from patrol, the families of her crew knew just that she had been lost 'somewhere in the x or y sea'. And often no one knew *why* she had been lost, or even on what day of the patrol. Even that minimal level of information was withheld until long after 1945, since the navy classified submarine operations as Most Secret. *Triumph*'s last set of operational orders gave her almost the whole of the southern Aegean Sea as her operating area after dropping Atkinson at Antiparos, an area of seven million acres, for a boat whose wreck would occupy just one quarter of an acre of seabed.

The size of this black hole was a source of prolonged pain for all the relatives of *Triumph*'s crew. Indeed, it was the inspiration for the research that led to this book. After 1945, the Royal Navy did make some efforts to fill the hole, at least partially. With the assumption that most of the submarine losses were due either to an enemy action or from a boat striking a sea mine, staff officers combed captured German operating records and war diaries to see if they could join up an Axis report of an attack on a submarine with the time, date and location of a possible or probable loss. This work led to a few mysteries being either wholly or partially resolved, with a 'probable' attribution of cause, place and time, but even today, some two dozen lost boats remain completely lost.

In *Triumph*'s case there were two reasons for the navy to make more than average efforts to join up the dots of her loss. First, Sammy Woods ended the war as a senior submariner – he retired as Flag Officer Submarines with a knighthood – and was able to focus the staff's research more intently on his old boat. The second reason was that the father of one *Triumph*'s officers was himself a retired naval officer who was able to use his personal network to bring gentle pressure to bear on the question. With these two spurs to action the Admiralty gave slightly more attention to *Triumph*'s fate than to that of her lost sisters. In 1952, a commander was despatched to re-visit the German staff records. He partially succeeded. In the war diary of the German Naval Staff[4] he found three references to the sighting of a submarine in the Aegean in the first ten days of January 1942. The first of these was a possible sighting of a periscope from a shore guard post. The second was the possible sighting of a torpedo track. Both of these may have been *Triumph*, or may have been sightings of logs, dolphins, or just imagined, for it is easy for a lookout to see what he is looking for, even if it is not there.

The third reference, though, left no room for imagination. The German Naval Staff war diary contains the report of an unsuccessful submarine attack on a cargo barge being towed by a tug around the tip of Cape Sounio, on 9 January 1942. This unequivocal report is supported by local reports that the attack was evidenced not just by torpedo tracks but included the detonation of a torpedo on the shoreline of the Cape. A Mark VIII torpedo warhead contained well over 600 pounds of high explosive and was generally set to run at a depth of eight feet. Hitting the rocks on the shore of Cape Sounio, at eight feet underwater, the warhead set off an enormous explosion, easily visible for miles around. With no other Allied submarine tasked to operate within 100 miles of Cape Sounio, the torpedo that detonated can only have been fired by Johnny Huddart in *Triumph*. However, at the time, the secrecy around submarine operations meant that civilians, even next of kin, were not permitted to know that only *Triumph* could have fired the torpedo. There is only a single source for the information on *Triumph*'s operating area for her last patrol, the Naval Staff History of the Submarine War, published for internal Royal Navy use in about 1950.[5] This book was classified 'Confidential' – one level below 'Secret' – and therefore completely inaccessible to *Triumph*'s next of kin, no matter who they were. It was only declassified in the 1980s, and today the only copy accessible to the public is the one held by the National Archives in Kew. These circumstances combined to hide *Triumph*'s last torpedo strike behind a veil of secrecy, which in turn meant that for forty years the *Triumph* families lived in their own black hole of sadness and unknowing. This experience of total loss is more or less unique to the submarine service. Thanks to the patient and persistent work of the Commonwealth War Graves Commission the vast majority of the relatives of men lost in the war know where and when their man was lost, and for the most part, exactly where he is now interred, so that they can visit, grieve and say goodbye.

We now know that the 9 January torpedo was *Triumph*, making her last attack, but that knowledge does not in itself answer the questions of where or how she sank. There are three possible reasons for her loss. First, and by far the most likely, was that somewhere between Cape Sounio and Antiparos she struck a sea mine. We met mines in an earlier chapter, but they are probably worth another look. In essence a sea mine was a sealed steel globe floating in the water column at a given depth, anchored by a thin wire to a heavy steel sinker on the seabed. Inside the globe was an explosive charge stored in something about the size of an oil barrel. Mines had a choice of detonation triggers. The simplest was a set of soft lead horns containing a glass vial of electrically conductive liquid. Hit the horn and you break the glass, the liquid flows onto two charged contacts and completes a circuit, which detonates the mine. A variation on this primitive (1914–1918) invention was to replace the lead horn with a spring-loaded horn. Any movement of the horn, in any direction, completed the firing circuit. Both of these relied on the ship or submarine actually colliding with the mine. The Axis extended the trigger range up and down by fitting some mines with long magnetically sensitive wires above and below the mine, to increase its detection range from six feet to around fifty feet. Yet more sophisticated mines could be triggered by the magnetic field of a large steel object passing by without physical contact, or by the sound of a passing ship. Some mines were laid on the seabed instead of floating in the water column, but these could only be used in shallow waters. Floating mines were set to float at a predetermined depth. A shallow-floating mine, say six feet underwater, was aimed at a surface ship. A deeper mine, floating at about thirty feet, was set for a submarine. A submarine could usually pass quite safely below a moored floating mine. Malta was surrounded by moored mine fields which were regularly passed by submarines dived at 300 feet.

The explosive charges in mines ranged from 220 pounds up to half a tonne. A large ship would often survive a single mine strike, though might have to be towed to a harbour for repairs. There are many incidents of warships returning home missing bows or sterns which had been completely blown off by a mine. Submarines, though, are designed to sink, and are not large. In order to dive, a submarine on the surface has to be designed with a very small margin of buoyancy, small enough for its buoyancy to be reduced to nil at will (when buoyancy is nil the submarine will sink below the surface where she controls her depth by using underwater wings at the bow and stern called hydroplanes). On the surface it takes very little damage for that small reserve of buoyancy to vanish, and when it does, the submarine will sink like a stone. Underwater, a submarine has no reserve of buoyancy at all (by definition) and an even smaller amount of damage will set her into a fatal dive to the bottom.

During the entire Second World War, there is just a single incident in which a submarine struck a mine and survived to tell the tale. With one of those ironies thrown up by history, that lucky submarine was *Triumph*, not in 1941 but in 1939. Patrolling at night on the surface off the island of Heligoland (250 miles due east of Hull) *Triumph* struck a large mine floating on the surface.[6] Later analysis concluded that the mine had over 1,000 pounds of explosive, making it one the largest mines used in the war. By chance she struck the mine almost exactly head-on. The detonation amputated the first eighteen feet of *Triumph*'s bows, but by some lucky chance failed to penetrate her pressure hull, whose forward end was another ten feet back. *Triumph* was unable to dive but was able to move under her own power and stay afloat, and two days later she arrived at Harwich for repairs. That time she was extraordinarily lucky, but it was commonly accepted by everyone in the submarine service that a mine strike was usually fatal.

Just a week before sailing for Operation Isinglass, *Triumph*'s crew received a painful reminder of the danger of mines when *Perseus* failed to return from a patrol off the west coast of Greece. No claims were made by the Axis, leading to the obvious conclusion that she had been sunk by a mine. Remarkably, there was a single survivor from *Perseus*, Stoker Capes, who found his way back to Alexandria in one of Michael Parish's Levant Schooner Squadron caiques several months later. Capes reported that *Perseus* had struck a mine at night while charging batteries on the surface. With all her internal watertight doors open (submarines only shut these doors during a depth charge attack), she flooded with terrifying speed and her bow hit the bottom 170 feet below in twenty seconds, before her stern had even left the surface. Capes was in the stokers' mess, the aft-most compartment in the boat. He and his fellow stokers managed to shut their watertight door before the wall of flooding sea reached it. Sealed into their mess on the bottom they prepared to escape through the small hatch provided for just that situation. Capes was the only man to survive the escape. When the wreck of *Perseus* was discovered and inspected in 1997 the hole blown by the mine could be seen clearly – just a three-foot long crack about six inches wide.

The waters around Malta, Sicily and Tripoli were occupied by a web of mine fields, but in 1941 the waters of the Aegean were relatively lightly mined. So, for about fifty years after 1941 other possible fates could not be ruled out.

The second-most likely reason for *Triumph*'s disappearance was simply a fatal accident. When dived, a submarine is buoyant and can keep her depth only by using the small hydroplanes – underwater wings – set in pairs at her bow and stern. These need a flow of water over their surfaces to operate, and that means a submarine, like a shark, cannot stand still.[7] *Triumph*'s class of submarines was designed for a maximum operating depth of around 400 feet, with a likely crush-depth of 900 feet, less if a boat was old, or had been severely stressed by past depth chargings, as *Triumph* had on frequent occasions. There was therefore a risk that a dived boat might experience a failure of her hydroplane control system which would set her into an unrecoverable dive to her crush depth. Hydroplane control failures were not uncommon, especially in a boat which had been in constant use for over a year and suffered multiple explosive impacts from near-miss depth charges. In the absence of any other information, there was a possibility, perhaps small but not zero, that a hydroplane failure, or a failure in some other of her critical systems, had simply caused *Triumph* to lose depth control and sink. Added to this small possibility was the risk of an internal fire, or the gassing of her crew by chlorine after a battery accident, or a torpedo malfunction. After mines and accidents, the list of possible causes grows smaller and less likely. It was distantly conceivable that *Triumph* was sunk by enemy action, but that the action had gone unrecorded; it was probably this possibility that prompted the second look by the Admiralty in 1952.

The mystery of what had happened to her hung around the families of *Triumph*'s crew like an impenetrable black mist for two generations. When the Cape Sounio torpedo attack came to light after the Staff History was declassified it gave a possible, but not certain, datum point for one end of the mystery. When the Antiparos files were declassified, they gave a datum point for the other end of the puzzle. *Triumph* was due to arrive at Despotiko Bay on the night of 9/10 January. Her normal operating procedure of spending the day before a beach landing inspecting the beach in daylight was not required, for Craig and Redpath were in occupation at Antiparos and would transmit a coded light signal that the bay was safe. Then, as now, the Royal Navy prided itself on its punctuality and reliability – if Johnny Huddart said he would surface off Despotiko at 1.00 am on 10 January, then he would be there at that time and date.[8] We can therefore work back from Despotiko to Cape Sounio to see if the time and distance calculation fits the time gap between the two datum points – the morning torpedo attack and the midnight arrival at Despotiko.

It does, exactly. The track from Cape Sounio to the southern entrance of Despotiko Bay is seventy-six nautical miles. Sunset on 9 January 1941 was at 5.21 pm. *Triumph* would have planned to surface at 7.00 pm, well after the grey half-light of Marine Twilight had passed into starlight, to sail fast on the surface and arrive off Despotiko at about midnight. Six hours on the surface at ten knots, heading a half knot set of the current, would cover sixty miles of her track. In the hours between the torpedo attack and sunset, six hours at a standard three and a half knots, less half a knot for adverse currents, would add eighteen miles of distance covered. Lieutenant Alf Peterkin, crouched over his tiny chart table in *Triumph*'s control room, would have done the maths and advised Johhny Huddart that they must turn southeast from the area of Sounio no later than 1.00 pm, to arrive comfortably on time off Despotiko at midnight with an hour in hand.

Calculation of *Triumph*'s likely track plan did not, though, answer the question of where she might actually have sunk, for two reasons. The first reason is that a submarine sailing dived at three and a half knots is very much a prisoner of underwater currents and tidal flows. Over a track of eighteen miles these might push her two or three miles off the obvious planned track, and it would make more sense simply to allow her to sail off track and wait for the turn of a tide to push her back on, than to try and make the exact track all of the time. Second, even narrowing down her likely movements to a box seventy-six miles long and six miles wide (three miles either way) still leaves 220,000 acres of seabed to search, and even that area depends on all of the earlier assumptions being correct. It is entirely possible that something came up to alter *Triumph*'s planned track on 9 January, or that Huddart decided for some reason to miss the 9 January rendezvous and make a 10 January rendezvous instead, since that possibility had been accounted for in the plan.

By the 1980s, the *Triumph* families had largely given up hope that the mystery of her position would ever be solved. The author began searching the records at the National Archives at Kew but had no resources to extend that search into the waters south of Cape Sounio. One man, though, did. A Greek diver and underwater explorer[9] began to follow *Triumph*'s footprints in 1990. Years of desk research, dragging of sonars through the Aegean and of diving on likely targets followed, without success. Until, one day in 2023, the diver and his daughter lowered a new and more powerful remotely operated vehicle (ROV) into the sea off the island of Saint George, ten miles southwest of Cape Sounio. Their target was a long thin echo on the seabed which they had first detected many years earlier but had discarded as a possible *Triumph* because it was some forty feet too short to be a T-class submarine.

Seven hundred feet below their dive boat the ROV drifted down into the black. At this depth no light penetrates, even in an Aegean flooded with clear Greek sunshine, but the ROV's on-board searchlights sliced through the permanent night of the cold black water as it swam towards the target. A moment later the conning tower of a submarine swam into sight on the monitors far above. The ROV's pilot had to struggle to keep it still against the constant seabed current, only one knot, but enough to drive the delicate machine against the wreck and permanently damage it. The wreck, heeled over a few degrees to starboard on the seabed, was coated with just a layer of marine life, giving it a stippled look but not obscuring its key features in any way. Forward of the conning tower was the gun platform, with its four-inch single-barrelled gun in the stowed position, fore and aft in its small rotating sponson. A few feet below the gun platform a single torpedo, the midships starboard Mark VIII, was seen sticking out of its tube by about four feet. Its presence was one of the unique distinctive features of the first batch of T-class submarines that marks her out as *Triumph*. On the wreck's bridge the ROV showed her bridge wheel, never used in practice as she was always steered from the control room, and the voice pipes down which Douglas-Don, Peterkin and Janvrin had spent hundreds of night hours passing commands to the helmsman. At the back of her bridge, the conning tower curves down to the casing deck like an American 1940s automobile – another of the distinctive features of an early T-class boat. Sadly, her name plate, mounted on each side of the conning tower, is completely buried under marine growth. Astern of her twin propellors her aft hydroplane is set in the horizontal position, showing that she was making no effort to dive or rise at the moment that she sank. Her death, however it came, was sudden. A few feet forward, the upper hatch of her aft escape compartment swam into view, firmly shut: no attempt at escape was made, or even possible given the 700 feet of water above her.[10] Forward of the gun platform the story changes dramatically. Where they were expecting to see *Triumph*'s forward pressure hull and casing, the ROV team found … nothing. Instead, the wreck's deck plating folds down to the seabed, and to empty space. On the seabed itself are the remains of the lower quadrant of a pressure hull. Everything above that and forward of it had simply vanished.

The wreck is unequivocally *Triumph*. All the remaining visible features tied in to a batch 1 T-class submarine, and the only T-boat that could have sunk in, or anywhere near, that location was *Triumph*, whose known movements on her last day also tied exactly into the location. But what had happened on that last day? At last, with almost every piece of the complicated jigsaw of her story assembled, it might be possible to reconstruct the last day of *Triumph* and her people in detail.

Chapter 16

Triumph's Last Day

With the deductions from the last chapter made, we can enter the mind of *Triumph*'s navigating officer, Lieutenant Alf Peterkin, to work out *Triumph*'s probable planned track from her patrol position off Sounio to the beach at Antiparos, with some confidence. A glance at the map shows that she had four choices of track from Sounio to Despotiko Bay. The northern track option passed between the islands of Kea and Kythnos. Two middle options passed between Kythnos and Serifos, and Serifos and Siphnos. The southern track option passed south of Siphnos.

What the map does not show is that the three northern tracks all meet a pronounced current, a 'set', heading westwards out of the central Aegean. At a steady speed of around 1 knot. A modern ship or submarine would not be concerned by a slight current but *Triumph*'s speed when dived was only 3.5 knots, making a 1 knot current 'on the nose' an issue because it cut her speed of advance by a third. The set seems to fade to zero south of Siphnos. A set matters even to a surfaced submarine. While *Triumph*'s two big diesels would propel her at a maximum speed of around 15 knots if pushed, pushing her was unwise (engines break if stressed and hers had been in constant use for over a year), so Huddart would not have wanted to make more than ten knots on the surface, if possible.

In the circumstances, *Triumph* planned to use only one main engine for propulsion, using the other (clutched to the big electric motor), as a generator to pump charge into her batteries while she steamed south. With one engine working at a comfortable rate, her speed was about ten knots. Working back from our deduced arrival time a few miles off Antiparos, some time before midnight on 9 January, gives a track distance from Sounio of seventy-six miles. The northern tracks are a few miles shorter, but have that adverse set.

The most southerly track offered another benefit – it needed just one course change, midway between Siphnos and the island of Kimolos to the south. The southern track also has no small islets or islands to avoid along the route. Submarine navigation was hard enough at the best of times, especially at night, to make a simple track without obstacles more attractive than one with several course changes that jinked around islands in the dark without radar. I believe that Johnny Huddart chose the southern track.

Triumph planned to surface about ninety minutes after sunset, when the half-light of marine twilight had faded fully to black. Sunset on 9 January 1942 was at 5.21 pm local time, so *Triumph*'s plan was to surface at 7.00 pm, when she would be about due west of the north end of Serifos. This would put her close enough to get a reasonable visual chart fix before firing up her diesels to sail at ten knots on one engine while charging her batteries on the other.

On the surface, with power now freely available, the cook, Leading Chef Cornelius O'Brien, would have time to make breakfast, for 7.30 pm, and lunch for 10.00–10.30. Her passage plan gave her about nine hours dived at three knots (allowing for a net half-knot of track offset for the current) – twenty-seven miles – and five hours on the surface at ten knots – fifty miles – to arrive south of Antiparos at midnight for her run in to the beach, with a little time in hand. By midnight her crew would be fed, rested, and ready for five hours at Diving Stations (action stations in submarine speak) while she brought the escapers aboard. After leaving Antiparos she would then have a late rum ration ('Up Spirits') as she slid out to sea, serve dinner around the watch change from 3.30 am to 4.30 am, diving by 5.00 am with a full battery.

Dawn on Friday 9 January 1942, found *Triumph* sailing at periscope depth on a course of about due west towards a well-known route for merchant ship traffic sailing out of Piraeus for one of Greece's many islands. Johnny Huddart was unhappy. This was only his second active service war patrol (he had spent his career as a submarine commanding officer doing short stints in boats for training and deliveries). On his first he had sunk a single ship – a small tug in the harbour of Suda Bay. *Triumph* was a crack boat with a year-long record of success against ships large and small all over the Mediterranean. This day was Huddart's last on offensive patrol – his orders were to sail to Antiparos that night, pick up whatever party of escapers he found there, and return quietly to Alexandria, attacking nothing smaller than an Italian cruiser en route. His navigating officer, Alf Peterkin, had just left the wardroom with the track chart for the journey to Antiparos, which must start no later than about midday. Huddart had just one morning to bring back a proper kill, and his best best chance of finding one in daylight, was to lurk off the traffic concentration point south of Cape Sounio and hope that something worth a torpedo would sail past his sights.

This was familiar ground to *Triumph*'s crew, and they knew that merchant traffic always kept very close inshore, no more than a few hundred metres off the rocks. Sailing that close to land made it harder for an attacking submarine to develop a target picture (because she would have to take sightings through the periscope against a shore background). It also allowed a ship to put herself aground if she was hit but not sunk. Another advantage was that near the ancient temple of Poseidon, a set of three concrete bunkers manned by sentries gave her many more eyes to see the periscope of an attacking submarine. Finally, of course, if she did sink the crew had less far to swim ashore.

Huddart's plan was rewarded. At about 8.00 am the officer of the watch sighted a small tug, the *Taxiarchos*, towing a large lighter eastwards close inshore. We know what happened at this point because the Greek dive team did not just discover *Triumph,* it also found three Mark VIII torpedoes on the seabed a few hundred yards south of Cape Sounio. The Mark VIII torpedo was powered by a small diesel engine which used an internal compressed air vessel to fuel its combustion cycle. The engine ran until the air vessel emptied, after which the torpedo (designed to be very slightly negatively buoyant) sank to the seabed. The range of a Mark VIII was therefore a function of the air pressure in its air tank and of the speed at which it was set to run. Speeds were always set to forty-four knots – the maximum practical speed for the size of engine – to make the aiming calculation easier and generate more hits. At this speed, with the air vessels charged to 2,400 pounds per square inch, *Triumph*'s torpedoes could run for about 3.5 nautical miles. Each torpedo's maximum range varied very slightly, with slight variations in its air vessel pressure, and the state of its engine and propellors. The presence of three exhausted torpedoes, lying on the seabed off Cape Sounio, tells us that they were fired at maximum range. Three ran out of air before reaching either *Taxiarchos* or the shoreline. The fourth missed the tug but hit the foreshore where it exploded with enormous and visible force.

The three exhausted torpedoes lie in a parallel line on a heading of 350 degrees – just a little west of due north. A Mark VIII torpedo ran straight on the track on which it was fired, which means that the heading of the torpedoes today, is the heading of *Triumph* when they were fired. That means Huddart turned his submarine from her westerly course onto a northerly course in order to fire at *Taxiarchos*. We can extrapolate back from the course and run-distance of the four torpedoes by measuring three and a half miles on the reciprocal course of 170 degrees to deduce *Triumph*'s firing point. This shows that Huddart fired his four torpedoes from just to the north of a single line of mines revealed by Italian mining records after the war. Huddart had sailed *Triumph* inshore of the line of mines on his port side because to have sailed outside the line would have put the shipping lane out of range (which is why the mines were laid where they were).

The range was extreme, which prompts the question: why did Huddart not try to move closer before firing to increase the chance of a hit? When one plots out the attack on a chart the reason becomes clear – the distances involved prevented him. *Taxiarchos* would have come into sight only after she emerged from the narrow channel that separates Cape Sounio from the islet of Patroklos (in 1942 called San Giorgio). Sailing at around six to eight knots (she was towing a 1,000 tonne lighter) it would have taken *Taxiarchos* just twelve minutes to sail from the channel, past Sounio, and reach the next channel that passes north between the long island of Makronisos and the east coast of Cape Sounio. During that twelve minutes, Huddart, dived at three knots, had to squeeze in three periscope sightings to generate a firing angle on the 'fruit machine', turn north, ready four tubes, and fire. When adding the three more minutes it took for the torpedoes to reach *Taxiarchos,* Huddart had just nine minutes to set up his attack. There was no time to close the range – if Huddart had turned inshore to get nearer, *Taxiarchos* would have been past and sailing away out of range by the time he could fire. To continue the attack from there, *Triumph* would have had to chase *Taxiarchos* from astern, with a speed advantage of just one knot. At that speed, *Triumph* would have exhausted her battery within an hour and been forced to surface in full daylight a few miles off Cape Sounio, which would have been suicidal. So, the attack was necessarily rushed, and it is no surprise that once it had failed, *Triumph* had to let *Taxiarchos* go.

The three torpedoes on the seabed are separated laterally by a few hundred yards. From this it is possible to deduce that Huddart fired them 'on the swing', which means that he fired while he was turning *Triumph* to starboard to bring her torpedo tubes to bear on *Taxiarchos*' track from west to east, or left to right, from Huddart's perspective. An attack 'on the swing' was known to be unreliable for aim but was a way of getting a shot off when a target suddenly presented itself and would be past and gone if a submarine invested time in lining up for a more deliberate shot. Just south of *Triumph* was the line of mines identified by the post-war declaration, which shows that it contained 120 mines laid sixty metres apart at a depth of twelve metres, intended to sink a dived submarine. The mines were small – only ninety pounds of high explosive each – but large enough to crack the pressure hull and sink a boat.

The Cape Sounio minefield was laid by the Italian minelayer *Barletta* on 6 December 1941, just a month before, which begs an important question. Did *Triumph* know they were there? The staff of the Mediterranean Fleet did know the exact locations of many mine fields, because their positions were signalled by radio in codes which the codebreakers at Bletchley Park could break. The positions of known minefield were distributed in signals with a 'QB' designation, a few of which have been preserved in the archive at Kew. The process of making the radio intercept, enciphering the intercepted (coded) five letter groups, sending the enciphered intercept to Bletchley, waiting for Bletchley to crack it, and then disseminating the decrypt in a secure way back to the Mediterranean, was slow. If *Barletta*'s mine-lay order at the start of December was sent by radio, it is quite possible that a decrypt had not reached *Triumph* when she left Alexandria just twenty days after the lay. If it was sent by Italian fleet radio, it would not have been read by the Allies because they had lost access to Italian naval codes several months before. It is also quite likely that the mine-lay order was not sent by radio at all. *Barletta* was probably based in Piraeus at the time, and the order might well have originated just ten miles away in Athens, and been carried overland, never touching the airwaves.

Whether or not Huddart knew the field was there from a QB signal, it is likely that he saw it on *Triumph*'s mine-detecting sonar unit as he sailed his boat west towards Sounio that morning. The mine detecting unit was referred to twice in writing that has survived the war, once in a patrol report and the second time by inference in a letter home from Robert Douglas-Don. It was a standard fit for Batch 1 T-class submarines. We also know that it worked reasonably well because patrol reports by other T-class boats refer to its successful use in action. *Triumph* approached her 'lurking' position off Cape Sounio from the east that morning at periscope depth – the same depth as the mines. An approach from that direction would have presented the line of mines at an oblique angle to *Triumph,* as an almost continuous line of pin-prick contacts on the cathode ray tube of the mine detecting unit. Other circumstances tend to corroborate the deduction that Huddart could see the Cape Sounio minefield. The standard operating procedure after a torpedo attack, was to reverse course and sail away from the firing point – the 'datum' – to open deep water as quickly as was consistent with remaining quiet and preserving battery power to frustrate a counterattack. The torpedo firing datum was marked by thirty-foot wide 'splashes' which could bring violent retribution from escorting ships or aircraft. It was best to clear off and out as quickly as possible.

The three exhausted torpedoes lie on a 350-degree heading, which means that *Triumph* was on that track when she fired them. From there, her normal evasion route would be south, away from the enemy and into clear, deep water. The Mark VIII had a facility which allowed it to be turned ninety degrees immediately after firing. This might have allowed Huddart to fire his torpedoes northwards while sailing westwards, but the system was considered by submarine commanders to be unreliable, and complicated the aiming calculation, so was almost never used. Even if he had used it, Huddart's evasion course would still have been south. But, south from the firing datum would have taken *Triumph* right across the mine-line. If Huddart could see the mine line on his sonar, he would instead have evaded west, parallel to the mine line. Greek sources report that *Taxiarchos* was escorted by a patrolling aircraft, which Huddart saw as he plotted the attack. What he did not know was that the aircraft was unarmed. Huddart would have assumed that it was armed and should be kept at a distance, which may be another reason that he kept at extreme range from Cape Sounio, because at periscope depth, *Triumph* was clearly visible to a passing aircraft as a large black shadow in the water. The aircraft immediately saw *Triumph*'s firing splash, and Huddart knew that it would close to attack within a couple of minutes. He therefore dived to eighty feet (to gain concealment, and he had 400 feet of water to work in), speeded up a little to 4.5 knots, and retired from the scene westwards with the mine-line to his port side.

The standard operating procedure after an attack was to evade at speed for thirty to sixty minutes to put some distance between the boat and her firing splash. An hour at 4.5 knots would take Triumph comfortably past the west end of the Cape Sounio mine-line. *Triumph*'s batteries would be starting to heat up from the high rate of discharge, so Huddart slowed down after ninety minutes and sailed cautiously on westwards, searching for other mines on her sonar and for new targets. With an aircraft patrolling behind her, and the likelihood that more aircraft or anti-submarine corvettes might appear from the north, Huddart kept *Triumph*'s speed up for longer than normal, knowing that his run would take him away from the search and towards water in which she might get lucky and encounter a new target sailing south from Piraeus.

Triumph ended her evasive run a little southwest of that small island of Patroklos off Cape Sounio. At about 10.30 am Johnny Huddart and Alf Peterkin crouched over the small chart table in the control room with a pair of brass dividers measuring off distances. Antiparos now lay seventy-five miles southeast. The question was, turn southeast now, or wait a bit? Peterkin pointed out that taking *Triumph* a little more to the west would offer two advantages. The first was that the start of their track to Antiparos would benefit from a good position-fix using the island of Patroklos, clearly in sight three miles to their northeast, the temple of Poseidon clearly in sight to the east, and the edge of land north of Patroklos as fixing points.

The second was that by starting a little further west, they would have just one course to steer (140 degrees) to hit the southern end of the island of Siphnos, where they would turn to port to make the easterly run to Antiparos. There would be no need to time multiple course changes along the way. This angle would also take them near enough to the island of Serifos at around to give a mid-track fix from periscope depth to eliminate the errors caused by currents and tides along the track. The plan looked good to Johnny Huddart, especially since it allowed him to sail another hour or so and three miles further west, past Patroklos, before turning onto a 140-degree track for Siphnos, and that hour might bring another target. No new target appeared, and *Triumph* turned onto her 140-degree course at about midday on 9 January.

Triumph had eight torpedo tubes – six inside her pressure hull, and one each side of the bridge outside the pressure hull. She usually fired her internal torpedoes because these could be withdrawn from the tubes during a patrol for checking and maintenance by the torpedo maintainers, which made them more reliable. At the start of the day, before the *Taxiarchis* attack, *Triumph* had her usual six torpedoes in her internal tubes, and probably four unused reloads in her fore ends. She fired four torpedoes at *Taxiarchis*, of which three are visible on the seabed today and the fourth blew up on the shoreline. After the *Taxiarchis* attack she therefore had just two loaded internal tubes, four empty ones, two loaded external tubes, and four reloads waiting to be hauled into the tubes. Two of the reload torpedoes were inaccessible, sitting on racks below the deck plating of the fore ends which would have had to be taken up for the reload. On patrol, the fore ends were a mess of provisions, hammocks, canoes, spare gear, clothing and anything else that needed a home, for it was the largest compartment in the boat, so the reload was not a trivial task.

Johnny Huddart concluded that there was little rush to reload. If a new target appeared on his run to the west, he would not want the work of reloading to get in the way of a snapshot with his last two torpedoes, so the reload could wait until after he had turned southeast towards Antiparos. After that the Flotilla's standard operating procedure forbade any attacks en route in case they alerted the enemy to the presence of the submarine, which would make the one a.m. rendezvous more dangerous. He therefore ordered a delay to the reloading, securing from Diving Stations at around 11.30 am to allow both watches to eat their lunch in turn, have a rest, and get some sleep. Huddart knew that a long and stressful night lay ahead. He also knew that men were asleep in hammocks in the fore ends and would have to be disturbed for the reload. Lunch on patrol was not a full meal but a snack of ham sandwiches and tinned fruit which was enough of a distraction to disrupt the complex and delicate task of heaving the one and a half tonne torpedoes into their tubes with ropes and tackles. Lieutenant Michael Janvrin, the boat's second-in-command suggested that they delay the torpedo reload to 12.30 pm, when the watch change and the midday sandwiches were out of the way, and by which time *Triumph* would be sailing calmly on a course of 140 degrees at 80 feet, out of sight, unbothered by the enemy, and with her crew rested and fed.

We can now fast-forward an hour or two and work back from the point at which we know *Triumph*'s life ended, on the seabed, 203 metres below the surface missing seventy feet of her forward pressure hull, four miles northeast of the island of Saint George. The wreck's heading is roughly southeast, which is consistent with her course of 140 degrees. Video of the forward part of her wreck shows that the pressure hull and casing forward of the gun platform has collapsed inwards as far as the torpedo loading hatch, and that the hatch itself, and all of the seventy feet of pressure hull forward of that, has simply disappeared, apart from a shallow 'scoop' of the lower fifth of the pressure hull, like a marrow spoon.

What could have done that much damage? The answer is not a mine, or rather not just a mine. Several wrecked submarines showing fatal mine damage have been photographed and we can use them as comparisons. When a submarine strikes a mine, the blast occurs next to its pressure hull, which is built from high-quality steel approaching an inch thick. Ninety per cent of the mine's blast energy vents away from the hull, harmlessly into the sea above, below and outboard of the mine. Only about one tenth of the mine's explosive power is absorbed by the submarine's hull. This tenth is still enough to open a small crack in the pressure hull. Water pressure rises by fifteen pounds per square inch for every thirty feet of depth. Water at pressure needs only a very small hole to overwhelm a submarine's small reserve of buoyancy, and when that happens, she quickly sinks. Even a mine with a large charge only just cracks open the hull. If *Triumph* had struck a mine we would have found her more or less intact, with a crack in her fore ends, like *Perseus* off Levkas. What the Greek dive team actually found is that *Triumph*'s entire forward third has gone – disappeared. There must have been a massive explosion to cause that to happen. The only candidate for that much blast is one of her torpedoes.

The Mark VIII torpedo was a powerful weapon[1]. At the front of the torpedo is the warhead – enough explosive to sink a merchant ship of almost any size, or to cripple a cruiser. Or enough to blow the front half of a submarine to pieces if detonated inside her. In that circumstance all the blast would be absorbed by the pressure hull, the weakest part of which (the upper three quadrants away from the reinforced keel), would give way, venting the blast upwards and leaving the lower quadrant still in place. That is what the dive team found. The blast would also destroy the watertight bulkhead between the fore ends and the rest of the submarine, which would then stop supporting the pressure hull and casing above it. Water pressure would cave the casing in downwards, which again is what can be seen on *Triumph*'s wreck.

But the explanation lacks a crucial piece – would, or could, a Mark VIII torpedo detonate unintentionally? While the Mark VIII Torpex warhead was extremely violent, it was also very stable and could only be induced to explode by detonating a smaller explosive charge inside it. This explosive, too, was relatively inert, and needed its own even more sensitive explosive charge to set it off. To explode a Mark VIII, it was therefore necessary to trigger not one but two prior explosions in a sequence of an exact number of microseconds. To ensure that this happened only when desired, the most sensitive trigger charges were held in four small brass tubes, like test tubes, by a spring *outside* the secondary charge, which was located inside the torpex main charge.

Four firing pins – strikers – were held on another spring outside the four trigger charges. So, to detonate the torpedo, the sensitive primary charge had to move (under spring power) into matching holes in the secondary, and then get triggered by the strikers. The whole assembly was called the Pistol and was screwed into the nose of the Mark VIII just before loading the torpedo into its tube. Before use, the Pistols were stowed in stout wooden boxes, well away from the torpedoes, in the boat's magazine.

This system was very stable. Even a violent shock to an armed Mark VIII would not set it off, for if the four sensitive trigger charges did detonate early, they would do so *outside* the larger second charge and not explode the warhead. We can see proof of this in *Triumph*'s own survival of the Heligoland mine, when a large charge detonated just eight feet away from eight armed Mark VIIIs. None of the torpedo warheads exploded.

The Pistol's double-spring firing mechanism was held in place by a shear-pin in the torpedo's nose. At the very front of the pistol was a four-armed steel cross two inches narrower than the torpedo's own twenty-one-inch diameter. When the torpedo hit something hard, ideally a ship, but also the seabed, irrespective of the angle of impact, the force of the blow would drive the arms of the cross backwards, towards the nose of the torpedo, against a retaining spring. This movement broke the shear-pin which released the firing springs. One spring then carried the primary charges into their slots in the secondary charge where, a millisecond later, the second spring slammed home the four strikers into the four primaries, whose detonation initiated the secondary charge, which in turn set off the main charge.

The shear-pin and the cross' retaining spring were designed to activate only on a very slight impact, about the same energy as a car hitting a wall at five miles per hour. This was obviously a significant risk factor when handling an armed torpedo, so for additional safety a strong brass collar was fitted around the external throat of the pistol to stop it from cutting its shear pin early. When dragging a 3,000-pound torpedo into its tube, a tough physical task involving six men, many ropes and tackles and much sweat, this collar was left in place until the very last possible moment, namely the last few inches of haul before the first eighteen inches of the torpedo, with its sensitive steel cross and its armed warhead, was sitting snugly inside its tube, safe from an accidental impact.

In 1941, Mark VIII torpedoes had no 'minimum run distance' safety mechanism. The torpedo was live in the tube and would detonate at any distance from the tube if it hit a hard enough target. Occasionally, torpedoes were reported to detonate a few seconds after leaving their tubes. Later in the war, a minimum-run trigger was installed, but *Triumph*'s Mark VIIIs didn't have them. The massive damage shown by the dive video can only be explained by the detonation of a Mark VIII warhead inside the boat. And that is where we return to *Triumph* at about 12.30 pm on 9 January.

The on-watch helmsman is steering a 140-degree course (southeast). The two men on her fore and after planes are keeping her at a steady eighty feet. Her twin electric motors are moving her along at a fast-walking pace – just over three knots. The forenoon watch (8.00 am to midday) has handed over to the afternoon watch (midday to 4.00 pm). Everyone on board has enjoyed a lunchtime snack of a ham sandwich and some tinned fruit cocktail. After fourteen days at sea the bread is turning green, but Chef O'Brien might bake some more that night on the way to Antiparos, to welcome the two or three dozen passengers that await them. The men off-watch are heading to bunks and hammocks in their messes, but the torpedomen have a task to do before they can get their heads down: arm and load four torpedoes into their tubes. By 12.45 pm they have rigged the folding arms on which the heavy torpedoes are moved around the compartment. They are ignoring the moans of messmates who want to sling hammocks and sleep.

It is heavy work, but this is something they have done a hundred times before, so they work swiftly. When it is lined up with its tube, the torpedo is given some basic checks. Its air pressure must be 2,400 pounds per square inch, its oil reservoirs must be topped up, its depth and speed settings set as ordered, fastenings tightened, screws, rudder and hydroplanes must be free to move. The man in charge of the boat's torpedoes, Petty Officer Frank Collison, gingerly removes a Pistol from its beige-green wooden box, painted with yellow stencils, and gently screws it into the nose of the torpedo. Frank is one of the handful of men in *Triumph* who are married. His wife, Doris, lives in Cosham, a part of Portsmouth. Fifteen years into his career, Frank is expecting to go home and complete the courses he needs to be rated up to Chief Petty Officer. In this rank, he is then likely to work ashore, teaching youngsters the dark arts of keeping Mark VIIIs in running order. This might be the last torpedo-reload of his career at sea.

The torpedo is hauled forward a foot until its steel cross is just a few inches from the circular steel opening of the tube. Frank carefully pulls away the red-painted brass safety circlip. The torpedo is now live, and the men's movements become gentle and slow. With ropes fastened to its tail, the seamen on the tackles are about to heave it gently into the open door of the tube.

'Steady lads, two six, hea…'

The only way in which *Triumph* could have lost her bows is if, at this critical point, the armed torpedo impacted hard on something inside the tube space, where the tube inner doors were open and waiting for their reloads. What could have dislodged a torpedo as heavy as a family car with enough force to throw its firing cross onto something solid? The mine-laying data recovered after the war provides the answer. We know from this post-war record that on 4 December 1941 *Barletta* laid another line of mines near Cape Sounio. This line of 108 large mines, set at forty feet below sea level, was laid exactly across *Triumph*'s 140-degree track to Antiparos. Our reconstruction of *Triumph*'s movements above sees her sailing across this mine line at about 12.45 pm on 9 January, just as Frank Collison removed the safety clip from a torpedo Pistol and gave the traditional naval order to haul on ropes together 'two six … heave'.

Combining her likely track with the known position of the mine line, it is almost certain that *Triumph* crossed the mine line at about eighty feet. *Barletta*'s mines were laid at just forty feet, about twenty feet shallower than *Triumph*'s most shallow part, the top of her periscope masts. The most likely course of events is that as she crossed the mine line, she snagged a mine mooring wire on her fore-planes. The mines were kept in place by a wire cable attached to a heavy sinker on the seabed below.[2] Normally, the noise of a snagged cable would penetrate clearly, and terrifyingly, inside the pressure hull – a horrible metallic grating noise that could only be one thing. But not always. One memoir recalls a boat surfacing at night and seeing, to the horror of all on her bridge, that she was towing a mine from her after planes and had been doing so for hours. A snagged cable might simply catch on the hull and not drag at all, making no noise. This is probably what happened to *Triumph*. Sailing on unknowing at three knots, *Triumph* would have drawn the mine down towards her hull. With just forty feet of the mine's mooring wire between her and the mine, it would have impacted at the aft end of the torpedo compartment or at the forward end of her mess deck.

Detonation.

A massive bang just a few feet above the heads of the men inside. A huge impulse shock to the boat, which leaps violently downwards away from the blast. As the hull cracks open and high pressure water floods in, the shock of the explosion throws the armed torpedo out of its loading slide, and sends it crashing into the rear end of the tube. The Pistol's steel cross hits the tube door violently. The shear pin is cut. The strikers spring down, chasing the primary detonators into their snug home in the secondary charge. The strikers hit the primary charges just as their designer intended, at the moment that they are fully inserted into their slots in the secondary charge. Primary detonates secondary, secondary detonates the warhead.

The shock wave from the warhead detonation, moving at the speed of sound, takes only one third of a second to propagate through the boat. The internal watertight doors are all open. The blast wave has an open path to the stokers' mess right astern. Any man standing up is thrown violently against a bulkhead. Every cup, plate, and spanner, becomes a high-energy missile flying around inside the hull. The men in the fore ends would have had less than half a second to process what was happening as the torpedo leapt from its rack. They were dead before they knew it.

The men settling down to sleep in the three messes aft of the fore ends, the junior rates' mess, the petty officers' mess and the artificers' mess, would have been hurled violently out of their bunks, probably killed almost instantly too. Aft of the messes the off-watch officers, asleep in the wardroom, and Johnny Huddart in his cupboard-sized cabin, were thrown onto the deck or the deckhead, but might have had a second or so more in which to realize that something terrible had happened, perhaps a moment to think of home, of regret that they were not going to survive the lethal Mediterranean war, before they too died. Men further aft will have had a few more seconds of conscious thought, but the next thing they heard, and then quickly saw, was a tidal wave of water powering aft, arriving only a few seconds after the explosion. The water wall first filled the control room, then the radio office, then the galley where Chef Cornelius O'Brien was kneading dough for his afternoon's baking. As *Triumph*'s deck angled steeply down, towards the bottom, the water continued to flood aft, slowing a little as the air in the stern half of *Triumph*'s pressure hull began to compress. The flood reached the motor room a few seconds later, short-circuiting the heavy electrical breakers that directed current from the batteries to *Triumph*'s two electric motors with vivid blue flashes. There was hardly time for her screws to stop turning before her bows reached the seabed just two hundred yards below. The last men to die were the stokers, mostly asleep, but perhaps playing cards or uckers in their mess, right at the stern of the boat. Stunned by the explosion, now in semi-darkness (for the water wall fused the main power circuit two seconds earlier) and with the deck tipping steeply under them, the stokers struggled to keep their heads above the freezing black water while trying to work out what was happening.

It only took twenty seconds for *Triumph*'s bows to hit the bottom. In that time, the air pressure in the stokers' mess rose from one atmosphere to twenty atmospheres, dramatically heating up as it did so. The stokers, in their mess, passed out within a minute as the partial pressure of the carbon dioxide in the compartment soared to over one atmosphere, and were unconscious when they drowned a minute or so later. By the time *Triumph*'s stern crashed to the bottom and lay still every man aboard her was already dead. And that is where the Thoctarides team found her eighty-one years later.

There is a painful question which echoes the one from earlier that day – did Johnny Huddart know about the second mine line?

Probably not. If he had, he would have taken a different track, probably west of the island of St George, or perhaps close inshore along its east coast, but *Triumph* took neither course. The two mine lines, off Sounio and off St George, were laid within a few days of each other and were probably ordered in the same signal, if indeed there was a signal at all, so if *Triumph* did not know about the first mine line from an Enigma decrypt, she would not have known about the second one either.

If *Triumph* didn't know about the second mine line, did she see it on her mine-detecting unit? The east-west line earlier in the day was denser than the St George mine line, and *Triumph* had approached it obliquely, at the same depth as the mines, making sonar detection much more likely. *Triumph* approached the second mine line forty feet below the mines (and possibly deeper still, she might have been as deep as 100 feet). The detecting unit's sonar transducer was located at the front of her keel, deep under her hull, and it is possible that its ability to detect contacts above the pressure hull was degraded by the blanking effect of the hull. It is also likely that the sound energy propagating from the transducer was designed to propagate in the horizontal plane, to prevent the unit from picking up false echoes from surface waves. We know from an earlier *Triumph* patrol report that the mine-detecting unit provided false echoes from the rough surface water, created by a rip tide off Rhodes when she was near the surface. It is quite possible that the unit simply did not reveal the mine line.

Another obstacle may have prevented detection. The sea does not have uniform salinity and temperature. As one descends through the water column from the surface, salinity (the amount of dissolved salt) changes slightly, and so does water temperature. The borders between different layers of temperature and salinity act on sound energy like mirrors – the sound literally bounces off the joins between two different layers. The sea has a pronounced surface layer where solar energy makes the water slightly warmer and where surface wind action mixes the water more actively. The lower boundary of the surface layer acts as a sonar mirror (which saved the lives of many boats under depth charge attack), and it is possible that the St George mine line was floating above or on the border of the surface layer, while *Triumph*'s mine-detection transducer was below it.

Another factor is that the number of mines, for the sonar to detect, was small. Approaching the mine line at a right angle, and with the mines laid 120 metres apart, even a fully functional sonar might only see one or two contacts ahead, which could easily be missed in the distraction of the watch handover and lunch, assuming a man was even watching the sonar screen. It is far from certain that this function was actively being carried out at the time since it is likely that an operator was only 'closed up' on the mine-detecting unit at Diving Stations. At lunchtime on 9 January, *Triumph* was at 'watch diving', a much lower state of alertness, with fewer men on watch. A final possibility is that *Triumph* did see the mine line but decided to dive below it. This was a perfectly normal procedure at the time. Indeed, the only way to get into Malta, which was surrounded by multiple minefields, was to dive below the mines.

We shall never know which precise combination of events applied, but we don't need to. The sad outcome is that *Triumph* did not survive her last patrol, and the sixty-four men aboard her rest still on the seabed, a few miles southwest of Cape Sounio. And here their story ended, until she swam into view on the dive team's monitors in 2023.

Epilogue

What happened to *Triumph,* and her men, was a tragedy, but it was not unusual for the Royal Navy's submarines between 1939 and 1945. In September 1939, approximately 2,650 men were serving in fifty commissioned RN submarines. By the end of 1940, 1,040 of this group had been killed in twenty-five sunk submarines. In 1941 and 1942, another 500 had died (plus hundreds more men drafted into submarines after 1939). The exact number becomes uncertain because by these years submarines were being manned by wartime draftees. About a dozen of the men lost in *Triumph* were wartime submariners. Including pre-war submariners lost in later years, a reliable estimate is that 1,700 of those 2,650 did not survive the war – a mortality rate of sixty-four per cent.

During the first three full years of the war, the submarine service was an extremely dangerous place. By the end of 1940, the navy had lost twenty-five submarines, usually with all hands (168 men survived to be captured). In 1941, it lost another ten. New boats were being built as fast as the yards could turn them out, and with larger numbers at sea, sinkings also increased. In 1942, nineteen boats were lost, including *Triumph.* Men in submarines were painfully aware of the lethal risks attending their trade, and it is a tribute to their cold-blooded courage that they sailed on patrol again and again, with every sign of good cheer, knowing that their lives were at extreme risk. In total, the navy lost seventy-eight submarines during the war. *Triumph*'s real tragedy is not her loss – the loss of a submarine had become a tragic norm – but that she was lost on the last operational day of her last operational patrol, having dodged the bullets, bombs and mines of the enemy for a year.

Many of the lost submarines are in known positions and have even been inspected by divers. Many are not. The wrecks of fifteen of the seventy-three can be located within about ten miles, but have not been found and exactly located. The wrecks of twenty-three more are lost completely, of which slightly more than half were lost in the Mediterranean. This lost flotilla is the source of prolonged and intense sadness, for the families of the men have nowhere to attach their mourning. In *Triumph*'s case, the research behind this book led to the creation of a Families Association; it now boasts some 200 descendants and relatives of the sixty-four men. If that proportion held for the entire Lost Flotilla it would mean that thousands of people still live with unresolved grief – while it exists in the background, at a low intensity, it is the sort of grief that catches one in the back of the throat when triggered by some associative event, but it is no less painful.

Triumph was lost for eighty-one years, but is now found thanks to the long and tireless efforts of a lone Greek underwater explorer. Every couple of years another member of the Lost Flotilla comes to light, and another group of relatives finds closure. It will be many decades before the last man is found. I picture their spirits sitting in their messes over spectral grog or milky tea, playing brag or uckers, looking up to the surface and the sunlight, wondering when their families are going to come and say goodbye.

In June 2024, the *Triumph* families did just that, sailing out to her wreck and laying sixty-four wreaths, one for each man. As these landed on the sea surface, they appeared to drift off in a line towards the shore, as if each man had been given leave at last and was heading off to the Dun Cow pub in Sliema for a well-earned pint.

This book is dedicated to their memory.

Notes

Chapter 1: *Salpa*, June 1941

1. *Salpa* is a species of fish known as the Dreamfish or Cow Bream.
2. 1,300 yards.

Chapter 2: The Mediterranean Theatre, January 1941

1. Grand Harbour on one side and Marxamsett Harbour on the other.
2. HMS *Oxley*, sunk by HMS *Triton* on 10 September 1939, with just two survivors.
3. Wingate, J., *The Fighting Tenth*, Stroud, Tempus Publishing, 2000, p 45.
4. *Submarine*, Jean Hood, p 27.
5. A detailed analysis can be found in the medical report into the sinking of HMS *Thetis* in Liverpool Bay in 1939, NA ADM 298/499.
6. The minelaying submarine *Porpoise* was fitted with tanks in her mine-laying racks that could carry 12,000 gallons of aviation fuel. *A Submariner's Story*, Joel Blamey, p 122.
7. Hezlet – *History of the Submarine War*, Chapter 5.
8. https://www.bp.com/en/global/corporate/who-we-are/our-history/through-world-war-two.html
9. *Cairo in the War*, Artemis Cooper, p 46.
10. Kershaw, Ian (2007). *Fateful Choices: Ten Decisions that Changed the World, 1940–1941*. London: Allen Lane.
11. Estimates suggest that some 15,000 tonnes of bombs were dropped on Malta, equal to one and a half Hiroshima bombs.
12. He is buried in the Capuccini War Cemetery on Malta.
13. At shallower depths than this a submarine was clearly visible to a passing aircraft as a long black shape.
14. Naval ludo.
15. Always referred to as a 'pipe', in homage to the use of boatswains' silver whistles for passing orders, still sometimes used today.
16. As opposed to a 'fan' firing where torpedoes spread out in a fan to bracket the target.
17. This can be contrasted with the Atlantic War in 1941, where a convoy of fifty ships would typically be escorted by five slow escorts and no aircraft.
18. In one of those circularities that categorized the familial nature of the Royal Navy, Horton had joined the service as a cadet in 1898 in the same class as the father of *Triumph*'s gunnery officer, Robert Douglas-Don.
19. The Battle of the River Plate, in *Exeter*. Douglas-Don was on the bridge at the start of the action. Graf Spee's first hit on *Exeter* killed every man on her bridge except her Captain and Douglas-Don.
20. Both were awarded VCs.

21. The Italian post-war history *La Guerra di Mine, 1966*, contains laying depths for approximately 4,500 mines off the coast of Sicily in 1940, of which the deepest was 450 metres, pp 88-89.
22. Letter from Lieutenant Douglas-Don to his father, November 1941, author's collection.
23. *The Fighting Tenth*, p 42.
24. Later the Lazaretto would be commissioned as a stone frigate – HMS *Talbot* – but in 1941 it was just the Lazaretto.
25. Lord Byron, *Farewell to Malta*, May 1811.

Chapter 3: Special Operations – A New Form of Submarine Warfare

1. The K-class was an operational disaster, with half of the class sinking in one accident or another.
2. *The Fighting Tenth*, p 25. The paradigm continues today. In exercises with the US Navy in 2004 and 2015 European submarines were credited with sinking US supercarriers multiple times.
3. This was not always the case. Some submariners maintained their physical fitness with sports. Sub-Lieutenant Brian Lloyd of *Urge* served as a Folboat paddler, and submarines ran sports teams when alongside, but for the most part submariners were not among the fittest of sailors.
4. John Wingate, *The Fighting Tenth*, p 44.
5. John Wingate, *The Fighting Tenth*, p 37.
6. Colonel David Smiley RHG and 52 Commando, quoted in *Middle East Commandos*, Charles Messenger, p 76.
7. *Triumph* had already been 'blooded' in Malta. One member of her ship's company, Stoker Harry Hague, was killed while she was in dock at Valletta during an air raid, firefighting on the neighbouring merchant ship MV *Essex*.
8. Robert Douglas-Don letter home, author's collection.
9. *Commandos*, James Owen, p xxi.
10. *Commandos*, James Owen, p xxii.
11. Willmott's lessons sadly appeared not to have reached Combined Operations Command a year later, when it was planning the Dieppe Raid. Here, the pebbly nature of the beach prevented tanks from moving at all, much less advancing. The German defenders of Dieppe had tested moving tanks on the pebble beach and discovered the same fact beforehand.
12. *The Secret Invaders*, Strutton & Pearson, p 19.
13. *Commandos*, James Owen, p xxiii.
14. *Commandos*, James Owen, p xxv.
15. *Commandos*, James Owen, p xxv.
16. The hotel is still operating as a five-star resort.
17. They were in fact Italians.
18. *Commando*, James Owen, p xxvi.

Chapter 4: Operation Marita, the Invasion of Greece

1. Prince Philip's uncle.
2. Beaton, p 264.
3. Stanley Casson, *Greece Against the Axis*, p 26. Casson, a classicist and archaeologist, was an intelligence major with the British Military Mission in Greece at the time, and was present.

4. Ibid.
5. Ohi is Greek for 'No'.
6. Hansard, 13 April 1939, Lord Halifax.
7. Hill, *Diggers and Greeks*, p 28.
8. Sepp di Giampietro, *Blood and Soil*, p 63.
9. These were attacked by Allied forces in 1942, the last time that British forces fought a land war against the French.
10. Casson, *Greece Against the Axis*, p 65.
11. *Barham*, *Valiant* and *Warspite*
12. HRH Prince Philip of Greece was the midshipman in command of *Valiant*'s searchlight battery. He received a Mention in Despatches for the action, and was the last member of the British royal family to fight in a war, until the Falklands War in 1982.
13. In fact, Churchill fought hard *not* to make a landing at Gallipoli, as described by N.A.M. Rodger in *The Price of Victory*.
14. Both numbers are from https://anzacportal.dva.gov.au/resources/greece-and-crete.
15. Marita's main force was the 18th Mountain Corps, made up of one panzer division, two mountain infantry divisions and the 72nd Infantry division – in all about 60,000 men. Its second element was the 40th Panzer Corps, containing one panzer division, one infantry division and one reinforced regiment – about 30,000 men. While the 18th Mountain Corps moved against the Metaxas Line and down the Vardar valley east of Lustre Force's prepared positions, the 40th Corps was responsible for the right hook movement into Yugoslavia, to be followed by the sharp left turn south to use the Strymon Valley to envelop Lustre Force's strong positions on the Aliakhmon range from behind. A third element, the 30th Corps of two infantry divisions (30,000 men) was to attack the eastern end of the Metaxas Line and hold the eastern border of Greece against a possible Turkish intervention, coming nowhere near Allied forces. A few days into Marita, two additional panzer divisions were added to the Strymon Valley advance.
16. The Greek 12th Division deployed with just six motor vehicles, five trucks and the general's personal motor car. Hill, *Diggers and Greeks*, p 76.

Chapter 5: Atkinson, Craig and the Fall of Greece

1. Richard Titmuss, *Problems of Social Policy* (1950) p 102.
2. https://www.bbc.co.uk/history/ww2peopleswar/stories/32/a2057032.shtml.
3. Their motto was 'Twenty second to none'.
4. http://www.22battalion.org.nz/publications/mclean/chap7.php.
5. http://www.22battalion.org.nz/publications/mclean/chap8.php.
6. Strictly speaking, before Pearl Harbour, the troops would have referred to themselves as Imperial rather than Allied, but I've used Allied throughout to reflect the presence of non-Imperial forces including Palestinians, Cypriots, Free French, South Africans and others.
7. The commander of Lustre Force, sometimes referred to as Force W.
8. A promise abandoned when Rommel's Afrika Korps landed in Tripoli.
9. Sepp di Giampietro, *Blood and Soil*, p 63.
10. Sepp di Giampietro, *Blood and Soil*, p 48.
11. Sepp di Giampietro, *Blood and Soil*, p 78.
12. Ibid.

13. Roald Dahl, *Going Solo*, Chapter 11.
14. Quoted in *Diggers and Greeks*, Maria Hill, p 108. Shortly afterwards, Tsolakoglou became the leader of the Greek government under the Axis, suggesting his fascist leanings were rather pronounced.
15. Sepp di Giampietro, *Blood and Soil*, p 127.
16. While they were waiting, they were variously used for minor sabotage operations against Italian merchantmen and to smuggle Jewish refugees into Palestine.
17. The Sele River Mouth was probably one of these.
18. The attack is narrated in detail in *Target Corinth Canal*, Platon Alexiades.
19. *Operation Mercury*, John Sadler, p 50.
20. https://ndhadeliver.natlib.govt.nz/webarchive/20210104000423/http://nzetc.victoria.ac.nz/tm/scholarly/tei-WH2-22Ba-c2.html.
21. Ibid, quoting Sergeant Sargeson.
22. https://ndhadeliver.natlib.govt.nz/webarchive/20210104000423/http://nzetc.victoria.ac.nz/tm/scholarly/tei-WH2-22Ba-c2.html.
23. http://www.22battalion.org.nz/war-diary/craig.php.
24. CWGC records indicate that some 162 Allied troops died on 2 June 1941, two days after the surrender.

Chapter 6: The Bardia Raid

1. White, William, letters home, courtesy of the White Family archive,
2. Hitler Directive 22, 11 January 1941. https://der-fuehrer.org/reden/english/wardirectives/22.html.
3. Ibid.
4. *Sonnenblöme.*
5. *British and Allied Submarine Operations in World War 2*, Hezlett, vol I, p 74.
6. Ibid, p xx.
7. 7, 8 and 11 Commandos (*Commandos*, James Owen, p 29).
8. At the age of 33, it made him one of the youngest full colonels in the army.
9. Referred to without naming *Triumph* in Mediterranean Intelligence. Reports NA ADM 199/255 of 20 April referring signal of 19 April from RAF. There was no come-back on the RAF. Submarines were as wary of attacks from the RAF as they were from the Axis.
10. In 1942 and 1944, making it hard to argue that this was a product of inexperience.

Chapter 7: Secret House, Cairo

1. M.R.D. Foot, SOE, p 6.
2. Norman Crockatt.
3. M.R.D. Foot, SOE, p 17. The charter was in fact negotiated and signed by Neville Chamberlain, whom Hugh Dalton loathed. Chamberlain retired sick a few days later and died in November, leaving Dalton in command.
4. Vacated by the Prison Commissioners.
5. This makes SOE research in the archives particularly hard.
6. Sweet Escott, Baker Street Irregular, quoted in M.R.D. Foot, SOE, p 43.
7. Alexiades, *Target Corinth Canal*, p 15.
8. M.R.D. Foot, SOE, p 211.

9. Ambassador in today's parlance.
10. He had married her that morning to head off any bureaucratic opposition to her arrival in Cairo.
11. Northeastern Greece – the lands bordering Bulgaria and Turkey don't fit this model, but are instead huge rolling arable prairies. However, being remote from Greece's political and military centres, these played no part in SOE's war, though they were the scene for horrendous genocidal treatment of Greeks by the occupying Bulgarians, from whom they had been wrested in 1912.
12. His memoir is *Within Four Walls*.
13. Foot and Langley, MI9, *Escape and Evasion*, p 88.
14. In the words of Admiral Cunningham in a signal to Churchill, 'worth their weight in gold'.
15. Lavatories at sea are called 'heads'.
16. Lieutenant Commander Francis Pool RNR.

Chapter 8: Return to Malta, and Another Special Operation

1. The action is described in Chapter 2.
2. Engineering work on submarines in Egypt had to be carried out by civilian personnel of the Suez Canal Company. They were willing enough but not always experienced in the complexities of pressure hulls and valves.
3. George Simpson, *Periscope View*, p 158.
4. George Simpson, *Periscope View*, p 145.
5. SM10 is the designator for the commander of the 10th Submarine Flotilla, Shrimp Simpson. SM1 was the commander of the 1st Flotilla, Captain Sydney Raw.
6. Dog watches are a pair of two-hour watches inserted into the schedule at 4.00 pm and 6.00 pm, designed to break the day-night pattern of a four-hour watch system. With six 4-hour watches, men would always be awake and asleep during the same hours each day. The dog watches flip this cycle daily to share the burden of the middle watch midnight to 4.00 am. They also allow men to eat at around 6.00 pm without coming off watch, in peacetime at least.
7. Patrol report, NA.
8. *Triumph*'s target was the heavy – eight inch – cruiser *Bolzano*. She spent three months in dock, then returned to service where she was hit again by HMS *Unbroken*, after which she spent the rest of the war in dock.
9. Unpublished memoir by Padgham, in the author's collection.
10. 549 RN submariners were captured during the war. About 300 of these were men serving in commissioned submarines in 1939. Of the 2,600 men in commissioned submarines in 1939, approximately 2,000 were lost, leaving just 300 survivors who served throughout the war.

Chapter 9: Escape into Athens

1. It opened its doors on 9 May 1941, staffed by Allied doctors and well equipped with medical supplies.
2. Stout and Duncan, *Medical Services in New Zealand and The Pacific*, New Zealand Official History of the War.
3. Roy Farran, *Winged Dagger*, p 105.

4. http://nzetc.victoria.ac.nz/tm/scholarly/tei-WH2Pris-_N75380.html.
5. In one of these lie the remains of the author's cousin, Lieutenant Archie Don, of the Black Watch who was killed during a Bulgarian attack on the Rodope Mountains.
6. 2nd Lieutenant Cooper escape report, NZ archives.
7. National Archives HS5/363, Agent Liquidation Files.
8. Roy Farran, *Winged Dagger*, p 109.
9. Renamed 28 October Street after the war commemorate the 'No' day on which President Metaxas refused to surrender to the Italians in 1940.
10. Miss Morris was not the only English nanny to remain at liberty. Mary Henderson, in Xenia, recalled seeing a group of nannies giving their charges their morning airing in the Royal Gardens, all wearing their uniform of grey felt hat and grey skirt suit. *Xenia*, p 53.
11. Mary Henderson, *Xenia*, p 50.
12. Graeme McLeod, *Two Home Runs*
13. After the war Atkinson's effects were returned to her. NA WO208/3391.
14. Rigas Rigopoulos, *Secret War*, p 36.
15. Rigas Rigopoulos, *Secret War*, p 25.
16. Quoted by Graeme McLeod in a narrative on John Redpath.
17. Sometimes referred to in files as Poumpouras. Allied reporters struggled to transliterate Greek to English.
18. Cooper escape report, NZ National Archives, Wellington WAII; Series 1; DA541.2/3.
19. Cooper named them as *Valiant* and *Barham*, but records of their movements do not fit the dates. They were far more likely to have been destroyers.
20. Cooper escape report, NZ National Archives, Wellington WAII; Series 1; DA541.2/3.

Chapter 10: Coney Island

1. Wingate was an avid Christian.
2. Private papers of Corporal Alan Hackshaw, AWM: 3DRL/6398.
3. NA Kew HS5/524.
4. NA Kew HS5/524.
5. In May 1943 the heads of SOE and MI9 in Cairo received a memorandum from HQ Middle East from an agent codenamed Yorker that the Italians had declared they would shoot any man found in Greece not in his service uniform. NA WO204/12952.
6. NA WO311/370, a translation of an Italian memorandum dated 5 January 1942.
7. At this time, back home in the United Kingdom, the Double Cross Committee was capturing every spy and saboteur being landed in Britain. Those who refused to be 'turned' were invariably hanged.
8. The archives don't reveal whether *Theotokus* found her way back to her owners, but after the war the British made intensive efforts to ensure that Greeks who had spent money during the occupation were compensated. These efforts are elaborated in detail in a set of files in the NA called Liquidation Files – liquidation referring to the settlement of financial debts rather than systematic murder.
9. Unlike in the army and air force, the Royal Navy did not allow the war to disrupt its normal and well-established system of promotions. Officer promotions were promulgated twice each year, on 31 December and 30 June, just as they are today. Field promotions were not used, though a lieutenant might be appointed in command of a destroyer if

considered capable. As far as the officer promotions system was concerned, the war was merely a distraction.

10. Bray is a village on the Thames which enthusiastic Etonian rowers still might reach on a summer's afternoon.
11. A later memorandum refers to Atkinson by the codename Robin, which is certainly more in keeping with his appearance. SOE's use of codenames was chaotic. Multiple names were allocated to men, and records of allocated names were either not kept or were themselves so secret that half of SOE did not know how the other half was naming its agents. Many codenames in the files today have no real name attached.
12. Redpath's full story is told in *Two Home Runs*, by Graeme McLeod. Redpath would make two escapes from Axis-held territory and survived the war.
13. Craig Operational Report, NA WO208/5584.
14. Their last names have not survived into the record.

Chapter 11: Just One More Patrol

1. Robert Douglas-Don letter home 15 November 1941, Author's family archive.
2. In the RN all Turners are automatically 'Topsies', alongside 'Wiggy' Bennetts, 'Dusty' Millers and 'Dinger' Bells.
3. Radford family archive.
4. Sydney Hart, *Discharged Dead*, p 76.
5. Swan family archive.

Chapter 12: Operation Isinglass

1. Redpath operational report, NA WO208/5584.
2. Probably by an individual called Bekes. *Attack on Corinth*, Platon Alexiades.
3. NA WO311/370, 1945 affidavit by the Bourbouras siblings.
4. *Attack on Corinth*, Platon Alexiades
5. 250,000 Drachmae, then valued at about £500, or £25,000 today. NA HS5/524.
6. The record does not show what the signal was, or how it was supposed to escape notice by a passing Axis caique, but it was probably a small, coloured flag in a prearranged spot on the southern slope of the hill where it could be seen through the powerful search periscope of a boat.
7. Redpath operational report. NA WO208/5584.
8. We don't have a reason, though it might well have been something to do with Harry's pre-war smuggling business and a possible Turkish arrest warrant.
9. History does not relate whether the future Mrs Grammatikakis was still in residence. She is not mentioned anywhere in later (very detailed) reports, so it seems likely that, when Harry left for Athens, she returned to Paros.
10. Francis S Jones, *Escape to Nowhere*, p 115.
11. Robert Douglas-Don. In a small ship like a submarine, officers are often addressed informally by their functions, Guns for the gunnery officer, Pilot for the navigator, Engines for the chief engineer, Torps for the torpedo officer. The first lieutenant, who is second in command, is often referred to as the Jimmy (for Jimmy the One), though by his subordinates and not to his face, being addressed as XO or Number One by his boss. In wartime submarines at sea, ranks were often dropped completely, with men addressing each other by first names, sometimes even ratings to officers.

Chapter 13: Disaster on Antiparos

1. Craig operational report. NA WO208/5584.
2. Redpath operational report. NA WO208/5584.
3. Slightly smaller than Dartmoor, and about as rough.
4. NA WO208/3253 Interview with Grammatikakis, 9 June 1942.
5. Francis Jones, *Escape to Nowhere*, p 115.
6. Parish report of an interview with Grammatikakis, 8 June 1942, NA WO 208/3391. Harry claimed to have climbed up a chimney to escape, but even a man as slippery as Harry would have been too wide to fit. He probably just climbed out of a window.
7. NA HS5/711 note 18 December 1942. This was probably another Grammatikakis lie, since both of his potential fathers in law were living in Paros, and neither of them had actually achieved the status of father-in-law.
8. Michael Parish, *Aegean Adventures*, p 48.
9. Film Plan Number One was a caique route between Athens and the Turkish coast near Izmir, to be run by Frank Macaskie. Later in the war, it was operated by Michael Parish and a squadron of caiques, nicknamed the Levant Schooner Squadron, and was running weekly collection runs.
10. Michael Parish, *Aegean Adventures*, p 160.
11. Michael Parish, *Aegean Adventures*, p 161.
12. Michael Parish, *Aegean Adventures*, p 162.
13. After the war Parish returned to one of these on an Aegean sailing holiday to see if his stash was still there, but was unable to find it, to his chagrin.
14. Italian High Command report of the trial of Captains Savage and McNabb in Athens in May 1942. NA WO 208/3391.
15. Atkinson's diary was tabled in evidence and quoted from at the later trial of Captains Savage and McNabb in Athens in May 1942. NA WO 208/3391.
16. At this time, January 1942, SOE had not made any useful contacts with the much larger communist-supported resistance and so had provided Atkinson with no names of left-wing guerillas to reveal.
17. NA WO208/3391 signal SOE Istanbul to SOE Cairo 5 February 1942.
18. NA WO208/3391 signal SOE Cairo to SOE Istanbul 8 February 1942.
19. Jean Hood, *Submarine*, p 41.

Chapter 14: Disaster in Athens

1. Affidavit by Wing Commander Angellopoulos to Advocate General's Office in London, 9 October 1945, in NA WO311/370.
2. A post-war war crimes enquiry revealed that the only man to win this leave managed to shoot an unwary German sentry who had looked out of a window.
3. Affidavit by Kevin Walsh to Advocate General's Office 21 November 1946, in NA WO311/370.
4. Affidavit by Wing Commander Angellopoulos to Advocate General's Office in London, 9 October 1945, in NA WO311/370.
5. Affidavit by Evangelos Averof, Royal Hellenic Navy, to UN War Crimes Commission. NA WO 208/3391.
6. NA HS5/524 memo 18 October to Colonel Simonds.

7. Memorandum from Colonel Simonds to Brigadier Crockatt MI9, December 1942, NA WO 208/3391.
8. Macaskie was held for a while with Roy Natusch, a New Zealander of Dutch descent who had the startling record of making no fewer than ten escapes and ended the war fighting in Yugoslavia alongside Tito's partisans. On his return to British hands he was debriefed by Major James Klugman, who was later revealed to be a lifelong KGB agent. Klugman had been at school with Donald Maclean and helped recruit John Cairncross. A member of SOE, he was based in Cairo in 1942 where his reports on Yugoslavia were instrumental in persuading Churchill to drop Mihailovich and support Tito.
9. NA WO208/3391 signal SOE Cairo to SOE London 3 March 1942.
10. Note dated May 1943, NA WO 208/3391.
11. Memorandum dated March 1943, NA WO 208/3391.
12. An anecdotal report without a formal reference.
13. WO2 T. A. M. Boulter who escaped from a PoW Camp in Greece, Australian War Memorial archive 54 781/3/2.
14. E. B. Turton, *I Lived with Greek Guerrillas*, p 73.
15. Mary Henderson, *Xenia*, p 48.
16. NA Kew WO 208/3391.
17. Memorandum 4 May 1943 to Major Packer, MI9, NA WO 208/3391.
18. Greek National War Crimes Office charge sheet 391/1946, NA WO 208/3391.
19. Letter from UNWCC to Judge Advocate General 13 May 1946 NA WO 208/3391.
20. Report of the Atkinson trial to SOE by Pilot Officer Vlassiou, NA HS5/285.
21. Memorandum to Captain A. W. Graham 7 July 1945, NA WO 208/3391.
22. The trial took place after the fall of Stalingrad. The court must have known that its sentences of imprisonment were unlikely to outlast the end of the war.
23. Report of the trial to SOE by Pilot Officer Vlassiou, NA HS5/285.
24. Report of trial of Private William Ditchburn, NA WO 208/3391.
25. He had six children to support.
26. The cemetery is still there. Atkinson's headstone carries Josephine's dedication 'in ever loving memory of my darling John'.

Chapter 15: Missing, Believed Sunk

1. Letter from Captain S. M. Raw to George Waterall's father, May family archive.
2. 350 men were captured.
3. There were some notable exceptions. The wreck of the cruiser HMAS *Sydney* was completely lost until found off the Australian coast in 2014, and that of her sister ship HMS *Neptune* in 2022 off the Tripoli coast.
4. Translated by US Naval Intelligence in 1948 and declassified in 1972.
5. NA ADM234/381.
6. The mine should have been underwater. Either it was laid with an incorrect length of mooring cable, or, more likely, had broken loose from its mooring and was drifting about on the surface.
7. In practice, in extreme circumstances, a submarine can stop in the water at depth, for a short period of time, something like a cyclist balancing at rest, but stopping while dived is difficult to achieve and to sustain. In some circumstances water temperature and salinity combine to create a pronounced density change at thirty or forty feet of depth,

and captains found that they could occasionally 'rest' their boat on this layer without moving.

8. Punctuality remained a key feature of naval life. Forty years after the war the author, navigating a destroyer into Portland Harbour, was required to ensure that the gyro compass stand on his ship's bridge passed exactly between the two stone piers of the harbour entrance, within three seconds of the exact announced arrival time.
9. Kostas Thoctarides of *PlanetBlue*.
10. The deepest possible escape depth, in theory, was about 200 feet. Stoker Capes escaped at 170 feet, but the toxic effects of breathing natural air at high pressure quickly kills men at greater depths. At 200 feet, once the escape hatch is opened, air pressure in the compartment rises to seven atmospheres, and the partial pressure of oxygen – twenty per cent of air – to 1.4 atmospheres, giving a man about half an hour before oxygen toxicity sets in. At 700 feet ambient pressure is 23 atmospheres, and oxygen toxicity would be practically instant.

Chapter 16: *Triumph*'s Last Day

1. The Mark VIII continued in service for fifty years after the war. It was a Mark VIII that sank the Argentinian cruiser *Belgrano* in 1982.
2. There are many accounts of mine wire snags in memoirs of other submariners.

Bibliography

Alexiades, P, *Target Corinth Canal 1940-1944*, Barnsley, Pen and Sword, 2015
Ballantine, I., *The Deadly Trade*, London, Weidenfeld and Nicolson, 2018
Beaton, R., *Greece, Biography of a Nation*, London, Allen Lane, 2019
Blamey, J., *A Submariner's Story*, Penzance, Periscope Publishing, 2002
Bradford, E, *Siege Malta 1940-1943*, London, Hamish Hamilton, 1985
Broome, R., *No Occupation for a Gentleman*, published privately, 1999
Bryant, B., *One Man Band*, Wellingborough, William Kimber, 1958
Carr, W.G., *By Guess and by God*, London, Hutchison, 1920
Casdagli, A.T., *Prouder Than Ever*, London, Cylix, 2014
Casson, S., *Greece Against the Axis*, London, Hamish Hamilton, 1941
Chapman, P., *Submarine Torbay*, London, Robert Hale, 1989
Clayton, T., *Sea Wolves*, London, Little Brown, 2011
Clogg, R.C., *Anglo Greek Attitudes*, London, MacMillan, 2000
Cooper, A., *Cairo in The War 1939 to 1945*, London, Hamish Hamilton, 1989
Coote, J., *Submariner*, London, Leo Cooper, 1991
Courtney, G.B.,*SBS in World War Two*, London, Robert Hale, 1983
Cremer, P., *U333*, London, Triad, 1986
Dahl, R., *Going Solo*, London, Jonathan Cape, 1986
David, S., *SBS Silent Warriors*, London, William Collins 2021
Dickison, A.P., *Crash Dive*, Stroud, Sutton Publishing, 1999
Farran, R., *Winged Dagger*, Adventures on Special Service, London, Cassell, 1998
Field, R., and Gordon-Creed, G, *Rogue Male: Sabotage and Seduction Behind German Lines*, London, Coronet, 2012
Foot, M.R.D., *SOE, An Outline History of the Special Operations Executive, 1940-1946*, London, BBC, 1984
Foot, M.R.D. and Langley, J.M., *MI9, Escape and Evasion 1939-1945*, London, Bodley Head, 1979
De Giampietro, S., *Blood and Soil*, Barnsley, Pen and Sword, 2019
Gibson, J., *Dark Seas Above*, Stroud, Tempus Publishing, 2000
Goodwin, P., *Royal Navy Submarine 1945 to 1973*, Yeovil, Haynes, 2015
Greentree, D., *British Submarine vs Italian Torpedo Boat*, Oxford, Osprey, 2016
Hart, S., *Discharged Dead*, London, Odhams, 1956
Hart, S., *Submarine Upholder*, London, Oldbourne, 1960
Henderson, M., *Xenia, a Memoir*, London, Weidenfeld and Nicholson, 1988
Hennessy, P., and Jinks, J, *The Silent Deep*, London, Allen Lane, 2015
Hezlet, A., *British and Allied Submarine Operations in World War II*, Gosport, RN Submarine Museum, 2001

Hezlet, A., *HMS Trenchant at War*, Barnsely, Pen and Sword, 2001
Hill, M., *Diggers and Greeks*, Sydney Aus, UNSW Press, 2010
Hood, J., (ed), *Submarine, An Anthology of First-Hand Accounts*, London, Conway, 2007
Howard, M., *British Intelligence in the Second World War Volume 5*, London, HMSO, 1990
Jones, F.J., *Escape to Nowhere*, London, Bodley Head, 1952
Kalfakakou, P., *Kakavia*, Edinburgh, Maclean Dubois, 2006
Kemp, P., *The T-Class Submarine*, Annapolis, Naval Institute Press, 1990
Lawrence, P., *A Century of Submarines*, Stroud, The History Press, 2001
Leigh-Fermor, P., *Abducting a General*, London, John Murray, 2014
Lind, L., *Battle of the Wine Dark Sea*, Kenthurst NSW, Kangaroo Press, 1994
Llewellyn-Jones, M., (ed) *The Royal Navy and the Mediterranean Convoys, a Naval Staff History*, London, Routledge, 2014
Mackenzie, H., *The Sword of Damocles*, Stroud, Alan Sutton, 1995
Mackenzie, W., *The Secret History of SOE*, London, St Ermin's Press, 2000
Mars, A., *HMS Thule Intercepts*, London, Frederick Muller, 1953
Mars, A., *Unbroken*, The True Story of a Submarine, London, Frederick Muller, 1953
Mars, A., *Court Martial*, London, Frederick Muller, 1954, London, Elek Books, 1956
Mars, A., *British Submarines at War 1939-1945*, Wellingborough, William Kimber, 1971
Masters, D., *Up Periscope*, London, Eyre and Spottiswoode, 1942
McGeoch, I., *An Affair of Chances*, London, IWM, 1991
McLeod, G., *Two Home Runs*, Waikane NZ, High Tech, 2020
Messenger, C., *The Middle East Commandos*, Wellingborough, William Kimber, 1988
Moss, W.S, *Ill Met by Moonlight*, London, Cassell, 1950
Neave, A., *Saturday at MI9*, Barnsley, Pen and Sword, 2010
Owen, J., *Commando, Winning World War II Behind Enemy Lines*, London, Little Brown, 2012
Padfield, P., *War Beneath the Sea, Submarine Conflict 1939-1945*, London, Trafalgar Square, 1995
Parish, M.W., *Aegean Adventures* 1940-1943, Lewes, Book Guild, 1993
Posses, T., *Kalamata Beach 28 April 1941*, published privately by the author
Prien, G., *U-Boat Commander*, London, Tandem, 1969
Psychoundakis, G., *The Cretan Runner*, London, John Murray, 1955
Redford, D., *The Submarine, A Cultural History*, London, Tauris, 2010
Rigopoulos, R., *Secret War*, Paducah KY, Turner Publishing, 2003
Robertson, T., *The Ship With Two Captains*, London, Evans Brothers, 1957
Rodger, N.A.M., *The Price of Victory*, London, Allen Lane, 2024
Sadler, J., *Operation Mercury, the Fall of Crete 1941*, Barnsley, Pen and Sword, 2007
Simpson, G., *Periscope View*, London, MacMillan, 1972
Sims, A. J., *'British Submarine Design During the War (1939-1945)' in Selected Papers on British Warship Design in World War II*, Transactions of the Royal Institution of Naval Architects, London, Conway Maritime Press, 1983
Smith, D. J.B., *Being Silent They Speak*, published privately, 2012
Submarine Memories, Hadley, Gatwick Submarine Archive
Submarine Memories (More...), Hadley, Gatwick Submarine Archive
Submarine Memories (Even More...), Hadley, Gatwick Submarine Archive
Trenowden, I., *The Hunting Submarine, the Fighting Life of HMS Tally-Ho*, London, Harper Collins, 1974

Ufficio Storico Della Marina Militare, *Volume XVIII, 'La Guerra di Mine'*, Rome, 1966
Van der Vat, D., *Stealth at Sea*, London, Weidenfeld and Nicolson, 1994
Wade, F., *A Midshipman's War*, Victoria B.C., Trafford, 2005
Wilson, M., *A Submariner's War*, Stroud, Tempus Publishing, 2000
Wingate, J., *The Fighting Tenth*, London, Leo Cooper, 1991
Woodhouse, C.M., *The Struggle for Greece, London*, Hart-Davis, MacGibbon, 1976
Young, E., *One of our Submarines*, London, Rupert Hart-Davis, 1952

Index